D1332356

NEW COLLEGE NOTTINGHAM
182014

The Fashion of Architecture

Bradley Quinn

BERG

For Michel

First published in 2003
by Berg

Editorial offices:
1st Floor, Angel Court,
81 St Clements Street,
Oxford OX4 1AW
UK

838 Broadway,
Third Floor,
New York, NY 10003-4812
USA

© Bradley Quinn 2003
www.bradleyquinn.com

All rights reserved.
No part of this publication may be reproduced in any form or by any means without the written permission of Berg.

Berg is the imprint of Oxford International Publishers Ltd.

Library of Congress Cataloguing-in-Publication Data.

A catalogue record for this book is available from the Library of Congress.

British Library Cataloguing-in-Publication Data.

A catalogue record for this book is available from the British Library.

Designed at
Wilson Harvey: London
(020 7420 7700)

Typeset by JS Typesetting Ltd, Wellingborough, Northants.

Printed in China by Hong Kong Graphics & Printing Ltd.

ISBN 1 85973 752 8 (Cloth)
1 85973 757 9 (Paper)

www.bergpublishers.com

06/08
New College Nottingham
Learning Centres
182014 720

Contents

Acknowledgements

This book would not have been possible without the support and enthusiasm of so many wonderful people. Kathryn Earle and Ian Critchley, along with the rest of the Berg team and the designers at Wilson Harvey, worked above and beyond the call of duty to realise this project. I am deeply grateful for all of their efforts. I would also like to thank Chris Moore, Anders Edström, David Lachapelle, Francesco Valentino, Michael Maier, Helene Binet and William Timbers for contributing with special photography, as well as thank Simon Thorogood, Lucy Orta, Paula Orrell, Stuart Veech, Karel Vollers, Millie P, Pia Myrvold, Yeohlee Teng, Brian Lam, Aurelie, Maria Friberg, Michiko Koshino, Krystyna Kolowska, Andromeda Nahum, Haruko Sekihara, Ewa Bakowicz, Sophie Quinn, Isabelle Peron and Montserrat Gigi for helping source the perfect images for the book. A special thank you to Patrik Shumacher, Arkadius, Hussein Chalayan, Adam Thorpe and Joe Hunter, Yeohlee, Simon Thorogood, Pia Myrvold, Lucy Orta and all the others who agreed to be interviewed for the book. I especially appreciated the support and practical advice I received from Robyn Dutra, Emma Shanley, Ana Avalon and Vivienne Bellamy as I researched the book.

Introduction

P01_P02

The shapes of fashion, in their extensive range of historical styles and streamlined modernism, are seldom independent of the architecture around them. As doorways widened during the Regency period, skirts reached delirious proportions as their hoops and panniers extended to unprecedented widths. The black silk top hats of the mid-nineteenth century came into fashion at the outset of the industrial revolution and grew in popularity to become the very symbol of industrialization. Also known as 'stovepipe' hats, their resemblance to tall manufacturing chimneys and factory smokestacks symbolized the industrialists themselves. Men's tailoring has always contained vestiges of their professional affiliations; the robes of priests, the armour of medieval knights and even the suits of Edwardian bankers were cut to echo the architecture of the institutions they served.

The metaphor of architecture as clothing can be traced back to Vitruvius and possibly even earlier. Historic costumes reveal the axis of fashion and architecture in period dress, in many garments that were ornamented and even constructed according to architectonic references. The ladies of Henry VIII's court wore headdresses in the shape of a Tudor arch, while male courtiers wore expressions of Gothic architecture in their hats, capes and padded court attire. The trunk hose and cod pieces of the Elizabethan era mimicked the columns, buttresses and even the table legs of the period. Architecture of the 1840s was dominated by blunted arches and rounded window frames, the same flattened curves conspicuous in the dress lines of the period. James Laver identified parallels between the steel domes of Sir Joseph Paxton's pavilion for the Great Exhibition of 1851 and the structure of the crinoline frame. Paxton had no intention of influencing women's dress, but his design inspired a voluminous device that continued to dominate fashion for the following two decades.[1]

Fashion has not always been so distinct from architecture. In the long journey of human existence, clothing first provided the body with wearable shelter, with architecture manifesting as a framework to support the animal hides and panels of fabric that became roofs and walls. Gottfried Semper described how essential these structures were to the production of social space, especially the spaces of domesticity.[2] As woven textiles designated spatial boundaries, they also introduced the idea that the owners of the textiles had the right to occupy the spaces they demarcated. According to Semper, these early textiles engendered the idea of family among the kinfolk who dwelt there, as well as the idea of community among the group. As clusters of dwellings also designated communal spaces between them, the boundaries of public space were also established through the textile patterns and motifs that characterized the community. Such motifs shaped and produced the meanings of public spaces, their signifiers worn on the bodies that occupied them.

Adolph Loos also identified architecture with clothing, following Semper's logic closely. In his 1898 essay 'The Principle of Dressing', Loos acknowledged the primacy of dress as a basic shelter, encouraging architects to first engage with textiles as a method of grasping the meanings and aesthetics of dwelling, then employ architecture to sustain these principles in built form.[3] 'This is the correct and logical path to be followed in architecture,' Loos wrote. 'It was in this sequence that mankind learned how to build. In the beginning was dressing.'[4] Loos was visionary in identifying the parallels between fashion and architecture as they unfolded over time. Both trace their roots back to archaic textile panels; those adapted for use on the body became clothing, while those fastened to fixed frameworks became buildings. Irrespective of their modern permutations and respective roles as micro- and macro-structures, both disciplines remain rooted to the basic task of enclosing space around the human form.
But while fashion draws heavily upon architecture to interpret the spatial needs of the modern human, fashion also plays a role in shaping modern architecture. Architects such as Le Corbusier, Hermann Muthesius and Peter Behrens coordinated modern

architecture like a tailored suit, deploying the logic of clothing to divest nineteenth-century architecture of its ornamentation. Likening building ornamentation and stylistic decorations to 'the ribbon and ruffles' of women's fashion, they called for an architecture that could be clothed in the spare functionality of menswear (the men's dress of the day was disassociated with the excesses of women's fashion). By the 1930s these principles were firmly established tenets of modernist architecture, equivocal in their appeal to both the architect and the inhabitant. According to F.R.S. Yorke, author of *The Modern House:* 'The men who cultivate the perfect trouser-crease abhor straight unbroken lines in building, and those who detest the vulgarity of a personal display of jewellery are inclined to judge architecture by its wealth of ornament.'[5]

Siegfried Giedion defined modern architecture as an ethical refusal of the seductions of fashionable clothing. At this point, the term 'fashion', used in architecture, became synonymous with the concept of short-lived style we regard today as a 'trend'. Giedion condemned the styles of nineteenth-century architecture as 'fashion-conscious' and, like Le Corbusier, called for a paradigm of minimalistic architecture that would have lasting appeal. Yet the strong aesthetic statements of the sustainable architecture they envisaged only exaggerated the sensibilities of their age. Ironically, in privileging the present to such an extent, modernist architecture is only sustainable to the extent that it is able to remain 'fashionable'.

Today, for critics to brand an architectural project as 'fashion' is tantamount to excommunication in architecture circles. Much of the discourse surrounding modern architecture reads as a pre-emptive defence against the accusation that it is itself a 'fashion'. Most leading architects systematically avoid using building styles, materials, compositions and details that can be described as decorative. Selections of colour, texture and form are rationalized as aesthetic choices rather than stylistic ones. For these architects, 'fashion' is a lethal poison, deadly in even the smallest of doses.

While architecture attempted to purge itself of fashion at the beginning of the last century, the dawning of this one is characterized by the relationship between them. For almost a decade, architects have been competing for fashion projects with the zeal they once showed for

[A]Pia Myrvold collaborated with Bernard Tschumi to give her fashion designs an architectural expression. Constructed at Parc de la Villette in Paris, Myrvold's textile panels were conceived as abstractions of roofs and walls to define the boundaries of public space.

[B]Hussein Chalayan uses architectural principles to create clothing more akin to wearable buildings than conventional fashion. The plastic panels of this dress form a dense structure that maintains its shape independently of the body.

(A)

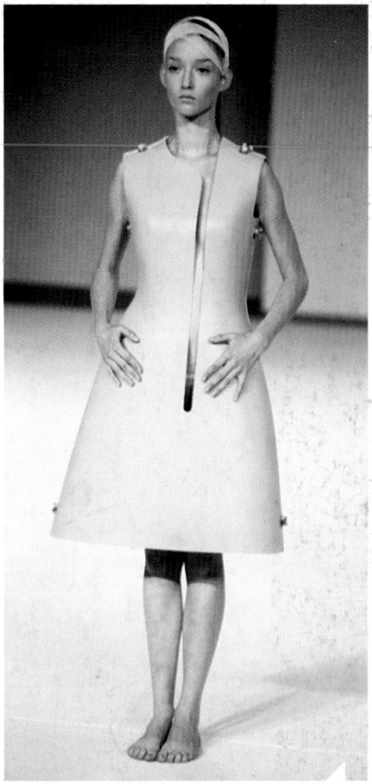

(B)

museum and gallery commissions. Leading architects such as Rem Koolhaas, Tadao Ando and Frank Gehry have made fashion statements in their building designs for Prada, Armani and Issey Miyake. Bernard Tschumi joined forces with Pia Myrvold to create a series of textile installations for Parc de la Villette in Paris, while architects around the globe are employing the principles of fashion design to create membrane structures and mobile buildings.

Renowned designers Pierre Cardin, Roberto Capucci and Gianfranco Ferre are also trained architects, and they make clothing according to architectural principles rather than following the rules of tailoring. Their use of structure and volume redistributes bodily proportions in a limpid, sculptural guise, yet the construction genius evident in garments that expand from flat forms into complex three-dimensional shapes recall architectural principles as precise as the buildings they are worn in. They position the wearer in forms that are at once radical and transcendent; their amplification of materials and proportions is extreme and even disconcerting, but subtle in its impact on the wearer as she becomes an agent of dress, art and architecture.[6]

Issey Miyake, an art graduate, appears to ignore fashion altogether as he produces works with proportions that vacillate between habitations and figurative sculpture; often it is only the wearablity of his design that designates them as fashion. At Gucci, Tom Ford studied architecture before switching to fashion, attributing his regard for clean lines and sleek panels to his awareness of architectural structures. Kei Kagami abandoned his architecture career in Tokyo to design fashions for Junko Koshino, then moved to London to work for John Galliano.

Married to an architect and once citing the Pompidou Centre as her sartorial equivalent, Rei Kawakubo said: 'From the point of view of finding possibilities, architecture and clothes-making share many potentials.'[7] Kawakubo conceives of 'interventions in space' based on architectural concepts rather than conventional clothing. Yohji Yamamoto designs structures rather than clothes; his complex designs leave the fashion world bemused, yet they are grasped immediately by architects. Hussein Chalayan says he has more in common with architects than fashion designers, and collaborates with architectural practices to realize his fashion innovations. These designers have moved far beyond the dressmakers of history who merely echoed the lines of architectural edifices in the cut of fabric. As cutting-edge designers assimilate the visual and intellectual principles of architecture into fashion, they interpret the two disciplines in terms of congruity of ideas.

Many of the collaborations between fashion designers and architects have been expressed through the arts. Zaha Hadid's costumes and set designs for the Metapolis Ballet performance infused garments with symbolic and allusive values that transformed architecture into fluid movement. Andreas Gursky, famous for his architectural photography, photographed a fashion campaign for Prada with the same eye for scale and proportion he would assign to a building. Ken Yeang exhibited his bioclimatic skyscrapers alongside Yeohlee Teng's tiered fashions, while Ben van Berkel's blueprints and models have been presented in exhibitions that also featured Issey Miyake and Donna Karan. The artist Lucy Orta's wearable structures have been likened to the nomadic sensibilities of C P Company and Final Home, her collections of reclaimed clothing the inspiration behind the deconstructed chic of Martin Margiela.

The connections between the two disciplines are significant: both rely heavily upon human proportions, mathematics and geometry to create the protective layers in which we cocoon ourselves. Fashion and architecture revolve around the scale of the human form to signify their dimensions, requiring an understanding of mass as well as space. They both operate within the same spatial frameworks to manage energy and material, and map the boundaries of the body by creating climatic environmental systems around it. Garments are wrapped around the body in successive layers of underwear, outer clothing and overcoats that define the outer core of the body, while tiers of sleeping bags, tents and shelters symbolically expand into houses and skyscrapers. Within this system the garments can be seen as more than mere clothing – they form part of a structure that negotiates the relationship between private spaces and public arenas, both defining our identity and place in society.

[A+B] Arkadius's use of volume reinterprets traditional dress proportions. By using the same design techniques an architect would use for a building, Arkadius takes garments beyond their traditional flat forms into complex three-dimensional shapes.

(A)

(B)

Egress is an essential concern for both disciplines. Designing a zipped jumper rather than a button-fronted shirt or planning a building with a network of entrances invariably reflects the equation of time with ease of movement. This equation is seldom reversed, but allowances are made in both disciplines for complex points of egress in highly aestheticized designs. The corset, for example, is notoriously difficult to append, but its aesthetic value overrides the impracticalities of putting it on. Likewise, circuitous staircases and sweeping mezzanines seldom facilitate direct egress, but they are designed to provide dramatic points of entry that enhance the building as a whole.

Principles of construction, design economy and conservation of materials are central to both disciplines, who create their respective structures according to the macro- and micro-systems they designate. Fashion designers are exploring the uses of the pliable metals, membrane structures, technological systems, lightweight glasses and the plastics used in building construction. The development of new technologized textiles gives clothing the potential to act as individual climate-controlled environments, or exchange information with sensors embedded into the environment around them. As fashion designers reflect on materials, the organization of information and the patterns of human interaction, they mirror the central tenets of urban architecture. Like architects, fashion designers produce environments defined through spatial awareness by working with and against the human form to create spaces whose meanings are inspired by a critical discourse or an evaluation of the natural landscape.

Fashion takes many forms, and can be imagined to take many others. Some designers make a comment on the body by dwarfing it within surreally large proportions, while others enhance it by engineering sleek fabric innovations that support and define the body. Issey Miyake creates moulded body casts that form a superstructure around the wearer, while Alexander McQueen encases his models in cages and tanks. London-based designer Arkadius says he cocoons his models in volume rather than material, enveloping the body in spherical forms or encasing the wearer in cage-like contraptions that seem to move independently of the body.

Many other designers work with volume to dramatic effect, creating dome-shaped dresses that seem to resurrect the silhouettes of the eighteenth and nineteenth centuries. Jean Paul Gaultier, Vivienne Westwood, Azzedine Alaïa, Rei Kawakubo and Yohji Yamamoto consistently created crinoline shapes throughout the 1990s and the early years of the twenty-first century. But unlike the hoop skirts and canework supports of previous eras, the spectacular figures they design are created through complex frames and technological constructions built with the precision of architecture.

Despite the exciting innovations that are created from interdisciplinary collaborations, many designers regard fashion as a difficult and unsatisfying craft. Although many classical designs endure, most garments become a thing of the past almost as soon as they are created. Many architects comment that the allure of fashion is its immediacy and its obsolescence; a building is judged by the sustainability of its design, and can take decades to plan and construct. Architects often lament the technicalities that arise during this process, ultimately excavating a vast chasm between their initial concepts and their constructed buildings. A built environment can only ever manifest as an imperfect model, an approximation of their ultimate vision. The same is true of garment design: the stages from sketchbook and pattern cutting to industrial manufacturing routinely eliminate refined details and tailoring innovation. Too often, the mass production of garments results in a decimated version of a design that promised to be a masterpiece on the drawing board.

In their dedication to the production of form, fashion and architecture both strive to create ideals of beauty and enduring designs. Notorious for its inherent elitism, the fashion elite dismiss many individual garments and even whole collections as 'trash fashion'. Although the vast majority of fashion designs are produced in multiples, it is typically the pieces made as 'one-offs' or as exhibition garments that receive the highest acclaim. These creations are often too intricate to be industrially manufactured, or deliberately made to express their

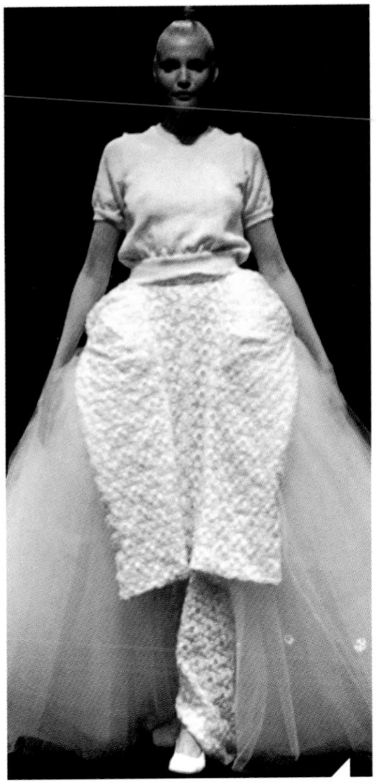

(A)

(B)

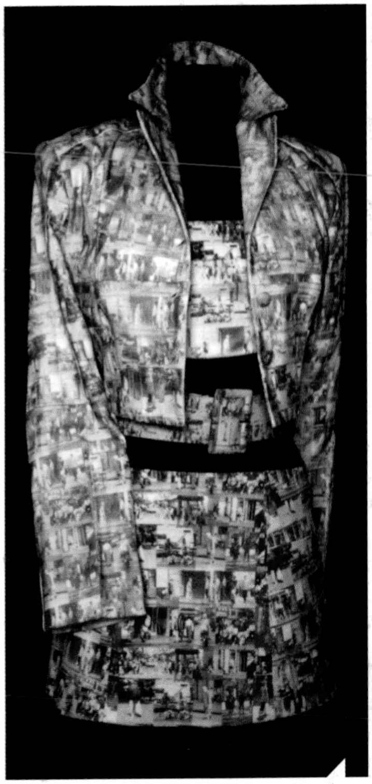

(C)

[A]Rei Kawakubo views the body as the common ground between fashion and architecture, and describes it as a site where she can experiment with expressions of space, volume and proportion.

[B]Alexander McQueen often constructs elaborate sets for his fashion shows, using an architectural backdrop to amplify the message behind the collection.

[C]Pia Myrvold transforms architectural details into a unique design signature by featuring images of structural supports as repeating motifs.

poetic guise. These are generally the fashions that express architectural principles most fully.

It is interesting to note that among architects, some structures are debased to the category of mere 'buildings', while historic monuments, iconic structures and the edifices acknowledged as poetic gestures are accepted as 'architecture'. The aesthetic elitism present in fashion is also pervasive in architecture, with critical acclaim lauded on visionary structures that redefine modernist strategies or outline new expressions of materializing spatial and territorial boundaries. Many of the buildings that suggest a congruency with fashion are those designed to take architecture in a new direction altogether, or revolutionize the fabric of the urban environment.

Despite the points of anthropological, historical and modernist congruency between fashion and architecture, it is not uncommon for architectural theorists and practising architects to refute any claims of their convergence. 'Fashion is all froth,' claims the architectural theorist Charles Jencks. 'It has no real convergence with architecture, it is merely an overlap.'[8] Other architectural theorists, when confronted with the myriad parallels between the two disciplines, point out that the principles of architecture have often been directed at contributing to the establishment of social, political and even spiritual mandates, expressing its ideals in enduring forms that they regard as the antithesis of the transience associated with fashion. Architecture also maintains complex networks with other discourses, generally aligning itself with the transcendency of art and the logic of science that are rarely realized in fashion.

Yet on a critical level, the same theories that provide insight into architecture also chart fashion's conceptual terrain. Deconstruction, post-structuralism, theories of the body and a range of other critical discourses reveal fashion's inextricable links with architecture, while also interpreting fashion's meaning in the wider context of society. As many architectural theorists believe the intangible content of architectural form to be the true potential for new architecture, so too are conceptual fashion designers applying theoretical models to reinterpret the

(A)

meaning of fashion. The contemporary architects who derive ideas from conceptual and philosophical sources rarely base their designs on tenets of architectural theory, tending to derive inspiration from analysis of literary theory, visual culture, computer-aided design, film sets, fine art and representations of the human form. In many respects, conceptual fashion designers are the only practitioners truly taking their discipline forward – ironically by working according to the principles of architecture, science and art.

The Fashion of Architecture is intended as a starting point from which the axis of fashion and architecture can be charted. Although this book is indebted to the historical accounts published by Susan Sidlauskas, Ulrich Lehmann, Mark Wigley and Deborah Fausch, it is not intended to reiterate them. By building upon the foundations established in these authors' texts, the interrelatedness of fashion and architecture are examined here in a contemporary context through expressions of cutting-edge fashion and new paradigms of architecture. While Wigley's and Fausch's compelling accounts revealed fashion's impact on architecture, *The Fashion of Architecture* is oriented towards identifying architecture's impact on fashion.

Nowhere are the dynamics of architecture more apparent than in the urban environment, itself a backdrop and an inspiration for the dramatic intensity of high fashion. For the majority of fashion designers, the industry is dominated by urban culture, and the cityscapes that provide a platform where identities can be created, dissolved and formulated afresh. The garments considered to be high fashions are undisputedly

[A+B] Fashion boutiques are being reinvented as architectural temples. In his projects for Prada, Rem Koolhaas is transforming the traditional retail environment into a public space with interactive capabilities.

(B)

conceived for the urban realm, and encode traces of architectural styles, the planning of public spaces and the logics of urban mobility within their designs. Often conceived as sculptural or artistic expressions, high fashions and couture designs also move between the boundaries of fashion and art.

A theme of urban space can be traced throughout this book, from chapter 1's investigation of the construction of urban space and the exchanges of place and non-place, to the subtle coding of architecture evident in contemporary fashion. Going on to examine surveillance and visuality, chapter 1 also charts the responses that fashion and architecture are making to the proliferating presence of these technologies. Chapter 2 also examines the meanings and locations of space, identifying the phenomena of fashion space and the sets of spatial relations underpinning the visual and material fabric of modern life. The chapter also focuses on retail architecture and fashion in cyberspace as each unfolds as a phenomenon of spectacle and a synthesis of form and fiction.

The third chapter explores the void, itself a point of fascination for fashion designers and architects alike, as it becomes tangible in urban structures and fashion designs. Theories of deconstruction, reconstruction and unconstruction are used to interpret the significance of the elusive void, examining it in the wake of the fashion designs and architectural aesthetics that it has inspired. The chapter concludes with an essay on the tragic, a classical trope encoded in memory, memorial architecture, mourning dress and statements of contemporary chic. This response also revisits the role of the void, whose representational value symbolizes individual tragedy and loss. The fashions of Arkadius reassign the tragic to the collective through their representational ability, demonstrating fashion's capacity to inject memory and transcendence into wider visual culture. As both fashion and architecture draw upon classical models, they encode their forms with memory devices that transform them into visual archives.

Chapter 4 tracks the movements of urban nomads. Drawing on the themes of chapters 1 and 3, the sense of mobility and freedom so essential to modern life unite both

(A)

disciplines. As urban planners and architects attempt to make the relationship between the city landscape and the city dweller as frictionless as possible, fashion designers such as Yeohlee Teng, Kosuke Tsumura and C P Company prove that garments can also compensate for the shortcomings of urban life. This is also the vision of Hussein Chalayan, outlined in chapter 5, whose works are more often described as dynamic structures than clothing.

Many of the exchanges taking place between art, fashion and architecture are outlined in chapter 6. These alliances are by no means a contemporary phenomenon: dress reformers, the British Arts and Crafts movement, the Russian constructivists and the Bauhaus all positioned dress within their visual and spatial systems. In the present day, these sensibilities continue in the work of both fashion designers and architects. Zaha Hadid's Metapolis project resurrected many of the tenets so central to the Bauhaus's collaborative designs. Artists also evoke these sensibilities as they create containerized dwellings and use fashion principles to create installations and habitations.

Chapter 7 focuses solely on the work of Lucy Orta, whose empathetic prototypes for social transformation forge an unexpected alliance between fashion, architecture and art. As Orta transforms our perception of urban outcasts and gives them visibility in the public sphere, her work redefines urban space and highlights the significance of individual identity.

Other artists link fashion and architecture through photo-based media, while the work of fashion photographers like Corrine

[A]Artist Maria Friberg 'dressed' this building in a Hugo Boss suit, in a trompe l'oeil installation that 'fashions' its architectural support.

[B]Zaha Hadid blurred the boundaries between fashion and architecture when she designed the sets and costumes for the Charleroi/Danses Metapolis Ballet performance.

(B)

Day and Anders Edström, featured in chapter 8, is recognized as an art form. As they use architecture to frame the fashioned body, architecture's role in giving garments meaning and context comes to the fore. Architecture often functions as a metaphor for the human psyche, revealing that the 'mood' created by fashion photography often relies more on the backdrop than the models or the clothes themselves.

Today, architectural visionaries and fashion designers are creating structures independent of pre-existing designs, defined only through their mandate to accommodate the human form. Chapter 9 reveals that clothing construction and architecture came together with the design of the spacesuit and the spacecraft, aligning their construction principles with technological innovation. Technology continues to underpin the style and form behind their construction processes as they move forward today. As fashion designers explore new expressions of physical space and materials, their garments parallel the blobs, folds, waves, spirals and twists of contemporary architecture. Applied to fashion, this architectural paradigm reveals a new visual language that outlines structural and aesthetical axes between them.

This account of the congruencies between fashion and architecture is by no means exhaustive; rather, the reader is encouraged to regard the text as an examination of their potentials rather than an inventory of absolutes. While fashion does not constitute an architectural paradigm in itself, its role within the larger spatial system of architecture reveals many revolutionary possibilities for fashion's rich future.

[1] See James Laver (1949), *Style in Costume*, London: Oxford University Press.

[2] Quoted in Mark Wigley (2001), *White Walls*, Cambridge, MA: MIT Press, p11.

3Adolf Loos's 1898 essay, 'Das Prinzip der Bekleidung', has been translated as 'The Principle of Cladding' by Jane Newman and John Smith (1987) in *Spoken into the Void: Collected Essays 1897–1900*, Cambridge, MA: MIT Press, p66–9.

[4] Quoted in Mark Wigley (2001), *White Walls*, Cambridge, MA: MIT Press, p13.

[5] Quoted in Mark Wigley (2001), *White Walls*, Cambridge, MA: MIT Press, pxx.

[6] Much of Roberto Capucci's work was inspired by the ornamentation, relief and sheer volume of Renaissance architecture and Baroque palaces. Retrospectives of his work are typically exhibited in grand palaces or in cavernous galleries to emphasize this link, such as his exhibition at the Nordic Museum in Stockholm.

[7] Quoted in Colin McDowell (2000), *Fashion Today*, London: Phaidon, p428.

[8] Charles Jencks was interviewed by the author.

Notes

Fashioning the Metropolis

The congruency between fashion and architecture did not manifest suddenly or spectacularly; throughout time they have been hovering on the margins of a mutual existence. As they conquered and consumed space in the form of clothing and dwellings, both disciplines evolved in tandem. The organization of space has always been the essence of both fashion and architecture; fashion's architectuality unfolds in its containment of space, while architecture continues to be fashioned by its relationship to the human form. Architecture's domination of space is widespread, while fashion's role in mediating space is generally regarded as secondary; yet fashion constitutes architecture's spatial and ideological equal.

Architects often think of fashion as the third layer around the body. 'You have the onion peel effect,' said Patrik Schumacher, of Zaha Hadid Architects. 'You have the cityscape which is organized into dwellings. Then the dwelling surrounds the human, who gets under the duvet wearing a pair of pajamas. There are different densities of space around the body in this system. Some near, some distant, but all have relative values to the human form.'[1] Just as architects design the interiors that we live in and adapt technological systems to monitor the human body, they bring the layers of architecture ever closer, shrinking the distance between body and building.

Like architects, conceptual fashion designers experience space as one act. By interpreting space as perceptual, intellectual and physical phenomena, they integrate fashion and form with principles of architecture and spatiality. As space is enclosed by garments, enveloped by architecture and occupied by bodies, it is made tangible in constructed forms. The cocooning folds of fashion garments and the dense membranes of architecture take on the meanings of havens and sanctuaries, while public spaces can generate a sense of human alienation or mediate social instability.

The concepts of space expressed in architecture and fashion are found where critical readings condense. With the dawning of modernism, critical discourses of space proliferated to the extent that Michel Foucault regarded modernity as 'the epoch of space'.[2] Space is consumed and commodified, summarily aligned with the polarities of idealism and materialism that dominate the West's understanding of space. Critical discourses of fashion and architecture are increasingly fascinated by this experience as they strive to map the visual and material transactions that create a sense of 'place'.

Fashion's impact on the built environment is too fundamental to be dismissed as merely a passing trend. Recent fashion innovations reveal that contemporary fashion can be considered to represent a built environment in itself or a component of a larger one, redefining the boundaries between clothing and architecture. Fashion's gradual integration with the built environment highlights its engagement with the systematic and theoretical tools underpinning the urban world. As fashion plays a greater role in determining the types of structures forming the urban environment, it also portends a new economy of space.

This chapter continues to examine the roles of fashion and architecture in shaping urban life, exploring the signifiers and meanings generated by the congruencies between them. The modern city, with its extreme spatial experiences, continually changes shape while reorienting humans within its margins. Expressions of the city manifest in fashion and architecture, their meanings penetrating further and deeper than mere codes of spatial exchange. By forging a dialogue with the urban landscape, both fashion and architecture charge it with the capacity to communicate in a visual language. As their roles in mediating urban space transcends their material boundaries, they reveal their ability to establish new systems and practices in the built environment and beyond.

Space, Vision and Power

'Visibility is a trap'

Michel Foucault[3]

Few people hesitate to flash their identification at the security guards or feed their swipe cards through the magnetic readers as they enter public buildings. Ultra-modern architecture facilitates a range of security measures by design, but shrewdly conceals the full extent of its surveillance regimes. From inside and outside, closed-circuit television cameras (CCTV), video monitors and face-recognition software screen those who approach its

façades or walk past its boundary walls. Movements within the building are scrutinized and routinely logged within a centralized database throughout the day and the during the night-watch. The occupants feel protected by the relentless technological vigil, without realizing that they never escape its perpetual gaze.

Several streets away and about four metres above street level, a security camera mounted on a tall metal pole rotates electronically as it films and records the people below. Sitting in a control room half a kilometre down the street, a security guard zooms in on groups of pedestrians or singles out individuals, recording the activities on the street in real time. The footage will be saved for six months and filed in a fireproof archive along with thousands of other video cassettes, or compressed into a digital database that can be recalled for viewing at a moment's notice.

The startling reach of surveillance capabilities in urban centres mirrors an exponential boom throughout the major cities of the world, which has lead many human rights organizations to equate the widespread installation of cameras with the diminishing role of the police to protect the public. Since video monitoring systems and CCTV were introduced in the 1980s, architecture has adapted to integrate surveillance objectives into its environmental systems. Security stations, restricted-access areas and plans to heighten visibility feature on blueprints for corporate architecture, while alarm-activated shutters, unbreakable glass and reinforced doorways are almost as prevalent in private dwellings as they are in civic domains.

The ability to monitor oneself and others electronically is a real and ever-present possibility as wiring and circuits are being factored into garment design as they are into architectural blueprints. Ultra-modern garments already feature the range of wireless Internet access, video relays and technical interfaces fitted into buildings. By concealing the systems within the garment's design and fabric, techno fashions fuse wireless technology with video-capture capabilities, mobile-phone communication and the Internet, making it possible for the wearer to contact databases and retrieve information from the interfaces fabricated into their clothing. Access is provided through the Internet, where video files can be transmitted in real time to view images from another place. As the wearer engages with systems beyond their immediate environment, they acquire the ability to interpret communication and surveillance in unequivocal terms.

Wearable surveillance technology blurs the boundaries between the shielding feature of clothing and the protection architecture provides. Garments have a distinct advantage in partnering surveillance technology with mobility and interaction, so that portable surveillance technology navigates the wearer through a matrix of CCTV, alarms and restricted-access areas. The ever-present gaze of 'Big Brother' is turned inside out as the wearer tracks the environment rather than being tracked by it. Techno fashions equip the wearer with the technological means to survey the environment and the activities of others, both near and remote. Vision becomes disembodied as it comes under the control of systems in fashion and architecture, aligning it with the sort of 'scopic regimes' observed by Martin Jay as he bemoaned the society of the spectacle identified by Guy Bourdin.[4]

Modern surveillance technology has absorbed and diverted centuries of methods of looking: the kaleidoscope, the camera obscura, microscopes, telescopes, panopticons and eventually infrared, thermal or satellite imaging practices. Until the 1990s, the power of commercial surveillance was largely confined to the architecture it was incorporated into. This changed with the launch of the Internet, as e-mail became one of the most pervasive information-tracking devices ever known. As mobile telephones grew in popularity and became more technologically advanced, intelligence operations and law-enforcement squads were quick to spot their surveillance potential.

As surveillance rewrites the rules of public and private life, distinctions between interior and exterior collapse, or vanish without a trace. While many of the icons of contemporary architecture strive to collapse the division between interior and exterior conceptually, surveillance gives them the means to do so literally. As the frontier between them is crossed to permit entrance and egress, the camera links the two separate spaces as it records them. While exterior surfaces signify the visual iconography of our time, the interior domain represents what is denied from sight, generating fantasies of inclusion and exclusion, knowledge and power as it facilitates the transmission of information and communication in urban space.

Surveillance relies on a legion of optical devices for capturing and imaging the world. As the dichotomous nature of space defines inner and outer, open and closed, public and private, technology provides the means to transcend them visually. The presence of television cameras, medical cameras, satellites, military aircraft and digital cameras ensure that we never escape the scrutiny of the lens. The fashion industry exploit these media to instil the desire to be seen, be visible and even pursued. As the body becomes increasingly monitored by the fashion world, it creates a parallel culture of self-surveillance, in which individuals must also scrutinize themselves to monitor their social acceptability.

The televisualization of people and events pervades the whole of society, as the popularity of webcams, the presence of CCTV and the Big Brother genre of television programmes reveal that surveillance is not the exception, but the norm. With this in mind, Prada have generated an atmosphere of heightened visibility in their New York flagship shop, surrounding the shopper with video monitors, electronic display screens and cinematic reels. Fashion shows, classic films and Prada advertising campaigns are projected throughout the shop. For many shoppers, the opportunity to be captured on film is to be glamorous and chic; the 'I know you're watching me' facet of the fashion experience reads as a willed pathology of surveillance.

In the changing rooms, video feeds stream grainy film images and fashion shows onto wall panels, while video cameras project the image of the shopper onto a screen inset within the mirror, simultaneously transmitting real-time and cinematic images. Distracted by the

(A)

allure of their cinematic 'other', the Prada shoppers forget that they are also under surveillance by the camera. As the camera records every movement and plays them back, Prada shrewdly manipulate our endless fascination with watching others and ourselves, amplifying the function of clothing as both boundary and margin in the ever-widening gap between public and private personae. Clothes, being the form in which the fashioned body is made visible, give the wearer a public identity while fostering the construction of the self, on screen or off it.

In a seamless web of interlaced visual conduits, Prada summons an ironic double vision fabricated and transmitted by the postmodern media world. Surveillance implies a certain distance between object and observer, creating distinctions of distance and nearness. The confines of Prada's changing rooms keep the shopper ever-present, producing a commodified image that can be objectified and consumed. Although televisuality can betray a profound anxiety about body image, this cinematic surveillance intends to subvert conventional modes of looking and seeing by paralleling the consumer and brand image in real time.

The televisual creates a universal visual market that generates the consumer publicity that Paul Virilio describes as 'comparative advertising'. Through global visual commerce, the market for trans-global concentrations of television and video becomes easier to understand. Traditional perceptions of the optic have changed. As Paul Virilio argues: 'Building the space of the multi-media networks with the aid of tele-technologies surely then requires a new "optic", a new global optics, capable of helping a panoptical vision to appear, a vision which is

In their New York flagship boutique, Prada surround the shopper with video monitors, electronic display screens and cinematic reels. Fashion shows, art films and advertising campaigns are projected throughout the shop, while the shopper's activities are under surveillance as they are monitored on CCTV.

(B)

indispensable if the "market of the visible" is to be established.'[5]

Televisual space can only be analysed as a cultural construct, as a space that can only be understood in terms of social relations of communication, and defined by the sense of place of its inhabitants. Akin to Foucault's heterotopias, televisual spaces can also function as countersites in their ability to simultaneously represent and invert several places within a single space, even sites considered incompatible with each other. The intention is often to blur the boundaries between local and distant cities and create the impression of a world meta-city; Fashion Weeks in Paris, Milan and New York merge into a single event rather than maintaining separate identities.

Both fashion and architecture presume the presence of a public that watches and must be watched. The fashion system is premised on visuality; a concept essential to the consumption of fashion but often underestimated in interpretations of it. As the cultural theorist Irit Rogoff explains: 'We actively interact with images from all arenas to remake the world in the shape of our fantasies and desires and to narrate the stories which we carry within us.'[6] Visuality is not the same as sight; it occurs when visual media and sensory perceptions intersect, where gaze meets desire.

Visuality describes the modern gaze, as was first articulated by the Impressionists as they charted changes occurring in the metropolitan character of Paris during the 1860s. Their paintings conveyed how changes in modes of production were redefining the infrastructure of the city's urban fabric and profoundly affecting the lives of its inhabitants. Visuality presumes transparency, as though assuming that all events occurring within the public domain are real and accessible to all viewers. Although the presence of surveillance can be ominous, its existence implies that visuality is enacted within it, that no event, however secret, can be unremittingly hidden from view. Controlling the means of visuality imparts power, and the concept of surveillance enables fashion and architecture to share this power between them.

Before the advent of surveillance technology, modern architecture was designed to exert regulation and control over individuals and the masses, a premise that ranked high on the modernist agenda. Beyond its aesthetic role, architecture's engagement with the visual is mediated by its ability to conceal and to reveal, to hide and to watch. Likewise, fashion is a form of masking within a system of transposing images within the eye, revealing and concealing, part reality, part illusory. Frame by frame, these images unfold cinematically, as garments circulate and become anchored to their surroundings kinaesthetically. Movement communicates visuality through the sensory realm of presence and tactility, in opposition to the absent gaze of the televisual. This creates a space of exchange where space is occupied by the gaze of the eye as well as the body.

For Foucault, all spatial expressions of power rely on such principles of visuality, in forms designed to give unmitigated surveillance free reign. Foucault regarded space in terms of its demarcation by structures of power, ultimately aligning with the juridical structures of society. He found its tangible expression in the model of Jeremy Bentham's 'panopticon', designed in 1786, which Foucault regarded as the architectural embodiment of the discourse he termed 'panopticism'.[7] Foucault reintroduced the panopticon into critical discussion, insisting that it serves as a model for the construction of power in the 'disciplinary society' of our era.

The panopticon methodically organizes individuals within a structure that makes it possible to view them at all times, a spatial system Foucault described as: 'At the periphery, an annular building; at the centre, a tower; this tower is pierced with wide windows that open on to the inner side of the ring; the peripheric building is divided into cells...they have two windows...corresponding to the windows of the tower. All that is needed, then, is to place a supervisor in a central tower...in which each actor is alone, perfectly individualised and constantly visible.'[8] Foucault emphasized the importance of intense lighting and a clear line of sight to each inmate, to ensure that the panopticon would 'induce in the inmate a state of conscious and permanent visibility'.[9] As the ever-present gaze of the 'supervisor' overlooks them, the inmates generate an atmosphere of self-surveillance, continually regulating their own behaviour to deflect the attention of the supervisor. Today this ethos extends far beyond the confines of the institution as the controlled space of the panopticon continues to be synonymous with the cultures and practices of surveillance that have so profoundly marked the modern world. Foucault concluded that, 'power should be visible and unverifiable', arguing that of Bentham's eighteenth-century model outlines the basis for an entire regime of twentieth-century technological power.[10]

With the panopticon now reconceived in terms of surveillance systems, the surveillance practices it initiated have social and political consequences for the built environment and a range of other representational practices, with fashion among them. Foucault's panoptical compression of visuality into a single view echoes Roland Barthes's examination of the term 'panorama', which identified the hypervisibility afforded by the view from the top of the Eiffel Tower. For Barthes the meaning of the Eiffel Tower is not generated through its subjective function as a monument, but through its capacity to facilitate a vast aerial perspective of Paris. The tower enables the spectator to attain 'an immediate consumption of a humanity made natural by that glance which transforms it into space', as their gaze encompasses the historical significance and spatial mass of the city.[11] 'The Tower is also present to the entire world. First of all as a universal symbol of Paris, it is everywhere on the globe where Paris is to be stated as an image,' wrote Barthes. Like Foucault, Barthes equated the exercise of power with spatial design, and ultimately, the ability to control and survey its boundaries.

Permanent surveillance is power perfected, and panoptical questions have had considerable impact on the canon of modern architecture. In *Delirious New York*, Koolhaas celebrates the needle and the globe as two emblematic forms that recur in various guises: the skyscraper and the helium balloon. Koolhaas considers the evolution of Manhattan to be a direct result of the dialectic between these two forms. 'Manhattan is the twentieth century's Rosetta Stone...occupied by architectural mutations,' he wrote.[12] While the skyscraper commands attention and reverence, the globe promises receptivity, their representations constituting potent metaphors for the exercise of power in the urban world. Like Foucault and Barthes, Koolhaas equates power relationships with spatial designs that facilitate wide panoramas and far-reaching gazes.

Taking its cue from the extensive arsenal of social control now integrated within architecture, fashion is reacting with its own solutions for reinstating anonymity. Surveillance can take place beyond optical devices; looks, visual exchanges and thwarted gazes play an important role in surveillance tactics. Surveillance, as a theme, has been widely explored by fashion designers since the mid-1990s. For his 1999 and 2000 collections, Paris-based designer John Ribbe gave women the means either to conceal their entire bodies or expose them at will. Creating a tiered system of fabric panels, Ribbe swathed his models in body-conscious sheaths that concealed the wearer's face, allowing her to draw the gaze of others while remaining anonymous.

Alexander McQueen has explored the effects of surveillance in his work, as a means of inciting terror and allure. From his *Dante* collection (autumn/winter 1996), masked models imposed a reign of terror on the catwalk as they stalked the audience. A red lace dress was rendered menacing as its mesh enveloped the head and face, merging dress and identity into one another. Another model wore a stiffened lace top that bracketed her face, its lapels flaring upwards from the sternum to conceal her nose, lips and jaw line. Members of the audience could never know for sure whether they were being watched, or what intentions lay behind the gaze. Like the panopticon's frightening supervisor, actual observation was replaced by the possibility of being watched. McQueen's panoptical subversion references the ever-expanding omnipresence of surveillance in daily life.

Exploring the sensuality associated with revealing and concealing the body, fashion innovator Hussein Chalayan has even placed

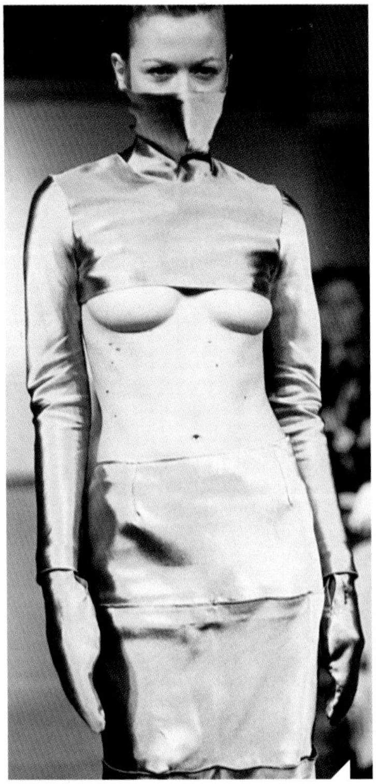

(A)

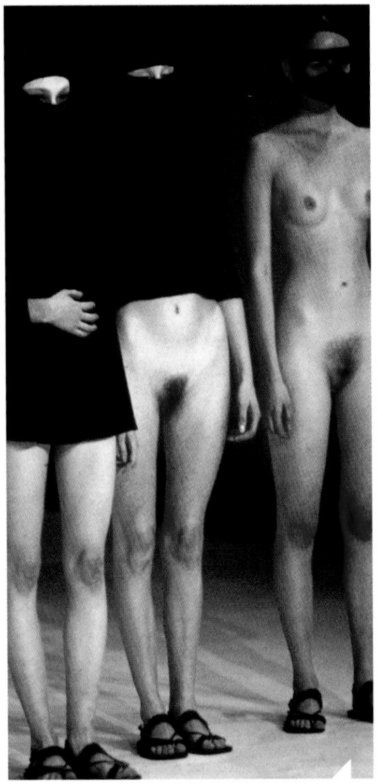

(B)

Fashioning the Metropolis

his catwalk audience under surveillance. In 1997 he sent models onto the catwalk wearing black chadors of varying lengths and nothing else, exploring the capacity of traditional Islamic dress to define and de-individuate the body by concealing the wearer's identity. The shortest chador exposed the model's body from the navel downward, while another model roamed the catwalk in only a yashmak. Both enabled the wearers to gauge the audience's reactions while remaining anonymous to the onlookers.

An expert on the social significance of veiling, Fadwa El Guindi points out that, 'dress form and behaviour...are not accompanied by withdrawal, seclusion, or segregation'.[13] With vision and mobility among the essential concerns of Islamic dress, the sense of privacy afforded by veiling is comparable to the refuge of a building, yet allows the wearer to wander freely. Chalayan's inversion connects contemporary modes of visuality with this long tradition, demonstrating the power that masking can provide for a wearer who wishes to see and yet remain unseen.

The London-based fashion visionaries Vexed Generation also create garments that counter surveillance. Their strategic design tactics give fashion the power to invert and deflect electronic surveillance by using visors, hoods, zips and collars to render the wearer anonymous. One of their most popular garments is the 'Vexed Parka', which they created as a commentary on the escalation of surveillance during the 1990s. The Vexed Parka is characterized by a hood and collar that covers most of the head and face, closing over the mouth and nose but leaving the eye area open. Adam Thorpe, who owns Vexed Generation in partnership

John Ribbe's 'Mummy' dress and Hussein Chalayan's 'Chadors' give women the means to either conceal their entire bodies or expose them at will. Both designers swathe the models in body-conscious sheaths that allow them to draw the gaze of others while remaining anonymous.

with Joe Hunter, explained: 'We made the parka in 1994 and launched it in 1995. It sums up all the ideas and concepts we had about fashion and social surveillance, which we include in most of the other clothes we have designed since.'[14]

During the 1990s, the British government and private industry is estimated to have spent around £3 billion to establish surveillance systems and equipment. 'For a fraction of the cost we made it pretty much redundant as the person wearing the parka can hide his face,' Thorpe said. 'The area in front of the mouth and nose is formed so it can take one of the filters normally used in special neoprene cycle masks.' Though the mask was designed to look and function as a filter, it also concealed the lower half of the face.

The political climate at this time was characterized by protests and civil disobedience in response to the controversial British Criminal Justice Act and the government's implementation of poll-tax reforms. 'At that time we felt that civil liberties were attacked. Freedom of expression, the rights to demonstrate, assembly or party were strategically cut short. Particularly during the poll tax riots it was apparent that although holding an equally valid proposition or opinion, people were confronted with riot police wearing protective kit,' Thorpe said. The parka embodied the difficult juxtaposition of civil liberties and CCTV, becoming a confrontational parody of police riot gear that protected the wearer. 'We were interested in the possible sartorial links between the extremes. For us the garment was a kind of modelling of social situations,' Thorpe said. This enabled the wearer to maintain a public presence and gather social and political information first hand, while remaining anonymous. Thorpe said: 'Our clothing is about communicating what we think that is essential or important. To give people enough protection for them to be able to go out and be active, more involved with their environment in a secure fashion and more individual.'

In the aftermath of 11 September, the scales have tipped heavily in favour of increased surveillance. In London and New York, measures have been taken to heighten security in the public arena, reconfiguring their characteristics into the military-like milieu Hal Foster regards as 'defensible space'.[15] As these systems spread, the search for 'real' enemies becomes a part of urban mythology, as technologies now monitor an unseen, invisible, unidentified and non-specific threat both within and outside the boundaries of the Western world. Our experiences of the urban realm has taught us to decentre our way of looking.

The US government's constant warning of future attacks has been pervasive and unnerving. Mounting fears now bill the skyscraper as a terrorist terrain, and in many respects New York's tall buildings are seen as sitting targets in the 'war' against terrorism. As architecture is no longer viewed as an ultimate refuge and a fortress, clothing is adapting to assume its protective function. US retailers are now stocking 'anti-terrorism' fashion in the form of jackets lined with anti-radiation materials, heavy suits fitted with hoods, masks and gloves to safeguard against biological and chemical warfare agents and 'fashionable' parachutes for the tenants and employees of high-rise buildings, apartments and hotels. According to Safer America, this clothing is intended to feature among the safety devices already commonplace in most homes and offices, such as smoke detectors, surveillance cameras, burglar alarms and first-aid kits.[16]

With garments now able to assimilate the capacities of surveillance devices, the voyeurism ascribed to fashion is moving beyond the act of watching. Brought under the control of the wearer, video and data portals embedded in the garment could record and share the scene with a network of viewers, or equip wearers with the means to evade detection. Anticipating this eventuality, new methods of social control are based on data systems that could soon render visual surveillance outmoded. Sensors, scanning devices and infrared transmitters can track movements within buildings and beyond them; even credit-card transactions can be relayed at a speed that pinpoints an individual's location even before they have left the shop.

As the visual exchanges of life now take place in a culture of hypervisibility, the possibilities detailed here offer a visionary glimpse of the role of surveillance in the near future. The ultimate vision of these technologists and fashion designers is to equip clothing with the elements of protection already afforded by the urban architecture around them. Like the techno fashions that interact with systems embedded in architecture, they form a link in the net gradually evolving into an intimate network capable of interacting with other systems. As visual media increasingly redefine the meaning of visibility in our society, fashion is making a clear response.

Place and Non-place

Urban space is a history of people bound together within the built environment as they struggle to define the territory around them. Rural folk would dress up to visit 'town', while urban dwellers donned their 'country' clothes as they escaped the confines of the city. The polarities of urban and rural dress are paralleled by the formal façades of the city and the rustic architecture of the countryside. The visual coding of fashion frequently corresponds to the type of architecture it was intended to be worn it, transforming the figures moving through urban space into walking signifiers of it.

Urban space underpins a set of relations between objects, products and intangibles such as style and taste in a surreal combination of fantasy and commercialism. The visual fabric of modern life is complex, and the fashion ideals associated with the urban place are frequently elusive. Often fashion represents a mythology of urban life, evoking the glamour of city nightlife and the prestige of social status, paying tribute to the classical woman of fashion rather than expressing the lived experience of the man in the street. This is the sense of artificiality that appealed to Baudelaire, who, in *The Painter of Modern Life*, was the first to equate the modern with the decadent.[17] Baudelaire even argued in favour of the artificial, asserting that such paradoxes lay at the very core of the social infrastructure. Baudelaire judiciously identified the essence of modern space by detecting how the visual transactions of modern life are conducted in social space. But as they occur, the realities underpinning them remain carefully hidden from view.

The artificiality, fragmentation and transience common to urban spaces are, paradoxically, the cohesive elements binding them together. As space is revealed to be hybrid, heterogeneous, adaptive and accumulative, it echoes the mutability that fashion and architecture assume as their mutual existence unfolds. Their combined impact on urban space guarantees that it is never determined by the rules of geometry alone, or shaped exclusively by its physical boundaries.

Modern architecture makes a revolutionary statement, declaring that the liberation of man and the open plan cannot be distinct from each other. As a public place, the ideological goal of urban space would seem to be the total transparency of information. Urban 'places' are organized as signifying spaces that attract or repel a public, who convey meaning through the events and rituals performed in them. In modern cities, public areas and open spaces frequently function in opposition to their intended purpose, fragmenting urban interactions or drawing unwanted habitués. This is especially evident in the zones sustaining leisure, sport, shopping and transport, which are interpreted as the 'non-place' by Marc Augé.[18] Non-places are often the transitional spaces of the urban realm, areas that facilitate the movement of bodies as well as the constant flow of information in and around urban space. In addition to increasing the accessibility of information, they also sustain social control, and the commodification of time through automated systems.

Disconcertingly transitory, non-places are often sustained by commercial activities, often evolving within the type of shopping-mall architecture described by Rem Koolhaas as 'junk space': 'We recycle and vomit all kinds of public space without the support of a public vision,' he explained, 'the private is generating public conditions and using it for branding.'[19] The architecture of junk space, usually dismissed by architectural theorists as aesthetically unappealing or theoretically unsound, organizes society's time and space in accordance with consumer agendas. Social control is emphasized by the presence of law-enforcement officers or surveillance technology. Roy Coleman, a criminology expert, explains: 'It gives the veneer of a sanitised, clean, healthy public space. We are turning our cities into glorified consumption zones.'[20]

The flow of human traffic these areas permit is essential for commerce and communication, while also designating non-places as the space where the visual exchanges of modern life are transacted. Augé believes that non-places have a profound affect on consciousness: they accelerate the consumption of physical space and psychological information while simultaneously increasing the need for physical and psychological protection. The architecture in these spaces is often planned with security measures in mind, and heighten the sense of visuality through the presence of screens, portals, interfaces and other digital modes. Surveillance systems, bright lighting and security centres shape the response of pedestrians, who may make fashion choices based on the senses of security or vulnerability these convey.[21]

Supermodern fashions are produced specifically for urban protection, outfitting the wearer in some of the devices they typically associate with architecture.[22] Jackets, for example, are designed to provide the wearer with a sense of refuge and a degree of protection. Made from bulletproof textiles and equipped with personal alarms and protective visors, they maintain a grim defence against the ever-present threat of violence in the urban environment. Garments like these are enhanced with greater functionality through technologized devices, enabling them to extend the body's mobility and allow it to interact with

Fashioning the Metropolis

other systems. The materials and design ethos behind them highlights their congruency with architecture as their signifiers speak of itinerant structures. Symbolically, they reveal architecture's potential to become mobile by evolving into vehicles that contain and enclose the human form.[23]

Fashion's arrangement of techniques and materials produces wearable shelters that can also be considered a component of social space. Like architecture, fashion demonstrates a capacity to respond to emotion as well as construct it, injecting the personal/individual into the social. Fashion is a representation of what inhabited space can mean, to the wearer as well as to the onlooker. A garment can entrap or protect, or generate an unsatisfied need for protection.

In an era characterized by technology's impact on cultural life, technology's potential to shape urban style and fashion trends outlines its role as the *genius loci* of urban space. Adapting technical systems for everyday clothing may alleviate the fear described by Ellen Lupton as the 'terror of the technological' – as their power is brought under the control of the wearers they appear less threatening.[24] In an ironic reversal, fashion's assimilation of technology could displace its presence in architecture, and decrease the individual's reliance on automated systems.

Jackets with hoods, face masks and visors are intended to redress the urban anxieties, contact phobias and feelings of exclusion that motivate individuals to seek the refuge of architectural space. These are among the first wave of self-contained environments that provide the wearers with heating devices, music systems and communication functions. Although these technological systems are new, the concepts behind them are not – dwellings are fundamental to bringing people together for warmth, safety and protection. As they amplify fashion's primary function as shelter, they also signal fashion's capacity to assume the functions of modern dwellings, as Marshall McLuhan surmised: 'Clothing, as an extension of the skin, can be seen as a heat-control mechanism and as a means of defining the self socially. In these respects, clothing and housing are near twins, though clothing is both nearer and elder; for housing extends the inner heat-control mechanisms of our organism, while clothing is a more direct extension of the outer surface of the body.'[25]

As technology accelerates the interface between fashion and

architecture, the synergy between them could even rearrange the patterns of human association and community, dislocating and dividing individuals into their own self-contained shells rather than unifying them in a single environment. This shift could also reverse architecture's domination of space as fashion gains the means to construct viable dwellings.

Non-places challenge the way we think about space, mirroring the phenomena identified by Michel Foucault as 'heterotopias'.[26] As a reconstituted concept of space, heterotopias are sites that appear to be incongruous or paradoxical, places that mediate socially transgressive practices and often facilitate a sense of danger and defiance. Places such as parks, theatres, galleries, museums and libraries are often designed with the goal of achieving absolute visual and functional perfection, typically based on a mode of social improvement or aesthetic sensibility, but ultimately voicing uncertainty and ambivalence due the multiplicity of meanings ascribed to them. Heterotopias are constructed as spaces that are simultaneously mythic and real, imbued with elements of fictional space and material space.

Foucault's concept of heterotopias has been applied to interpret a range of other spaces, events, geographies and territorialities, leading Foucault to suggest that heterotopic spaces are universal in scope. In an urban context, the presence of heterotopias questions architecture's ability to organize space, as its controls do not include sites of alternate ordering. Heterotopias do not exist in isolation, but become visible through their differences with other sites as they upset spatial relations or provide alternative representations of them.

The fragmentation of heterotopias mediates ambivalent and uncertain expectations among its inhabitants over the meanings and functions of the space itself. Often, heterotopias originate from a mandate of social improvement, and usually continue to bear traces of their original fashioning. As centres for alternative culture (including those of 'outsiders' and the socially disenfranchised) they are places where rejected knowledge is legitimated. Many are reclaimed by urban dwellers and fashioned by graffiti, the constant presence of individuals, groups and events, or even the planting of flowers and trees. The appropriation and reclamation of everyday spaces cuts through the institutional fabric of the urban environment, constructing spaces that stand in opposition to dominant culture. Members of urban subcultures typically inscribe their bodies and clothing with the signs and symbols that manifest as graffiti, re-fashioning the space as they self-fashion themselves. Martin Margiela demonstrated the potency of heterotopias in his early work, charging his collections with spatial and social signifiers. The early 1990s were characterized by the collapse of social orders, as the economy declined and war erupted in the Balkans and the Middle East. Margiela drew parallels between second-hand or abandoned clothing and the derelict urban areas described as 'war zones' or 'wastelands'. He recognized that while an existing space may outlive its original purpose and the social parameters that determine its forms, functions and structures, it is still possible to reappropriate it for use as it is – without necessarily modifying the architecture remaining on it.

Margiela temporarily regenerated some of the spaces in the Paris area by staging fashion shows in their midst. In October 1989, Margiela staged a fashion show on an abandoned plot in Paris's 20th arrondissement. The following spring he presented his collection in a vast warehouse, followed by a fashion show in a derelict car park near Barbés in October 1990. By using fashion to communicate resistance and renewal, Margiela fashioned new identities for both the spaces and the clothes themselves. The fashion space typically ascribed to haute couture (detailed further in chapter 2) took on new meaning as it was deployed in an arena with conflicting meanings and values.

(A)

Fashioning the Metropolis

The concepts of recycling and regeneration expressed in Margiela's garments made a strong comment on the potential uses of heterotopic spaces, while the fashion show itself conveyed the message in a literal sense. As Margiela's innovations highlighted an area of interrelatedness between fashion and architecture, they also identified the degree to which fragmentation pervades many levels of urban material culture. Urban space often exists in different phases simultaneously, as interstitial spaces, as modern conversions designed to preserve eroding buildings, or in developments where old architecture coexists with new structures. Reclaimed, recycled and vintage fashions mirror this paradox, expressing the optimism that urban wastelands can also be redeemed and reconstituted.

Staging a fashion show in a wasteland reveals another layer of social exchanges that can be identified in such heterotopias. Couture fashion's presence in such spaces is ambiguous or unconventional, transforming them into the zones that the cultural theorist Nikos Papastergiadis dubs 'parafunctional spaces'.[27] This term refers to urban spaces in which 'creative, informal and unintended uses overtake the officially designated functions'. Such space can be found in urban space, for example, in the legacies of the 'shanty towns' that existed in New

Martin Margiela often stages fashion shows in subversive venues. Warehouses, car parks and derelict urban spaces amplify the messages of resistance and renewal expressed in his collections, fashioning new identities for both the spaces and the clothing.

(B)

(C)

York until relatively recently. The encampments of displaced people erected in the wastelands of the Hudson River and in Tompkins Square Park resulted from the breakdown of urban space, but invariably signified a resistance to capitalist spatial arrangements. The last of these was demolished in 1997 to make room for multimillion-dollar riverside developments that attempt to erase or even reconcile the fragmentation that existed on the sites previously. As architectural theorists such as Leon van Schaik and Andrea Kahn identify the potentials of such spaces, they outline a new form of urban discourse that interprets them as discarded objects or the modern equivalent of the romantic ruin.

Surprisingly, parafunctional spaces have a history of romantic associations. In the early 1960s, artists began to explore urban junkyards, condemned buildings and abandoned warehouses to reconstitute the debris they contained as artistic materials. As a result, they generated a counter-narrative for urban life as they expanded the scope of artistic practice, incorporating urban relics and rubbish into the genres of modernism and abstraction. In the manner of modernist art aligning itself with urban discourse, Margiela's foray into these spaces establishes a dialogue between the narratives of space and the construction of fashion. To a certain extent, this traces the legacy of past fashions as it recalls the punk sensibilities of ripping, slashing, distressing and piercing clothing and its irrefutable alignment with the 'street'.

While the recent vogue to photograph fashion amidst urban decay is a subtle attempt to refashion these spaces, it is also a trend loaded with deeper ideological significance. Cutting-edge fashion photography rarely sets out to engage with the meaning of clothing, usually intending to make a strong comment about the body, sexuality, or urban life. The ruin associated with industrial areas and urban social housing is typically attributed to poor planning and lack of maintenance, but for many fashion photographers their form and style creates an irresistibly edgy backdrop. As a setting for fashion, non-places and heterotopias are intended to generate a realistic feel, beckoning the viewer into an urban wasteland whose inhabitants have salvaged their clothing, but not the world they live in.

Fashioning the Metropolis

[1]Patrik Shumacher was interviewed by the author.

[2]Michel Foucault (1967), 'Des espaces autres', translated by Jay Miskowiec as 'Of Other Spaces' in *Diacritics* (1986), Baltimore, MD: Johns Hopkins University Press, p22–27.

[3]Michel Foucault (1977), *Discipline and Punish*, London: Penguin.

[4]Martin Jay in Hal Foster (ed) (1988), *Vision and Visuality*, New York: The New Press, p3–20.

[5]Paul Virilio (2000), *The Information Bomb*, London: Verso, p61.

[6]From Rogoff's book *Terra Infirma* (2000), London: Routledge, p30.

[7]Jeremy Bentham (1748–1832) was a British philosopher and founder of the doctrine of Utilitarianism.

[8]Michel Foucault, *Discipline and Punish*, p200.

[9]Foucault, *Discipline and Punish*, p201.

[10]Foucault, *Discipline and Punish*, p201.

[11]Roland Barthes (1997 edition), *The Eiffel Tower*, Berkeley, CA: University of California Press, p8.

[12]Rem Koolhaas (2001 edition), *Delirious New York*, New York: The Monacelli Press, p14.

[13]Fadwa El Guindi (1999), 'Veiling Resistance', in *Fashion Theory*, 3(1), p58.

[14]Adam Thorpe was interviewed by the author.

[15]Hal Foster (2002), *Design and Crime*, London: Verso, p44.

[16]See www.saferamerica.com

[17]See Baudelaire, 'The Painter of Modern Life' in Jonathon Mayne (ed) (1995), *The Painter of Modern Life and Other Essays*, London: Phaidon.

[18]See Marc Augé (1995), *non-places*, London: Verso.

[19]From Rem Koolhaas's talk at the Institute of Contemporary Arts, London, 26 April 2002.

[20]Roy Coleman is a lecturer in criminology at Liverpool's John Moores University, quoted here in Esther Addley's article 'Why the Camera Loves Us' in *The Guardian*, 14 September 2002.

[21]This refers to the garments known as 'techno fashion' which are equipped with wearable technology. The garments typically integrate communication devices, sensors and software into clothing design. Some are equipped with hoods, masks and visors to conceal the identity of the wearer.

[22]See Andrew Bolton (2002), *The Supermodern Wardrobe*, London: V&A Publishing, p 71.

[23]Note that 'vehicle' here is not intended to evoke the transportation function of an automobile. As portable architecture, these clothing structures would remain specifically within urban centres.

[24]In her book *Skin* (2002), London: Laurence King.

[25]Marshall McLuhan (1994), *Understanding Media*, Cambridge, MA: MIT Press, p119–20.

[26]Heterotopia is derived from Greek, meaning a 'place of otherness'. This sense of the term originated in the study of anatomy where it refers to parts of the body that are missing or out of place, or extra growths like tumours.

[27]Nikos Papastergiadis (2002), 'Traces Left in Cities', *Architectural Design* 72(2), p45.

Notes

Mapping Fashion Space

We think about it, talk about it, wear it and perform it. The ubiquitous space of fashion takes shape at precisely the point where traditional definitions of public space – as an urban site, a physical place, a democratic arena – fail. Fashion space is a palimpsest of projects sedimented in time; constantly rewritten, but never erased. It is a field of action for an endless exchange of codes and interpretations, demonstrations of predatory sexuality, promiscuous styles and fleeting identities. Fashion space reflects structures of economic power, social interaction, and commodification, yet provides sites for curiosity, exploration and resistance, routinely deconstructing image and object. It is a stock exchange of status and chic, where the kudos of labels and the reputations of designers boom and crash. A vast territorial sprawl that extends to strange and uncertain destinations, fashion space unfolds in virtually every culture. It travels.

P33_P34

Michiko Koshino's pleating and folding techniques mirror the structures and surfaces of modern architecture. Many of her designs are based on architectonic principles that underpin traditional garment construction with an architectural framework. In this promotional photo, Michiko makes this connection explicit.

(A)

Mapping Fashion Space

Dominated by the ideology of the public sphere, fashion space, like fashion itself, produces a sense that there is something more, some more intense experience, or a wider horizon to be found. Fashion space is both a written source and a visual representation, read like a text and decoded in cinema-like images. Imbricated with fantasy and desire, as well as suffused with memories and nostalgia for other places, fashion space is always heavily romanticized, and imbued with fiction, fetishism and ideals. Unpredictable, immense, uncharted, condensed; lived, performed, directed, reformed – it weaves in and out of public and private, or unravels among theorists and critics like a loose stitch in the conversation. Fashion space is not a given, but a spectrum of possibilities to exploit.

Fashion space distances itself from the 'real'. Preoccupied with manufacturing how reality should look, it produces a wide range of 'looks', trends and body aesthetics; it provides the space for self-fashioning and the ultimate means for mindless conformity. In these spaces, fashion is consumed visually – though it is created for wear on the body, it is conceived and given form as a visual exchange. Many conceptual designers give primacy to theoretical content and visual signifiers, as though the garment's visual significance is intended to outweigh its wearability.

In *The Fashionable Mind*, Kennedy Fraser located the spaces of fashion where 'political strategies are planned, movies made, books published, art exhibits mounted, critical columns turned out, dances danced, editorial polices formulated, academic thesis germinated, wherever people think, speak or create shared forms of expression'.[1] Indeed, fashion space is always pressed into the service of cultural consumption, itself a domain for the production of material culture. Fashion space is inextricably aligned with the dominant modes of production, effectively overlapping into capitalist spectacle, the complex relationship between them unfolding as an emerging rapport rather than a pre-existing given. Henri Lefebvre's foray into such spectacle revealed an insidious ideological force, which he was keen to expose: 'People look, and take sight, take seeing, for life itself. We build on the basis of papers and plans. We buy on the basis of images. Sight and seeing, which in the Western tradition once epitomized intelligibility, have turned into a trap.'[2]

Fashion is not constructed as an object to which movement is added. Movement and garment are

[A]As gallery presentations of fashion become increasingly popular, fashion is encroaching on the spaces traditionally allocated to fine art.

[B]There is a trend among contemporary designers to reveal the process of fashion construction, even moving the tailoring workroom onto the shop floor.

(A)

(B)

conceived as a single act. Like architecture, fashion exists in the dimension of time and movement. A building is conceived and experienced in terms of sequences; it is a modernist transaction of movement and form premised on representing and experiencing. Both architecture and fashion articulate the dimensions and essence of existential space; both create experiential scenes of individuals moving through urban life. In the same way that buildings and cities preserve and reconstruct representations of society, fashion space juxtaposes an archaeology of the era that it references along with the signifiers of the present.

Fashion shows combine the artificiality of the catwalk with the affected movement of the model, presenting garments in a hyperreal context that radically dislocates them from their intended environments.[3] What takes place on the catwalk is fictitious, but it is not experienced by the viewer as artificial, because it appears divisible and repeatable. In the context of everyday life, the garments in a collection continue to be animated by a multitude of wearers against many different backdrops. In this abstract sense, fashion space is intensely cinematic; as the frame of a film is replayed many times and the action reconstituted, the circulation of garments through fashion space repeats these movements.

Fashion space is a synthesis between fiction and realism. In the fusion between them, the act of shaping and forming social identities is constructed and performed. Fashioning a sense of self through clothing, as Iain Borden explains, 'is above all searching for a sense of one's own identity, for a layer in which to drape one's self-image in relation to the city outside'.[4] Looks are created or reconfigured as individual social realities take on new contexts. But the fashioned identity is seldom a constant. It exists as a work in progress: unfinished, incomplete, mechanical, serviceable and renewable. It confronts the imagined with the real, affirming or negating the prevailing assumptions about individual social identity and relative positions in social space. Fashion space represents the means to affirm or deny these convictions though clothing alone, constantly tempering new versions of self-fashioning through other garments.

Expansive in scope, yet fashion space shrinks the distance

between body and building. Conceived as space, garments are designed and constructed as three-dimensional entities rather than façades, and are simultaneously thoughtful and sensual. The spatial enclosures that garments and buildings provide are produced by a convolution of vision and tactility. Numerous sensual transactions occur between the body, the eye and the building as the wearer traverses the space. Fashion space is felt, seen and travelled, implying a kinetic way of experiencing the garment as well as the space itself. In fact, fashion space is premised on mobility, a key consideration of architecture. One of the functions of fashion space is to broker the connection of opposites, in this case bridging the static with the movable, merging privatized space with public existence. Buildings are designed to predict and anticipate the effects of the contrasts and linkages through which the individual must pass; as garments anchor the space around them, they become signifiers of the body's connections to the spatiality of lived experience.

The concept of space presumes the presence of a public. And fashion space is characterized by a distinctive audience with different and often conflicting sensibilities. Michael Warner emphasizes the degrees of fragmentation between them: 'Some publics are defined by their tensions with a larger public. Their participants are marked off from persons or citizens in general.'[5] Multiple publics take shape in fashion space as style tribes form and disperse. Individuals may circulate among several publics simultaneously, or clearly demarcate themselves from the outsider 'publics' who do not conform to the conventions of 'their' space. When fashion space is enacted in built form, it is framed by the kind of architecture that elevates the commodities of fashion to a space that is easily accessible to its patrons but capable of filtering the foreign, alien, unwelcomed 'public'. Retail architecture is one such 'filter', providing means for fashion to manage space and construct it into an enduring image of desire.

The spectacle of fashion takes shape in many forms: the urban place, the retail environment and the virtual world of the Internet. Fashion space masses in and around the garment, itself constituting space and a component of a larger spatial structure. But as the spaces of fashion extend beyond their physical confines, they also draw in sets of relations corresponding to wider social structures. In his

^Fashion retail is being redefined as an interactive forum that allows customers access to some of the designer's databases and stock information. New architectural techniques are employed to make fashion boutiques visually spectacular, so that shopping becomes an event rather than a routine

(A)

analysis of space, Henri Lefebvre wrote that, 'Social space is an encounter, assembly, simultaneity... social space implies actual or potential assembly at a single point, or around that point.'[6] Applied to the spaces of fashion, Lefebvre's model highlights the mechanisms of self-organization and territorial transformations typical of architecture, and their role in constructing classifications of such spaces.

With the new-media revolution of the early 1990s, retail architecture was reconceived as interactive, entertaining event spaces intended to generate a strong brand identity and dynamic experiences between the consumers and the clothing. Fashion websites, in their creative imaging, mirrored these retail environments and formed ephemeral links between them. The global presence of fashion on the Internet reveals that fashion is a vast invisible network. As fashion retail takes shape in the virtual realm, the set of connections it creates mirrors the event space of their physical counterparts.

Today fashion is establishing itself as a space for both speaking and listening, as an open forum where individual expression can connect with the broadest political issues. It is establishing itself as a vehicle for collective reflecting and a site for protest. Fashion space reframes the way we understand and engage with advertising campaigns, virtual space and retail architecture. As the consumption of fashion begins to find new audiences and forge new identities, we can no longer draw a demarcation line around fashion's space.

Shopping for Architecture

Notoriously described as 'the last remaining form of public activity', and 'the terminal human condition', few activities unite the human race like shopping does.[7] Just like fashion, shopping is constantly reinvented, reformulated and redefined, mirroring even the most subtle changes in society. It pervades virtually every arena known to man, to the extent that many social activities are now sustained through shopping. Clothing boutiques are merging with cafés, sports centres, web exchanges and even museums, while public spaces are being reconfigured to incorporate retail units into their development. Urban centres are increasingly characterized by the proliferation of fashion labels and

Mapping Fashion Space

brand logos fixed to buildings, advertisements and shopping bags. Retail architecture is, effectively, rebranding urban space.

Fashion's ability to shape urban space is not a recent phenomenon: Walter Benjamin's fascination with the urban realm drew him closer to social activities like shopping, and he submerged himself in the environments that sustained them. Although unfinished, his remarkable *Arcades Project (Passagen Werk)* updated the functions of both private and public spaces, articulating their importance to fashion, architecture and the role of consumption in constructing identity.[8] Benjamin was quick to identify the porous nature of urban architecture, as he observed that the shopping activities it sustained collapsed the boundaries between private, interior realms and the external world of public space. Intrigued by Charles Baudelaire's somewhat contemptuous appraisal of Second Empire Paris, Benjamin identified a new mode of urban experience as he traced the movements of the rambling dandy he described as the '*flâneur*'.

The *flâneur's* stroll through Paris connected a variety of different sites, introducing the interrelatedness of place as an urban narrative. The flâneur traversed the public spaces built by Haussmann, who rid the capital of its intricate web of tiny streets and replaced them with broad, clean avenues and wide pavements. Haussmann linked the great train stations with the wide avenues, effectively decongesting the city centre and designating open spaces for commerce, leisure and shopping. 'The arcades were a cross between a street and an intérieur...the street becomes a dwelling for the *flâneur*; he is as much at home among the façades of houses as a citizen is in his four walls,' wrote Benjamin.[9] The *flâneur's* daily jaunts negotiated a sphere of intense visibility, one in which the fashions he wore in public attested to the private domains he frequented, drawing attention to his style and position.

Historically, shopping was segregated according to products. Over time, stalls became markets, markets became streets, streets became arcades, arcades became gallerias, and gallerias became department stores.[10] As department stores brought together a variety of goods previously dispersed throughout the city, architecture encompassed the functions of the street, in effect constructing a place without a city. 'The city was now landscape, now a room,' Benjamin wrote. 'And both of these went into the construction of the department store, which made use of the *flânerie* itself in order to sell goods. The department store was the *flâneur's* final coup.'[11]

While women also traversed urban spaces on their shopping jaunts, the city street was predominately a masculine space. Feminists writers have identified the *flâneuse*, the female counterpart of the *flâneur* who enjoyed immersing herself in the city, noticing and observing urban sites and taking pleasure in her seemingly purposeless stroll.[12] The nineteenth-century Parisienne was reluctant to venture into the street without a sense of purpose – shopping, for example, provided an excuse for the idle pleasures of window-gazing and strolling. According to Janet Wolff, 'There is no question of inventing the *flâneuse*... such a character was rendered impossible by the sexual divisions of the nineteenth century.'[13] Like the *flâneur*, the *flâneuse* was creating a space or a path between architecture and place.

In his experience of the city, Benjamin identified many of the parallels between fashion and architecture as they generated representations of space. He regarded urban architecture as an expansive and complex assemblage of objects, people and events – all united by the mores of capitalism – able to transform the possible orientations to life as they contributed to social practices.[14] Benjamin – whose surrealist sensibilities are among the most profound of anyone's on record – documented the diverse objects and strands of information he found in the retail domain, considering their significance in a wider context. These observations foreshadowed the range of uncanny experiences found in retail architecture today: themed environments, surveillance systems, indoor landscapes and the architectural juxtapositions of contemporary styles with period styles. Architectural superlatives have become a commercial need, with retail environments designed to generate spectacular identities, upholding the market economy's drive to create spectacle.

The axis between fashion, architecture and identity is highly topical but, until recently, relatively unexplored. Throughout the world, a new paradigm of retail architecture is reassembling the range of images and identities characteristic of fashion space, changing its perception among consumers as well as designers. As a socioeconomic activity, shopping is also an area of interest among anthropologists and geographers, whose contributions are shaping the type of experiences architecture is designed to evoke. Architects like Rem Koolhaas are redefining the shopping landscape in accordance with such input, and rethinking the identities of those who inhabit it and the meaning of shopping in material culture. This shift in identity even extends to the role of the architects themselves. In their manifesto *Move*, architects Ben van Berkel and Caroline Bos state that 'the architect is going to be the fashion designer of the future' – a move for architecture to become more populist and less elitist.[15]

The 1990s witnessed significant shifts in fashion's business strategies, which emerged as prestigious fashion houses were acquired by global retail conglomerates. The fashion retail environment became increasingly corporatized by marketing initiatives to create strong brand identities with global appeal. Aware of architecture's role in shaping consumer consciousness, fashion's new business tycoons forged an aesthetic dialogue between retail architecture and high fashion. Fashion space began to echo the minimalism of art galleries and modernist museums, and even shadow their geographical locations. Some sites even included exhibition spaces for contemporary art on their shop floors.

The architects behind this new generation of fashion retail openly acknowledge their acquiescence to corporate culture. In this context, retail display, style subcultures and architectural design all seem to have been pressed into the service of commodity capitalism, despite architecture's goal of tran-

Mapping Fashion Space

scendence and fashion's ability to voice resistance. But this has not necessarily been to either industry's detriment: architects such as Koolhaas, Frank Gehry, Future Systems and FAT have interpreted this approach to fashion space with characteristic flair, moving away from the finely detailed minimalism that prevailed in retail architecture for more than a decade. They continue to challenge the status quo of retail architecture, creating twenty-first century environments that collapse the boundaries between public and private space, invert the norms of fashion space and explore a variety of new techniques and materials.

Like fashion itself, a retail boutique is premised on constant renewal, in many respects the antithesis of sustainable architecture. An architect working with fashion retail 'has to understand the marketing of brands, and in particular the need for those brands to constantly to develop and reinvent themselves'.[16] Prada, Gucci, Burberry and Louis Vuitton have all updated themselves as ultra-modern visionaries rather than traditional classicists. The new market they have created directly reflects changing perceptions of luxury and status. Fur coats, ostentatious jewellery and chauffeured cars belong to another era, and fashion designers are changing their products and their public images in line with contemporary sensibilities.

While the goal of architecture is to achieve sustainability, it also maintains a fashion-conscious concern for 'the look' – a principle that serves the interests of its fashion client far beyond the material structure of the shop. Fashion is characterized by its attention to the image it projects and its never-ending quest for new media. Its engagement with architecture signals the use of space as a medium beyond the confines of the garments, extending its reach to a spatial system that transcends the literal function of the garment as well as the boutique. Although this move may appear to integrate the two, it has the effect of distancing them from each other. Architecture remains in dialogue with the objects it encloses or incorporates into its design, and its engagement with fashion space says less about the message of the designer and more about the dynamics of space.
The symbolic incorporation of the garments into architecture is not limited to visual expression alone, but also materializes in the wearer's spatial experience.

The retail milieu reinforces the fashion label's identity through its alliance with architecture, defined in

^Fashion showrooms and flagship shops create an important message about a label's image. Many fashion boutiques are being designed with the same considerations given to an art gallery, using architecture to maximize the impact of the clothing.

(A)

terms of the city surrounding it or within a system of architectural styles. According to Borden, their designs typically conform to several characteristic styles: the utilitarian 'Homeliness' architecture popular with high-street firms such as Marks & Spencer and Next in Britain the period architectural styles common to the 'City Quarter' of neighbourhood areas such as Nolita in New York, 'The Haight' in San Francisco and London's Westbourne Grove; the distinctive 'Narrative' styles of Comme des Garçons and Vexed Generation; the 'Blankness' of austerely minimalistic shops; and the 'Heritage' style of old, established fashion houses.

These distinctive styles create signature identities for both the retail site and the garments they stock. Future Systems' bold concept for the Milanese fashion label Marni follows the seasonal changes of the fashion collections. Marni own prime retail locations in London, New York and Milan, each fashioned in an identical concept that gives the label a signature aesthetic in each shop. The floor is conceived as a floating island, enclosed within a grotto of sloping walls and contoured surfaces. Interior paintwork is intended to change colour each season to compliment the new colour palette expressed in the clothes. Polished to a high sheen, the ceiling juxtaposes flatness and depth, softly mirroring the shop beneath it.

Interiors like this are described as 'promotional architecture', a term introduced by Dietmar Steiner.[17] In this context, the architecture is a commodity in itself, designed to attract a particular consumer identity, as Jane Rendell explains: 'It is the "acting out" of shopping in and through architecture, and the "acting out" of the purchase and use of architecture, that identities are continually constructed and reconstructed.'[18] Rendell also points out that the process of consumption extends to the transaction between client and architect, resulting in the finished design of a building: 'A shift from producing towards consuming has changed our understanding of the environment, resulting in a new focus on the ways in which buildings are used and experienced after completion.'[19]

With mass consumption in mind, promotional architecture targets specific ranges of people by creating an architecture of difference; cultural affiliations, ethnic backgrounds, age demographics and style tribes are all signified within its aesthetic. Conversely, promotional architecture can also bridge the variety of diverse identities evident within the retail market. Pierre Bourdieu, in his examinations of taste and distinction, describes this type of consumption pattern through the social dynamic of negative distinction, in this respect mediated by a pre-existing grammar of material signs.[20] Invariably, these signs register as signifiers of 'high' or 'low' values, as well as a range of values in between; the distinctive identities they mediate are not so much created as they are selected and consumed.

Retail Temples

Flagship shops are a relatively new phenomenon, the most dramatic statement a designer can make about their label. Like the traditional maison de couture in Paris, the building is most likely set in an exclusive area, its exterior architecture and interior design carefully chosen to amplify the image and status of the label. Generous proportions, size and scale are important, as vast expanses of space and a cathedral-like atmosphere never fail to impress.

Jil Sander's showroom in Hamburg signals a return to this tradition. Sander's clothing has often been compared to the Bauhaus architecture of the 1920s, as her designs are characterized by simple lines and a highly sophisticated cuts of fabric. Sander's collections are typically Spartan in print and coloured in muted tones rather than vivid hues, and she is equally economical in her approach to accessories.

After designing a series of critically acclaimed boutiques for Jil Sander world-wide, New-York-based architect Michael Gabellini renovated a nineteenth-century villa outside Hamburg. Gabellini restored the villa's historic rooms (which had suffered bomb damage during the war) to their former glory, renovating the plaster reliefs and repairing the woodwork. The villa's period features created a grandiose backdrop, which Gabellini restored to their original splendour. Gabellini carefully updated the interior with stark and modern lighting and contemporary furniture, and designed a dramatically futuristic glass and steel spiral staircase. The edgy minimalism Gabellini invoked is an essential visual link to the designer's cool, disciplined style and ethos. By successfully juxtaposing the two periods and conflicting style matrices, Gabellini is associating the label with

'Paul Smith converted a Victorian townhouse in London into his flagship shop. The building's heritage emphasizes the 'Englishness' associated with the label, creating a nostalgic backdrop for the collections that brings the nineteenth century dandy to mind.

(A)

Mapping Fashion Space

a history and a pedigree that makes it appear to be a continuation of old-world elegance.

The British heavyweight Paul Smith mirrors Sander's approach in the London town house he converted into his flagship shop. Smith commissioned Sophie Hicks Architects to transform a Victorian mansion in Westbourne Grove into a retail showroom, but structured according to its original purpose as a dwelling.

Accordingly, the house is separated into themed rooms – the Play Room for children, the Archer Room for menswear, the Kensington room for women – fitted with domestic shelving, freestanding wardrobes, pictures, photographs and furniture reminiscent of a family home. Like Sander, Smith's choice of a period environment may initially seem to conflict with the image projected by his other outlets. Yet he is a far cry from the fashion labels that mine the nostalgia of historical association. Liberty, Laura Ashley, Gieves & Hawkes are installed within period architecture to escape the modern world, attracting a consumer that can be likened to a 'heritage tourist'.[21]

In Smith's case, Victorian architecture reinforces the 'Englishness' of his collections, an aspect that adds cultural cachet to his label in countries like Japan and the US. Part of the success of Smith's menswear is its stylized neutrality; his garments have a chameleon-like ability to project a variety of images: the carefree British 'lad', up for a night out; the edgy, urban bohemian donned in cool, casual attire; and the British innovator and sophisticate dressed in design classics. Given the class values associated with a town house and its period décor, Smith is completing his palette of styles by conjuring up the image of a Victorian dandy and connecting with the long tradition it recalls.

Donna Karan, with the city of New York inextricably connected to her label, opened her flagship shop in Manhattan. Set amid other prestigious labels on Madison Avenue, the shop Janson Goldstein designed captures the spirit and energy of the city itself, and features materials typical of the urban scene outside it. Concrete floors, exposed ducts and tubular stainless steel create an atmosphere almost antithetical to the quiet temples of minimalism favoured by Calvin Klein and Cerrutti down the street. Rectilinear forms, glowing Plexiglass cubes and wooden boxes mimic the shapes of the architectural landscape, suggesting that DKNY

[A]While the Prada shop at 575 Broadway boasts an ultra-modern interior, the nineteenth century façade has been preserved. The traditional architecture gives the impression that the label has a long heritage, despite its contemporary image.

(A)

are equipping the city dweller to blend into an urban backdrop.

Issey Miyake's showroom in TriBeCa opened long after the gentrification process had taken hold. Miyake chose his downtown location for its strong industrial aesthetic, which he reconfigured to amplify his fashion ethos, attempting to collapse the structure and surface of his garments into an architectural milieu. Formerly a loft space, Miyake's New York showroom was designed by Gordon Kipping, who exposed the rough ceiling joists and opened the space to the basement displays with walkways of reinforced glass. Frank Gehry was commissioned to fill the space with his signature architectura, fitting the shop with a broken stream of metallic ribbons hovering at ceiling height or placed vertically among the column supports and the staircase. Gehry acquired cachet as an 'art' architect following the critical acclaim of the Bilbao Guggenheim, prompting cultural institutions around the world to clamour for similarly curvaceous buildings that will generate as much publicity for the occupants. Visually, Gehry's signature curvilinear peels succeed in imitating the irregular forms of Miyake's folded, pleated fabrics.

Gehry's fractals and wave formations produce the illusion of movement that characteristically imbues his façades with a continuous surf of gleaming metal. Fragmented into pieces and installed in the Miyake interior, the flow of light and reflection is broken by the titanium panels sitting awkwardly among the deconstructed architecture of the loft. Gehry's sculptural pieces subvert Kipping's architectural design, neither reconstructing the interior in a fresh direction or enhancing its reductionist aesthetic. If the metal ribbons are interpreted as abstractions rather than loose architectural details, they are convincing in their casual, seemingly arbitrary positioning around the shop. In this respect they can be equated to the random placing of safety pins and fastenings in deconstructed fashion. Their floating characteristics bring to mind fabric panels secured with Velcro fastenings – easily attached and removed, reconfigured and replaced.

Any conceptual links between Gehry's design ethos and Miyake's pioneering fashions remain

(A)

(B)

unarticulated, their congruency limited to the mutual contours evident in their twisted forms. Gehry, like Miyake, has produced the equivalent of architectural multiples in the architectura he has displayed throughout the shop. Architecture is packaged like fashion here, reinventing itself as a commodity and engaging with economies of scale.

Prada

Although Koolhaas likens the contemporary practice of shopping to an incurable disease, his retail designs for Prada effectively make him the fashion industry's house doctor. Prada tried to turn its shops into the subject of serious intellectual inquiry when it unveiled plans for new stores in Japan and the US from Koolhaas and Jacques Herzog. Herzog designed London's Tate Modern museum; Koolhaas has just completed the Las Vegas branch of the Guggenheim. The message suggested by Prada's choice of architects and the type of venues they are commissioned to create is far more significant than the clothing designs themselves. The role of architecture goes far beyond subliminal means to relate the type of status with which consumers are expected to regard the clothes, physically designating the monumental significance of the Prada brand.

Both Koolhaas and Herzog are architects who, in a previous age, would have been unlikely to consider planning retail shops and carried on designing art galleries. Koolhaas has revealed plans for Prada 'epicentres' in New York, Los Angeles and San Francisco, three visionary retail units that allow shoppers to traverse their uncongested spaces with distracted ease, supposedly unfettered by the usual signifiers of shopping, and perhaps the

[A] The SoHo Prada shop has been designed as a public space with zones for fashion shows and performances. The display units shown here are suspended from ceiling tracks and moved away when events are planned.

[B] Fashion motifs adorn the walls as well as the clothing.

[C] In a fantastic manipulation of volume and space, Rem Koolhaas scooped out an area below the ground floor to create a performance arena.

[D] Glass and reflective materials channel daylight into the core of the shop.

(C)

(D)

relevance of fashion altogether. Koolhaas's work offers astute critical insights into the sensibilities of the fashion consumer and their perception of architecture.

The first Prada shop to be completed opened in New York in spring 2002, located in the SoHo space previously occupied by the retail shop of the downtown Guggenheim museum.[22] The connection with the art world continues even though it is an uneasy one; Koolhaas's new space upholds the union between fashion, consumerism and art as though they are an indissoluble trinity. By structuring the shop to incorporate seating and a performance space, sales points and the sort of access and egress common to public space, Koolhaas seems to be suggesting that culture is virtually inseparable from commerce. The sweeping expanse of ground-floor space is uninterrupted by walls or false ceilings and retains its original industrial features, attesting to the building's former life as a manufacturing site. Koolhaas's design signals a move away from the white walls, bare surfaces and clean lines of the gallery-inspired retail environment, incorporating the principles of loft culture into his aesthetic and vision of urban chic.

Koolhaas reverses the trend of bringing commerce to art by bringing performance to commerce. In a fantastic manipulation of space and volume, most of Prada's actual sales space has been banished to the lower ground floor, accessed via an amphitheatre of stepped seats that function simultaneously as display surfaces and a performance ring. To create this arena, Koolhaas scooped out an area beneath the ground floor, creating a rolling wave of zebra-wood sweeping from the front of the shop to its centre. Its hollow was conceived as a single spatial gesture, a void within an expanse of linear space, undulating downwards to an abrupt stop before a cinematic projection. After hours, the shoes and accessories usually displayed on the amphitheatre's steps are removed, and the parade of wire cages floating overhead regroup at the back of the store, out of culture's wake.

The interactive technology featured in the lower floor transforms the sales area into a mechanical ballet. Vintage bookcases constitute movable display units; as they glide on tracks, wireless technology guides them into new configurations. Customers engage with the interactivity when they step into the changing rooms. A panel of environmental controls adjusts lighting or surfs Prada's database for stock availability and store location of the current collection. The shop's interactive technology and obligatory promenade through the real-life fashion ramp of the amphitheatre adds a new dimension to the shopping experience. Deliberately charged with energy and amusement, it takes on the characteristics of the 'event space' Koolhaas had in mind. It is surprising that the garments actually play such a small role in the space; rather than designating it as a realm of fashion, the site transacts the consumer's engagement with the architecture of shopping.

Prada seem to have fallen prey to the notion that dramatic physical form is now the most important aspect of the retail environment. While the architecture of Koolhaas, augmented by high levels of media stimulation, is certainly an effective means of drawing in their target audience, what their audience will actually encounter once it starts shopping for clothing seems to have been given much less thought.

Comme des Garçons

Rei Kawakubo has often described the garments and furniture she designs as architecturally inspired, with the architecture of her Comme des Garçons boutiques contributing to the meaning of her work. Kawakubo is married to Adrian Joffe, an architect and the managing director of her business. Kawakubo opened her first Comme des Garçons boutique in Tokyo in 1975, which she developed with the designer Takao Kawasaki, and with whom she continues to collaborate. The early shops were designed as angular, minimal environments, resembling interconnected boxes containing clothes that echoed the architecture. Many of them reflect the enigma of her collections, with one boutique notoriously remaining completely empty, although the collection could be brought out by special request.

Since then, Kawakubo has opened shops throughout the world, each one adopting its own identity, but sharing a consistent treatment of space and light. Kawakubo's interest in architecture has little to do with current trends for brand identity, but results from her mission to create an environment as evocative of her ethos as the clothes themselves. 'I've always tried to create as complete an environment as possible for my clothes,' she told Rasshied Din.

[A–B] Comme des Garçon's showrooms are often as enigmatic and poetic as the clothes Rei Kawakubo designs. One boutique was so strictly minimal that it initially remained completely empty, with the collection brought out by request only.

(A)

(B)

'Comme des Garçons has always been about a complete environment.'[23] Kawakubo does not seek to align the label with high or low culture, but uses her work to negotiate the spaces between them. In Kawakubo's vision, the architecture she commissions is not intended to be separately commodified, but incorporated within the complete environment she strives to achieve. For Kawakubo, the interrelatedness between the intellectual content of the individual clothing, the conceptual themes behind the collection as whole and the spatial experience of the architecture is a single expression.

The Comme des Garçons shop that opened in Tokyo in 1999 juxtaposes the sculptural interior composition of the New York shop. It is not a fashion space conceived with a traditional retail formula in mind, but an environment more in tune with artistic sensibilities than consumer culture. The wall installations were designed by Sophie Smallhorn and Christian Astrigueville, with many sculptural references that recall the work of artists such as Richard Deacon.

The boutique's boundary wall consists of an undulating glass ribbon that tilts outwards as it winds its way around the shop's perimeter. Designed by the London-based architectural firm, Future Systems, the textured surface of the glass is intended to invert the physical distinction between interior and exterior, introducing an element of translucency that makes the garments and products visually accessible to all who pass by. The interior fixtures follow the contours of the glass wall, creating a dialogue between the sinuous outer wall and the inner components of the shop.

The Comme des Garçons shop in New York's Chelsea gallery district is a seamless fit between two cultures of elitism. Kawakubo's use of architecture has moved it beyond the confines of retail and into the domain of art, creating a space that is at once a gallery and a work of art in itself. The shop is accessed via a tunnel of curved steel designed by Future Systems. As tunnel gives way to interior, various volumes of white forms divide the spaces within it, suggesting a series of intimate structures evocative of Richard Serra's 'Torqued Ellipses'. This was especially apparent at one point

Mapping Fashion Space

when Serra's Ellipses were actually being exhibited across the street in one of the Gagosian Gallery's early spaces. They introduce shapes and abstractions that appear arbitrary yet collude with each other to generate positive and negative tensions throughout the space. The structures do not represent any conventional retail design but present customers with a unique environment that tantalizes the eye and displays the garments in a sculptural guise.

Comme des Garçons choice of premises in the West Chelsea area may have cemented the label's alliance with the art scene, but it also represented a larger trend to operate outside conventional fashion locations. During the past decade, lower Manhattan has shown signs of triumphing over Madison Avenue by attracting a number of designer boutiques. The opening of the fashion emporium Jeffrey in the meat-packing district initiated a move to hide in the fringes of Manhattan and be discovered by those in the know, but its gleaming façade flashes as brightly as any Madison Avenue fashion beacon. Alexander McQueen's choice of location further down the street mirrors the edgy, underground venues he chooses for his shows – usually bus garages, warehouses and derelict buildings – and reflects his rebellious image.

For fashion designers seeking a connection with the art world, the celebrated 'funkiness' of the downtown art scene in the early 1990s presented a striking contrast with the bourgeois feel of the Upper East Side, attracting taste makers from the worlds of film, art and music. Many young designers were lured by inexpensive rents and the bohemian romance of downward mobility, or felt that their brand had more impact set amidst the urban decay of TriBeCa, West Chelsea, the meat-packing district and (then) ungentrified SoHo. The dereliction of these areas also invoked a sense of urban authenticity and realism that seemed to authenticate the edgy, urban 'looks' in fashion at that time.

In New York, lofts have been catalysts for movements in visual art, fashion, performance and architecture for several decades. The ultimate in deconstruction architecture, lofts are unique in their intrinsic ability to dissolve the high/low distinctions between urban spaces. They are spaces for living and working, exhibiting art or holding performances, symbolically collapsing boundaries between the domestic, the public, the private.

When renovated as fashion showrooms they invest high fashion with the meaning of the city itself, creating a distinctive urban style. As architecture takes a symbolic step toward reconciling space with the logic of urban cultural centres, it takes fashion with it. The fashion spaces created from former lofts are also a component of bigger projects to 'revive' the city by providing spaces for shopping, egress, cultural activities and the expression of architecture itself. With fashion now fully encompassing these elements of urban place, it questions the extent to which public space will continue to exist independently of retail – or be forever sustained by shopping for fashion.

As fashion boutiques opened downtown they appeared to promote the early steps of urban renewal that had been initiated by community-minded activists in the 1970s. Activists attempted to reclaim derelict housing and improve some of the more unpalatable and problematic spaces in cities to enhance the quality of urban life. Ironically, fashion's role in this movement seems to have undermined it by participating in a gentrification project that ignored pre-existing community values and the needs of the original residents. Sensing a change in the potential of these areas, Manhattan real-estate magnates bought up vast tracks of property and evicted many of the tenants as they redeveloped the area for shopping, restaurants and other commercial amenities.

Vexed Generation

Vexed Generation have always worked outside fashion conventions. The concept behind their shop in Soho, London set out to present fashion in a public forum rather than through insider PR events. Conceived as a public space rather than a boutique or showroom, Vexed Generation created an environment where buyers, press and public could be in dialogue with the clothes and gain a sense of the concepts behind them. Adam Thorpe, one of Vexed Generations designers, explained: 'We put all of our energy in communicating the ideas through the space, through our shop because it is open all year long, anyone can walk in and experienced it. Meanwhile if you do a catwalk show you rely on the press or on those who attend to communicate what they've seen or they've felt to other people.'[24]

In architecture things are generally built to be longer lasting than they are in fashion, but Vexed Generation's garments and shop design inverted this concept completely. The high-durability techno textiles they use make clothes that are almost impossible to wear out are far more durable than the paint, carpet and wallpaper that inadvertently wear away. Rather than constantly renovate and redecorate like most shop owners do, Vexed Generation decided to create an interior based on thematic installations, collaborating with designers, artists and musicians to create unique environments for each collection.

The first of these, opened in 1995, reflected Vexed Generation's strong commentary on the escalation of surveillance as discussed in chapter 1. The front window was rendered opaque with several layers of white paint, with only a video monitor left visible. Onlookers could observe the shop's interior by looking into the video screen. By placing the shop under the surveillance of passers-by, Vexed Generation reversed the normal security measure of recording customers by placing the screen in the public gaze.

The following year environmental themes were featured. Vexed Generation moved their shop upstairs to the first floor, where walls and display units were made from inflatable bags powered rhythmically by an air compressor. The effect was that of 'breathing' walls and 'breathing' clothes, echoing the role of trees functioning as the 'lungs of the planet'. In its next phase, the shop was transformed into a grow room. The garment displays were aligned in rows, like fields of crops waiting to be harvested. Around them fast-growing ivy, clematis and

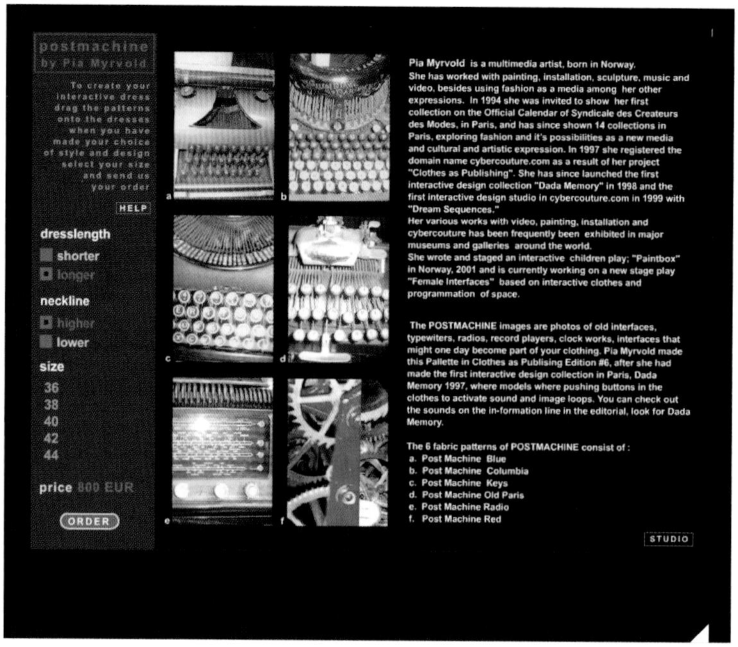

(A)

passiflora grew up through the clothing, sprouting from necklines and cuffs, drawing attention to nature's bounty. Blackboards lined the walls, inviting customers to share their personal details as a statement encouraging public access to information.

The plasticine floor in the gallery space started off as pure blue surface that would be worn down with each footprint, recording the traces of each visitor and accelerating the process of erosion day by day. 'We were interested in its weathering capabilities and in concepts of quality and tradition and longevity,' Joe Hunter explained. 'It was also our Luddite approach to surveillance, because we were tracking people without using digital technology,' he said.[25] At one point the floor was covered in £750 worth of one-penny coins to illustrate the concept of safety in numbers: large sums of money could be accessed by the public yet not be removed.

The shop was later themed 'A Stitch in Time', featuring an installation called 'The Label Database'. Rather than fitting conventional heating insulation and concealing it with a flush surface, the shop's interior was padded with the same quilting used in the garments. 'We did that to slow things down,' Thorpe explained. 'Before that people could scribble their names and orders on the wall, but we put the padding up so that they could embroider their names, which took them longer to do. Later on we printed out labels for each order that had the customer's name on it. One was sewn into the clothes, the other was sewn up on the wall, mimicking the way big retailers build a name and address database to keep records of their customers,' he said.

Vexed Generation's work tends to ignore short-term trends,

^Web architecture often mimics built environments, with 'galleries' and 'rooms' where e-commerce transactions can be made. Cybercouture.com goes a step further by creating an interactive 'studio' where visitors can design their own garments in cyberspace.

notions of exclusivity and product branding by placing emphasis on protection and durability. They also innovate by guaranteeing high performance standards for their clothes, achieved through hi-tech textiles and functional design. 'With our garments, and as a philosophy, we go against the main stream of production where the products are designed to last a determined period of time through concepts of cheapness and disposability. We are fundamentally against that and that's why our garments are intended to endure keeping their qualities,' Thorpe said. Vexed Generation's uncompromising perspectives on the standards and values of their designs outlines a durability of materials and structure more common to architecture than fashion. As they eschew the transient styles of fashion and the use of outmoded fabric, they inject fashion with an element of sustainability that promises to extend its value long after its shelf life.

Virtual Re(tail)ity

> 'What is an ideology without a space to which it refers, a space which it describes, whose vocabulary and kinks it makes use of, and whose code it embodies? What would remain of the Church if there were no churches?'
> Henri Lefebvre[26]

The answer is nothing, of course, since the Church not could guarantee its survival otherwise. Indeed, the institution of fashion would not survive without its retail temples...or could it? When Lefebvre wrote these words, it is unlikely that he conceived of a virtual space on the scale of the World-Wide Web or the global impact of e-commerce. In its mission to conquer the space around it, fashion is transacted within multiple realms, both physical and virtual. Fashion's virtual 'existence' defies containment by garments or architecture, but is no less potent in its ability to construct identities and mediate physical transactions. In fact, the boundaries between the real world of fashion and its virtual counterpart have already begun to blur.

Websites, in their creative imaging, are conceived as built environments. Although the digital frameworks are known as 'web architecture', the concept of architecture used in the Web context defines a new architectural language, designating ethereal spaces as 'rooms', 'floorplans', 'frames' and 'departments' (many US e-commerce sites refer to their opening page as the 'storefront'), accessed via navigation tools that move between the 'floors', 'levels' and 'voids' of the site's infrastructure. As the new-media revolution took hold in the early 1990s, fresh approaches to retail architecture gained momentum, and fashion boutiques were reconceived as interactive, entertaining event spaces able to generate a strong brand identity and dynamic experiences between the consumer and the product. These principles are paralleled on the Internet, where the storage, circulation, marketing and classifications of fashion amplify the consumption of its material counterparts.

The relationship between physical and virtual architectural forms charts the power that the image has over those who perceive it. Digital technologies arbitrate a climate of 'technical territorialisation' that gives digital architecture the capacity to exert what Mark Goulthorpe describes as, 'not so much an architecture, as the possibility of an architecture, a "reverie" as to a new (digital) condition'.[27] Images of this type are used in architecture to map the project's scale and proportion by means of digital technologies, generating a virtual mode that enables the spectator to 'tour' it. This is one of many creative platforms leading to the final architectural form, but one that is fully resolved within itself. In the thinking of Gaston Bachelard, this type of uninhabited domain constitutes the image of a habitable shell with the capacity to reconstruct architectural images, inviting 'daydreams of refuge'.[28] Written in 1958, Bachelard's text on 'Nests' seemed to anticipate the conditions of the digital image, describing a spectral environment that can continually adapt and be recalibrated to suit other needs. Likewise, the fashion website deploys texts and images representing the habitable spaces of garments, displaying showrooms and workshops that the visitor is symbolically invited to conquer and consume.

Mapping Fashion Space

While cyberspace forms ephemeral constructs between sites, they continue to be bound to physical spaces. Had Foucault been alive to navigate fashion websites he might have interpreted such online spaces as heterotopias. Although they are not lived spaces, they have the curious ability to link to all other fashion spaces in a way that contradicts, neutralizes, inverts or reflects the sets of relations they designate, in ways that are difficult to gauge fully. While fashion's presence on the Internet continues to gain momentum, fashion websites are also laboratories where new ways of understanding the ephemera generated by fashion images and architectural representations can be attempted.

Most fashion sites are analogous to their retail counterparts, their tone and image often constituting annexes to the shop's architectural style. The categories of retail architecture Iain Borden outlined earlier are reflected in the type of web architecture retailers apply to their e-commerce sites. The 'Homeliness' of retail locations owned by such high-street firms such as Marks & Spencer is reflected in their conventional appearance and the user-friendly structure of their websites. Just as their clear-glass façades and signposted shopping areas effect an image of normality to the world, their navigation tools and search engines make shopping straightforward and easy. The 'Blankness' of the minimal architecture styles favoured by Jil Sander and Issey Miyake is reflected in the streamlined chic of their web counterparts.

Hedi Slimane, Dior Homme's chief fashion designer, directed his web team to design a site that mirrored the architecture of the studio at 40, rue François 1er in Paris. 'We do not want it to look like a fashion site,' Slimane explained, and developed a site consistent with the design ethos channelled into the retail space where they are presented to the public.[29] The sounds, visuals and information made available on the site are designed for the visitor to 'discover' rather than navigate, echoing Slimane's manifesto to create menswear based on his intuition rather than traditional processes.[30]

It is insightful that Slimane is re-creating the feel of his studio, charging the label's virtual component with a sense of urban place. While it is physically anchored to the prestigious 8ème arrondissement – an area associated with exclusivity and elitism – its virtual dimension unfolds in a less elitist realm. Entering the website permits visual access to the collection and to the transmission of a message direct from the designer. But as the site includes images of the retail showroom and scrolls '40, rue François 1er' across the screen, the collection is never liberated from its physical confines. Neither is the message from the designer, although the world-wide access afforded by the Internet may allow it to reach an audience far beyond the 8ème arrondissement. Emphasizing Dior's real-world location, though distant in place and time from the site's visitor, reinforces the 'real' experience by grounding both clothes and designer in a legitimated or 'real' place.

Helmut Lang prefers virtual environments to 'real' ones, transcending the legitimacy and prestige that physical locations confer to his collections. Lang's clothes project a utilitarian, often futuristic aesthetic that stands in opposition to the period architectural surroundings of his retail outlets. In 1998 he decided against a catwalk show, instead sending journalists videos and CD-ROMs of the collection during New York Fashion Week. By 2001 the Internet had become Lang's primary show platform, broadcasting his spring/summer collection to an international audience. This move forward mirrors the recent shift to hold fashion shows in urban wastelands or derelict buildings (à la McQueen and Margiela) instead of holding them in showrooms or the official venues designated by Fashion Weeks in New York, Paris and Milan. The range of signifiers inherent in such spaces often creates a startling contrast to the designer's work.

As retail environments and fashion-show platforms are 'fashioned' by architecture to create both real and perceived boundaries, so too must a fashion website demarcate its limits. Web designers use spatial elements to set the initial terms for the visitor's experience, ultimately trying to locate the virtual within signifiers of the 'real'. Each feature of the site's architecture fulfils a specific purpose beyond its aesthetic value, designating the site's function, contributing to the mood and atmosphere associated with the collections and projecting a specific image to attract a target audience. The site condenses the visual transactions of fashion space – catwalk shows, retail display, photography, cinematic presentations – and projects them onto an international platform for a global network of viewers.

Choosing web design, like finding a compatible architectural style, is a question of expressing the label's image in a visual vocabulary of signs and images. Despite the extreme importance that fashion retailers attribute to brand image, fashion websites are often a series of flat, static catalogue pages. Leading web designers make sites visually stimulating through their choice of web architecture, savvy texts, audio tracks, slide shows, animation sequences, eye-catching pictures and special effects. Like a magazine spread, web images also produce a sense of texture and depth that mimics a three-dimensional world of surfaces. The best fashion websites are viewed as a fragment capable of representing the whole, strategically engineered to incite the visitor to interpret the label's sense of identity and product image.

Laird Borrelli, author of *Web Fashion Now*, documented three basic types of fashion websites.[31] Fashion's first presence in cyberspace manifest as the 'vanity' sites created to boost the image of the brand and communicate the feel of the latest collections. Next came the editorial sites that produce cyber 'e-zines' (many of which are set up by published magazines), followed by the 'sale' sites established to attract e-commerce trade, taking the visitor on a virtual tour of garments and merchandise exactly like their retail counterparts. These images turn viewers into virtual architects, who

Mapping Fashion Space

erect rooms, buildings and entire neighbourhoods in their imaginations as they progress through the site.

As technology progresses, multimedia websites have been created that engage with fashion rather than merely selling it. Websites featuring collaborations between fashion designers, visual artists, architects and product designers emphasize fashion imagery as a genre rather than a promotion. Diagnostic sites present a platform for discussions of fashion as a medium, looking at industry ethics, body aesthetics and documenting the changing meaning of fashion itself; these differ from editorial sites in their 'open forum' approach, and almost never feature advertising. Interactive sites invite the visitor to participate in garment design by selecting and customizing their choice of garment. Other interactive sites provide video-game entertainment: 'Shooting Supermodels' is a high-fashion Space-Invaders-type sport, 'Dress Up Jesus' outfits Christian icons with both summer and winter wardrobes and 'Shopping Rangers' challenges the visitor to bag designer goods as they take on the mall maze. Visitors to these sites develop respective identities as shopper, audience and participant, or all three simultaneously.

For many consumers, shopping is the ultimate social experience, an activity that Rasshied Din points out has, 'created trade routes across continents, and been the reason for the growth of market towns and gathering places'.[32]

The Internet's capacity to locate goods provides an efficient means of marketing brands that do not offer mail-order distribution, making them available far beyond urban locations. To Hal Foster, mail-order shopping initiated the expansion of urban identities, a move that the Internet continues to facilitate. 'Suddenly there was a Saks or a Brooks Brothers in your hometown too, and you no longer had to go to Manhattan physically or vicariously via *The New Yorker*, to appear metropolitan,' he wrote. 'You could get it at the mall and now at the website.'[33]

'Virtual retaility' holds fantastic potentials for advertising and promotions that even encourage visits to retail shops that were previously unknown to the shopper. However entertaining it may be to surf the Internet, the virtual interface between the garments and the shopper cannot replace the excitement and stimulation encountered on a shopping trip. Fashion boutiques are sensory realms, where consumers can gain a tactile experience of the product, feeling its tex-

[A–B] Pia Myrvold launches a new cybercouture collection online each season. Virtual visitors use their mouse to choose from a range of motifs, such as this pattern based on images of architectural structures.

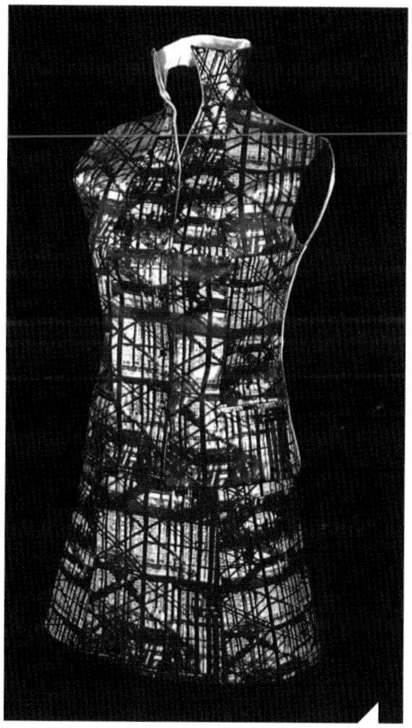

(A)

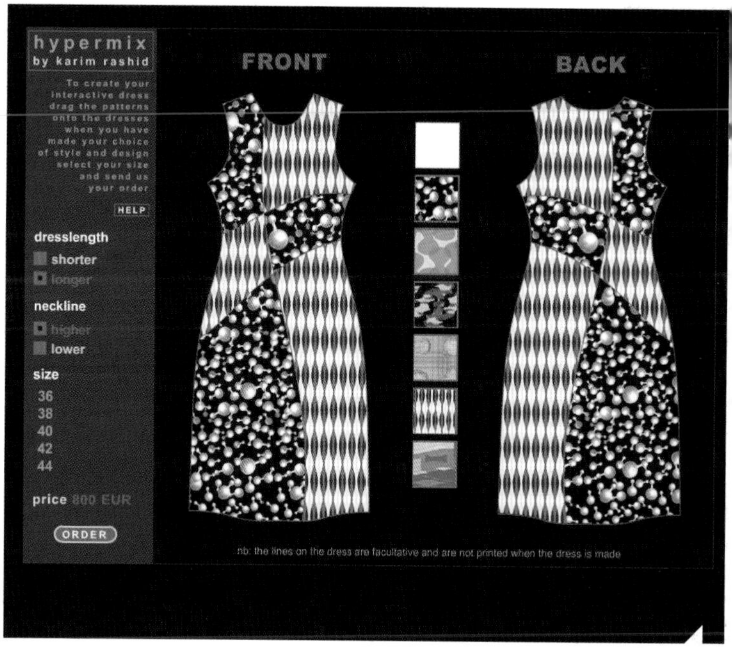

(B)

ture and finish while trying it on. Such stimulus is absent in the virtual world, as it is in the mail-order shopping catalogues that established a precedent for home shopping more than a century ago. In the United States, the Sears Roebuck catalogue is practically a national institution.

Many designers prefer to exist as an electronic entity, investing their website with many of the commercial attributes they would assign to a retail location. Others, such as French designer Dorothée Perret, use their website as a gallery for showcasing works-in-progress, collaborative projects and a range of information about the inspirations behind the collections. Canadian hat designer Alison Howell is based in Los Angeles but sells her collections world-wide. According to Howell, few shoppers actually buy hats online because, 'buying hats is a vanity exercise, people need to try it on and view it from several angles,' she said. 'It is essentially an architectural experience too, because you need to reference its scale in the context of a room or a building to make sure its proportions work for you.'[34] Howell launched her website, www.alisonhowell.com, to establish a dialogue with her customers around the globe and transmit their feedback into her collections.

The Paris fashion vanguard Collette supplements its sales-oriented main site with a sister site, www.ilovecollette.com. The site invites viewers into 'the world of Collette', a virtual world representing its material counterpart through line drawings of the shop's interior. The shop's architecture has been redrawn to scale in a cartoon-like environment that gives it a free, young feel. For the designer, Craig Robinson, the idea was 'to do something that represented the phrase "I love Collette" and to make the store look like it was alive, not a showroom'. Robinson's vision for Colette's virtual shop presents a Utopian dreamscape that gives consumers an idealized new world, streamlined and undisturbed by other shoppers, long queues, loud music or rude sales assistants. The site provides the ultimate in-store experience that even the most cunning e-commerce websites are unable to replicate.

While the interactive potential of the Internet is still relatively uncharted by most e-commerce sites, the Paris-based fashion designer Pia Myrvold has identified the possibilities that cyberspace holds for fashion. Myrvold set up her website, www.cybercouture.com, as an interactive fashion forum in which her clients can design and order a range of garments. She operates within the traditional horizons of fashion design and manufacture, but reconfigures them into her own system of web interactivity. For Myrvold, cyberspace is both process and agent: 'The Internet had none of the limitations of other media; sound, image, film, text or voice could overlap freely and create new contexts,' she said. 'I also realised that a truly interdisciplinary universe could be linked by technology to the clothes and from the clothes into practical reality.'[35]

Myrvold launches a new collection on cybercouture.com each season. Each Cybercouture garment is initially displayed in white; once selected, the image rotates three-dimensionally to display the garment's construction and detail. Clients can browse among the current range of prints, or drag them onto the garment to get a scaled view of how the pattern will look on their choice of garment. While they are 'shopping', clients are free to experiment with a range of options. Some garments can even feature several different prints – the sleeves can be made in one print and the body in another. Each order includes the precise measurements of the client, as each piece is made to a custom fit. The clients email their orders to Myrvold's centralized workshop, where the garments are cut according to specification, printing the selected patterns via a heat process. Skilled craftspeople then sew the garments together and ship them to the client more or less immediately.

Myrvold's departure from conventional fashion resulted from her mission to circulate the ideas behind her collections – essential to grasping what each garment represents – simultaneously with the clothes. Parallel to the fashion collection is the editorial space on the website titled 'Clothes as Publishing' that expands Myrvold's ethics and concepts textually through her collaborations with artists, writers, musicians and architects. Cybercouture collections have featured the work of visionary architects like Winka Dubbeldam, Jean Nouvel and Bernard Tschumi, who contributed blueprints, drawings, photographs and writings that Myrvold configured into fabric prints. Myrvold's collaboration with Tschumi began in 1992, when he commissioned her to create an installation as part of an architectural event held at Parc de la Villette. Myrvold stretched scaffolding and textile panels for five hundred metres along the canal in an interactive structure that mimicked a garment's role in containing and surrounding space.

Aspects of cybercouture.com's interactivity can be related to the rules and components of a video game, with clients adopting the role of a player or a 'gamer'. Myrvold's online discussion forums, together with the interactive garment construction, gives Cybercouture the potential to function as a social device that facilitates individual expression and network communication. The site's parallels with public space are obvious; as architecture shapes and defines spatial forums for social interaction, cybercouture.com also brings individuals together in its virtual forums. Over time, this ethos will forge alliances with other interactive websites as they evolve, perhaps enabling the fashion user to create a customized wardrobe from head to toe.

Fashion's foray into the virtual domain signals a significant shift in the modes through which clothing is produced and consumed, potentially revolutionizing its value and meaning. Giving the wearer direct involvement in the construction process makes the interactive platform a hands-on creative process that dislocates the immediacy that characterizes fashion. It also invokes questions of authorship, where the designer no longer assumes responsibility for the finished product. As a new fashion culture emerges, the idea that fashion can be a communicative device as well as an interactive platform in itself is driving both its physical and virtual components forward. And with the delivery of customized garments to the Web user's home, reality has never seemed less virtual.

As the physical space of the crossroads now gives way to the virtual space of the Internet, the pervasiveness of the built environment is challenged by fashion's expanding consumption of urban space and Internet domains. As these disparate realms divide human activity they also signal significant shifts in the modes through which clothing is produced and consumed. In the retail environment, the emerging role of art and performance suggests fluidity between fashion space and the role of the gallery. For decades, exhibitions featuring historic dress have brought fashion into the spaces of galleries and museums; now art forms and cultural artefacts are reversing this trend in a movement to blur fashion and art – at least in the eyes of the general public.

Like the flâneur's stroll through Paris that connected different sites within a spatial framework, the interrelatedness of place continues to be a narrative that depends on the role of the public. The presence of the public in fashion space unites action and contemplation, including a multiplicity of regimes and conflicting forms, embodied movements and sensations. Such actions are monitored by structures of knowledge that chart their mobility and responses in cyberspace as well as urban space, creating strategies to regulate and frame the encounters, assemblages and systems of representation that map fashion space.

Mapping Fashion Space

[1]Quoted in Susan Sidlauskas (1982), *Intimate Architecture: Contemporary Clothing Design*, Cambridge, MA: The MIT Committee on the Visual Arts.

[2]Henri Lefebvre (1991 edition), *The Production of Space*, Oxford: Blackwell.

[3]Although many garments are created specifically for the fashion show and never manufactured, they are generally conceived for wear in public space.

[4]Iain Borden (2000), 'Fashioning the City', *Architectural Design*, (70)6, p14.

[5]Michael Warner (2002), *Publics and Counterpublics*, New York: Zone Books, p56.

[6]Lefebvre, *The Production of Space*.

[7]From Rem Koolhaas's talk at the Institute of Contemporary Arts, London, held 26 April 2002.

[8]Drawing specifically on the sections titled 'Fashion', 'Flâneurs' and 'Dolls', in Walter Benjamin (1999 edition), *The Arcades Project*, Cambridge, MA: Harvard Belknap Press.

[9]Walter Benjamin (1999 edition), *Charles Baudelaire*, London: Verso, p37.

[10]Benjamin marks this transition as occurring in the aftermath of the July Revolution, when 'for the private citizen, for the first time the living-space became distinguished from the place of work' (Charles Baudelaire).

[11]Benjamin, *Charles Baudelaire*, p171.

[12]See Deborah Parsons (1999), 'Flâneur or Flâneuse? Mythologies of Modernity' in *New Formations* 38, p91–100.

[13]Janet Wolff (1990), 'The Invisible Flâneuse: Women and the Literature of Modernity' in *Feminine Sentences: Essays on Women and Culture*, Berkeley, CA: University of California Press, p34–50.

[14]Benjamin regarded architecture as a dialectical image, rooting his philosophical understanding to a historical concept.

[15]See Ben van Berkel and Caroline Bos (2001), *Move*, Rotterdam: Nai Publishers.

[16]Rasshied Din (2002), *New Retail*, London: Conran Octopus, p13.

[17]See Steiner's article 'Promotional Architecture' in *Architectural Design*, (70)6, p20–3.

[18]Jane Rendell (2000), 'Between Architecture, Fashion and Identity', *Architectural Design*, (70)6, p11.

[19]Rendell, 'Between Architecture, Fashion and Identity', p9.

[20]See Pierre Bourdieu (1984), *Distinction: A Social Critique of the Judgement of Taste*, London: Routledge.

[21]See Borden, 'Fashioning the City'.

[22]See Rem Koolhaas, Miuccia Prada, Patrizio Bertelli and Michael Kubo (2001), *Projects for Prada Part 1*, Milan: Prada Foundation Editions.

[23]Din, *New Retail*, p156.

[24]Adam Thorpe was interviewed by the author.

[25]Joe Hunter was interviewed by the author.

[26]*The Production of Space* (1991 Edition).

[27]Mark Goulthorpe (2002), *Architectural Design*, 72(2), p20.

[28]Gaston Bachelard (1994 edition), *The Poetics of Space*, Boston, MA: The Beacon Press, p107.

[29]Quoted in Laird Borrelli (2002), *Web Fashion Now*, London: Thames & Hudson, p43.

[30]www.dior.com/diorhomme.

[31]See Borrelli, *Web Fashion Now*, p43.

[32]Din, *New Retail*, p8–9.

[33]Hal Foster (2002), *Design and Crime*, London: Verso, p5.

[34]Alison Howell was interviewed by the author.

[35]Pia Myrvold was interviewed by the author.

Notes

Dressing the Void

The search for hidden meaning mines the labyrinth of spaces between theory and form, exposing a vast rhetoric of distances, destinations, habitations and voids. Spawned by post-structuralist discourse, investigation of the gaps between culture and meaning reflects a modernist drive to identify the metaphorical and material cores underlying the 'true', the 'real' and the 'beautiful'. This mission reveals a double logic of conservation and demolition, as both physical and philosophical principles are deconstructed and reconstructed, or remain unconstructed in the limbo between void and space. Deconstruction, reconstruction and unconstruction are essentially spatial concepts, capable of contextualizing several incompatible sites within a single framework. Each has the capacity to function as a dialectical crowbar, applied to interpret a range of aesthetics, forms, installations and events.

Locating these sites is a point of fascination for architects and fashion designers alike. Nowhere are the stakes higher for deconstructive discourse than in the congruencies between them. As theorists and conceptual designers work in a method almost antithetical to construction, structure and technique provide a rich source of innovation that surpasses traditional modes of decoration and detail. In fact, the void seems to have emerged out of architectural discourse's long-standing engagement with the anti-fashion movement in clothing design. Revealing the void already hidden within deconstructive discourse opens up more radical possibilities for both architecture and fashion, offering a means of rethinking the institution of architecture, while using architecture to rethink the meaning and construction of fashion.

Few contemporary architects are content with concepts that interpret space as strictly internal and external; a variety of structures within a building transmute space into internal and external divisions throughout. While the boundary wall traditionally designates one surface as interior and the other as exterior, it simultaneously separates and links inner and outer spaces. This principle extends throughout a building, dividing its spaces on a smaller scale during the course of construction and habitation. To fashion designers, fabric also creates a boundary wall, positioning access points at collar and cuff as space flows from an outer surface to an interior void.

The construction of both garments and architecture creates spaces that are denied from sight, generating fantasies of inclusion and exclusion. Techniques of deconstruction, reconstruction and unconstruction can be deployed to penetrate such structures and invert their contents, making all spaces visible in a single view. In this respect they further the modernist ambition to eliminate 'excessive' details, purging extraneous features to convey a sense of the essentials. Exposing the structure's framework imbues the garment with a new sense of integrity based on the transparency it projects. This juxtaposition unites garments and architecture in a continuous panorama linked to other deconstructed sites: regenerated urban spaces, avant-garde fashion, virtual environments and fashion photography.

Revealing the void implies that there is nothing left to view. But paradoxically, exposing the void does not dissipate it, but only dispels the ambivalence and uncertainty previously attached to it. This manifests as the 'otherness' ascribed to the void, which is established via its relationship of difference to other spaces. Yet the void actually fills a role as an event space, as the devices of deconstruction and reconstruction uncover some of its meanings. Exploring the void highlights its capacity to function as a repository of knowledge and a measurement of time, as it is studied, examined and theorized with the scrutiny typically assigned to archived objects.

The current fascination with the void can be interpreted as an attempt to explore the limits of material and intellectual expression. The drive to eliminate excessive or extraneous ornamentation and leave almost nothing behind focuses the process more directly on gauging what the true essentials of form may be – ironically exploring the formless to do so. While these analytical perspectives on some of the principles of space and construction relate to fashion and architecture, they also reflect a wider move in society to control space, define it and designate a comprehensive model of spatial ordering. Architecture has long had a frame of reference for these principles which are mitigated by postmodernist theory, post-structuralist discourse and through the insights of architectural theorists. But this discourse dawns on fashion's horizon more recently, moving investigations of fashion space beyond the surface of the garment and into the void it subsumes. In the guise of reconstruction, deconstruction and unconstruction, discourses of space present a means to excavate critically the hidden reaches of fashion's depths.

Reconstruction

> 'Without any deformation or transformation we have only information.'
> Peter Eisenman[1]

The unspoken assumption of all design activity is that it results in a 'finished' product. Yet fashion designers and architects continually question this principle, asking if an object can ever be considered wholly complete? Undeniably, there comes a moment when design methodology and construction activity stop and 'habitation' begins; wear and tear quickly take hold, ageing and deterioration are inevitable. But what may appear to be a finished building is often merely a stage in the structure's evolution. Architects attempt to counter urban decay by regenerating existing spaces, preserving their historical features and expanding them with modern extensions.

Such spaces can be understood as interstitial: they are spaces in-between stages, buildings in transition, architecture under renovation and places subjected to reconstitution. Interstitial spaces often voice reconstruction, a concept employed by architects to describe their efforts to preserve derelict structures. As they reconfigure outmoded styles or introduce new aesthetics, new architecture appears to triumph over old, ensuring that vestiges of obsolete architecture are given a certain definition and identity they might not have had otherwise. The structures that result are imbued with inherited knowledge, imbricating their present and future with intertextual narratives.

Reconstruction does not necessarily present an authentic sense of history; it can also be a means of eliminating disgraced monuments, flawed ideology and unpopular architecture. Fredric Jameson was quick to point out that the role of reconstruction exists 'not merely as a matter of rebuilding but also as a matter of strategic demolition', presenting questions of historicity as architects determine which vestiges of the past are allowed to survive and the form in which they will be retained in.[2] Reconstruction may also generate a vogue for classical styles and historical features unrelated to the period of the structure being preserved. As old buildings threaten to collapse or disappear, nostalgia for them arises, as Svetlana Boym pointed out in *The Future of Nostalgia*: 'The stronger the loss, the more it is overcompensated with commemorations, the starker the distance from the past, the more prone it is to idealisations.'[3]

Urban space is an open system of rules transformed by additions, accumulations, renovations and reappropriations of existing structures, characterized by successive cultures of habitation and reinterpretations of function. In Europe, urban space is rarely transformed by outright replacement or elimination; recent trends to 'gentrify' poor neighbourhoods and regenerate industrial areas exemplify the tendency to redistribute power and space rather than construct it anew. These urban interventions and new typologies of habitat are not reliant upon tabula rasa, as they may be in other cultures, but demand the reconstruction and reuse of existing urban materials.

Reconstruction emerged in fashion at a time when projects were launched to rebuild Berlin, retrofit the earthquake ravaged harbour area of San Francisco and restore war-torn Beirut and the ruins of Sarajevo and Dubrovnik. The framework for architectural reconstruction evolved against a socioeconomic and political backdrop to which urban projects responded. As construction sites became a prominent feature in the urban metropolis, fashion designers began echoing the reconstructivist theme in their collections. Reconstruction first appeared in fashion as garments that appeared to be in mid-manufacture, transformable fashions that literally reconstruct other forms, or in reclaimed clothing and vintage materials given new life as modernist chic.

As spaces change and transpose between phases of development or social use, their classifications and representations hang in limbo. Typically, they are liminal realms, conspicuous in their lack of signification. Excluding spaces of historic ruins, these areas can be understood as interstitial space – their symbolic meanings and practical functions remain unfixed and ambivalent while they are being redeveloped. They project multiple meanings but rarely ever manifest as event spaces or spectacle. As they progress from one phase to the next, their temporary transition blurs their meanings, signifying interstitial space as ambivalent, unrepresentative and uncontrolled. Not only does this constitute their apparent difference to adjacent sites, but also their contrast to spaces established for the control of disorder, such as prisons, hospitals, schools and asylums. The disorder of interstitial spaces does not derive from the sites themselves, but is established via their relationship of difference to other spaces.

Just as abstraction and conceptual thought, two of the overriding tropes of the twentieth century, cast doubt over architecture's value of representation, reconstruction attested to architecture's ability to symbolize the contradictory relationship between the old and the new, the abandoned and the developed, the imagined and the real. The union of the old with the new presents an enigma, suggesting that this type of architecture will always be imbued with historical meaning despite its modern form.

Ruins are satisfying to the eye because of the memories they evoke. Whether real or imagined, they indulge the viewer in the fantasy of creation, suggesting that what was once there could be reconstructed and redeemed in contemporary vision. But when ruins are physically reconstructed they reflect an aesthetic crisis, the reconfiguration of their

Dressing
the Void

(A)

'Rei Kawakubo's garments are never created as static objects, but as designs that evolve within the fashion continuum. Reconstructed fashions are made complete and yet remain 'undone', often morphing previous styles and traditional motifs into contemporary designs.

crumbling forms suggesting modern architecture's failure to articulate the origins of pure expression.

Derelict architecture and reclaimed buildings can be viewed as a form of cultural refuse appropriated for its exchange value. Like the reconstruction of abandoned clothing, base materials are converted into precious commodities. Reconstructed objects, whether in the form of buildings, clothing or symbolic capital, connect the rag picker with the modern preservationist, transforming reconstruction into a contemporary cultural practice. As Hal Foster explores the links between them, he asks: 'Are postmodern pasticheurs any different from modernist bricoleurs in this ambiguous recuperation of cultural materials cast aside by capitalist societies?'[4]

Reconstruction surfaced in fashion after deconstruction had already taken hold, and was sometimes misinterpreted as the second wave of a look described by the media as 'urban decay'.[5] Although both aesthetics project a message of resistance, the differences between them are vast. Deconstruction explores the interiority of garments by slicing them open, rearranging their ornamentation, turning them inside out and sewing them back together in a new form. Reconstruction heightens the contrast of the interior and the exterior – the unfinished features of the outside do not necessarily mean that the garment's interior is unfinished – making the garment more dynamic as the relationship between the two is examined. The term deconstruction refers to taking apart, and actually shows the process of tailoring by dismantling it. The intention is to uncover, reveal and simplify, creating an unconventional garment but one considered to be 'finished'.

Reconstructed garments can be based on vintage clothing that have been re-cut, restyled and reprinted, and given a fresh lease of life as a new garment. Just as old fabrics have acquired unique texture and patina that cannot be simulated in new ones, their forgotten histories bring the past into the present, evoking narratives of the garment's lived experience. In this respect, reconstructed clothing becomes polydimensional in form and content, appearing to disrupt linear or chronological time. Their construction processes are often staggered in time, overlapping event formats and even metamorphosing from one event chronology to another. They can represent intersections of various temporal pathways; like the fashion moment itself, reconstruction is premised on the incomplete and the outdated.

Reconstructivist designers view the construction process as the starting point of the garment, rather than its completion. The finished garments are completed and yet 'undone'; this process continues as the clothes are 'lived in' – i.e. worn on the body – simultaneously figuring and disfiguring the body in defiance of the traditional signifiers mediated by codes of dress. As clothing passes from designer to consumer, it moves into a new phase of existence where it is interpreted visually, then augmented by the styling and lifestyle of the wearer. This process continues until the garment gradually deteriorates or falls prey to deconstruction, redefining notions of the garment as a static object to that of an entity in continual flux and construction.

Anthropologist Claude Lévi-Strauss outlines a model for creative activity that he terms 'bricolage', a form of production-oriented activity that does not rely upon traditional materials or methods to produce form.[6] Bricolage recalls the activities typical of children as they 'build' houses out of sand or mud bricks, fashion doll dresses from fabric scraps and pieces of string, or transform debris into tiny sculptures. Lévi-Strauss's model of bricolage extends beyond these analogies to apply to reconstructivist fashion. As designers consciously engage with unconventional materials and untraditional techniques, they revert to a basic form of creativity that rejects the myth that fashion results only from great skill and expertise. This departure from pre-

(A)

established methodology challenges preconceived views of high fashion and the roles of the designers and wearers in constructing it.

Simon Thorogood, one of Britain's most progressive designers, parallels the machinations of bricolage in an activity he terms 'materialisation'. Exhibited in the *Material/Izations* exhibition at the Unit-F Gallery in Vienna in May 2000, Thorogood, in collaboration with the design group Spore, projected an image of a fashion garment from a digital camera recessed into a 'light desk' to create an interactive fashion-design tool. Visitors interacted with a selection of design instruments placed on the work surface, enabling them to deconstruct the image or even redefine it according to their individual creative visions as their assemblages were captured in real time and projected over a larger version of the fashion garment.

Reconstructed garments are best understood as works in progress, as interstitial forms moving within a trajectory of rebirth and decay as they are transfigured over time and space. To this end, Vexed Generation developed their tectonics range of trousers, jackets and coats made out of high-performance denim. The garments are crafted from non-stretch plates of denim fabric positioned within a stretch framework. As they are worn against the body they move apart, mimicking the abrasion of tectonic plates moving in nature. The body's own movement generates friction between the denim plates and the surrounding fabric, effectively creating fissures along the edges of the plates and smoothing their surfaces together. The effect is that of suede as it gradually turns into soft leather with wear and tear. Rather than deteriorate, the

^The shredded chic of Robert Cary-Williams's fashion designs mirrors a broader trend in architecture. Just as deconstructed buildings expose their supports and elements of their interior structure, deconstructed clothing reveals its seams, fastenings, stitching and lining.

tectonic garments transform into something new over time, and also give the wearer a role in personalizing them.

A criticism of reconstruction fashion is that it falls beyond the parameters of fashion at all levels by failing to create something new. Reconstruction also describes certain types of transformable fashions that literally reconstruct other forms: jackets that become tents or mobile shelters, and garments that transform into bags or even furniture and reassume their original form again. The icons of fashion reconstruction are the garments that voice practicality and poignancy in equal measures, such as Hussein Chalayan's furniture-cum-garments for his *After Words* (autumn/winter 2000) collection. The collection demonstrated the literal expression of the reconstruction aesthetic in five pieces of 1950s-style furniture designed to transform into dresses and skirts, complete with suitcases to pack away the clothes taken off. Chalayan's chairs functioned as both pieces of furniture and wearable garments; the upholstery could be taken off and worn as dresses, and the chairs folded into suitcases by collapsing their frames. A round table transformed into an accordion-like skirt by removing a rounded disc from the table's centre and pulling the inside edge up over the hips and attaching it to the waist. By transforming the furniture into clothing, the models were able to wear them as they moved off the stage.

After Words expressed a political reality that articulated relationships between garments and cultural narratives, charging elements of historical tragedy with a narrative of fresh optimism. The collection was based on the idea of having to evacuate home during a time of war, hiding possessions when a raid was impending, and using the agency of clothing as the means to carry away possessions more quickly. The theme was painfully close to real life; it was an autobiographical expression of Chalayan's Turkish Cypriot roots and the political events that impacted upon his childhood. Chalayan was born in Cyprus and later educated in England; the collection recalled the 1974 Turkish military intervention that divided the country in half and displaced both Turkish and Greek Cypriots from their homes.

Reconstruction takes on a special context in this thought-provoking situation. Is Chalayan's work a reminder of an abject past, like the colonial architecture and the monuments to fascist rulers that continue to voice legacies of oppression? Or was it an attempt to repress the historical reality of these events by rewriting the past? It seems less of an attempt to restore the past, and more of a gesture that reconsiders how the evacuations would have unfolded if the population had had cunning means of concealing and carrying their possessions. It demonstrated fashion's ability to conquer the spaces of domesticity and reconstruct them elsewhere.

Reconstructivist designs can also take on the symbolism of monumental structures, poetically re-creating and memorializing abandoned styles, lost motifs or forgotten designers. They can construct an archaeology of dress that coexists with contemporary fashion, imbuing the present with the absent. British design duo Antoni + Alison, whose whimsical collections combine nostalgia for the past with the irony of the present, printed photographs of demolished nightclubs on T-shirts in their 'Dead Disco' series. Although the T-shirts protested against the destruction of period architecture, they did not necessarily voice the buildings' preservation. Instead, they called for their reconstruction in any form that would prevent their demolition.

Reconstructed architecture is in part a monument to the antecedent style it preserves, highlighting the role of architecture as a repository for collective memory. Reconstruction fashion also shapes memory into constructed form, albeit for another purpose. As both garments and buildings convey these abstract messages within specific spatial frameworks, they forge new links between memory and space.

Deconstruction

'For Margiela, the garment is an architecture that "fits out" the body, and thus he shares an architectural inquiry into the process and mechanics of construction,' wrote Alison Gill, as she explored the deconstruction trend that swept through fashion in the 1990s.[7] As Margiela reversed sartorial techniques and literally turned conventional garment construction inside out, the shredded chic of his early work seemed to have more in common with architecture than fashion. In fact, the term itself was appropriated by fashion from architecture, where deconstruction charts a horizon of contemporary thought and design innovations, deployed theoretically and materially to dismantle architecture's purpose, function, syntax and aesthetics.

Deconstructivist fashion can be traced back at least thirty-five years: Sonia Rykiel's visible seams were sewn on the surface of her garments in the 1960s; Karl Lagerfeld's *'le flou'* dresses were free-flowing with unfinished hems; Zandra Rhodes's interpretation of Punk fashion resulted in her unfinished 'ad hoc' creations. These all have resonance with the dresses patterned with *trompe l'oeil* rips and shadowy tears created by Schiaparelli in her surrealist alliances of the 1930s. These garments heralded the prevalence of self-fashioning, later identified with the cut, pinned and slashed clothing of Mods and Goths, many of whom also subscribed to a lifestyle of dwelling in 'squats', abandoned buildings and using furniture reclaimed from skips and junkshops.

Helmut Lang's work was influential in bringing the Punk style to the catwalk. Outfits in his 1994 collections disrupted the expectations of luxury and glamour associated with high fashion, using a retro Punk look to express a stark resistance to established fashion ideals. Just as Punk fashion had provided an expression for disgruntled youth to represent their desires and dissatisfaction in fashion, Lang treated fashion as visual warfare, showing the battleground upon which it is fought. Deconstruction's moment came as Rei Kawakubo and Yohji Yamamoto also conspired to take fashion apart, closely followed by Margiela, Ann Demeulemeester, Victor & Rolf, Junya Watanabe and Dries Van Noten. The tattered tailoring of Robert Cary-Williams, whose use of zips, fastenings, straps and linings feature as explicit design motifs, also sparked off the deconstruction trend among young British designers.

Parallels can be drawn between these designers' deconstructive technique and that of the architect Gordon Matta-Clark. Matta-Clark proclaimed that he inscribed himself into architecture by cutting a line through building walls to reveal and explore their hidden spaces. His cuts made the interior voids of the buildings visible, allowing light to enter their recesses and making visible the domains underlying their surface. Matta-Clark's work, like that of the deconstructivist designers, has been highly influential in generating new construction possibilities and inverting traditional understandings of the division between the visible and the unseen.

Deconstruction has been deployed by a number of high-profile architects to dissect the modernist grid, revealing fresh narratives, new signifiers and uncovering new meanings. Deconstruction constitutes its own rhetoric, voicing attempts to disclose the forms of distortion, error and domination that have been embedded in current perceptions of architecture. With its agenda to renounce these power structures and establish new visual and spatial hierarchies, deconstruction makes a powerful statement of resistance. By revealing the failures and limitations universally imposed by modern architecture, deconstruction foils the proliferation of the hegemony Augé describes as 'the worldwide consumption (of) space'.[8]

This colossal leap forward imbues architecture with unprecedented optimism and democracy. Architects are now re-examining urban space in response to Jacques Derrida's call for a new mode of 'architectural difference' that would enable the built environment to comprise 'places where desire can recognise itself, where it can live'.[9] Together with the work of other theorists, Derrida exposed the value of deconstructing canonical texts to probe their meanings further, producing a format that can also probe other disciplines. Although Derrida did not consider deconstruction in philosophy to be a style – he even refuted its congruency with deconstruction in architecture – the value of its application as a powerful conceptual tool for interpreting architecture is obvious.

Deconstruction emerged at a moment when Bernard Tschumi proclaimed 'the new Europe needs a radically new architecture, an architecture of disruptions and disjunctions, which reflects the fragmentation and dissociation within culture at large'.[10] Tschumi's agenda paralleled a similar development in philosophical thought, articulated in the deconstructive approach of Bataille, Derrida and Deleuze, all of whom work on the brink of philosophy and anti-philosophy, literature and non-literature.[11] As a dialectical device, deconstruction generates an anti-fashion critique, revealing its peripatetic ability to travel between literal forms and their conceptual counterparts that invert the empire of signs designating the high and the low in fashion.

Margiela charts the conceptual congruency between these visual tectonic plates, challenging the value and function of fashion as he creates rifts between them. Margiela creates new clothes from old ones by taking them apart, rearranging the pieces and sewing them back together in a new form. By exploring destruction as a process of investigative creation, Margiela's work represents a nihilistic reaction against traditional tailoring methods and paragons of body consciousness. A theme of transparency emerges as fabric is slashed open or whole panels are removed, revealing or concealing the human form with brutal precision. Seams are split open to reveal the selvedge ends of fabric or the presence of lining fabric, exposing the flesh beneath it. Margiela goes far beyond fashion's subtle and suggestive fascination with the body's erogenous zones, blatantly exposing them with the maliciousness of a sexual predator.

Margiela reconfigures body parts: knee socks are spliced open and stitched together with the rounded heels positioned at the breasts and elbows to create body-hugging jumpers; gloves are sewn together in surreal waistcoats that mimic roving hands grasping the breast and torso; 1950s ball gowns are violently slashed down the front and worn open as long waistcoats. Margiela challenges the norms that restrict ball gowns to formal occasions rather than the everyday casual. The hierarchy that persists between the exclusivity of designer fashion and the everyday casual wardrobe is reversed by reconstituting eveningwear as second-hand separates.

Deconstruction is also a metaphor for the dilapidation and disintegration associated with urban decay, voicing a strong comment on urban culture. The fragmentation evident in the non-place is echoed in the unfinished-cum-destroyed aesthetics of Margiela's garments. Rebecca Arnold regards such work as 'a signifier of a type of fashion held back from the abyss of continual repetition, where the hell of (post)modern city life might exhibit mortality and a reunion with the realities of the decay of the body'.[12] This experience of urban life is characteristic of non-places and heterotopias, where the violence of contemporary life presupposes the ruin of the body. Mediated through indiscriminate sex, drug use, alcohol abuse and radical dieting, the decadence associated with the 'fashion' lifestyle mirrors the breakdown of social structures in wider society. In the face of anxious times, deconstructivist fashions transform these uncertain signifiers into an urban identity confronting the unease they evoke.

Rei Kawakubo juxtaposes urban decay with luxury and elitism, rearticulating the vernacular of Western tailoring in her highly successful Comme des Garçons collections. Kawakubo characteristically calculates the proportions of conventional garments, then radically inverts them as she reconfigures the distances between neckline, waistline and hemline. Not that she places them in the usual areas anyway – her models are often required to drape or loop the clothes around themselves rather than wear them conventionally. She once made a dress that had no openings, making it impossible to put on. But Kawakubo insisted that it could be worn, and decreed that it could be tied on like an apron. Kawakubo also deconstructs the models themselves: their hair is often unkempt or brushed into straw-like configurations. Make-up is applied to look like bruises or blistering, highlighting the face with bold colours or erasing the mouth and eyebrows altogether. She interprets the body as the common ground between fashion and architecture, a site where their cohe-

A–B Kawakubo seldom adheres to conventions of scale as she rethinks the conventions of Western clothing. Sometimes she morphs panels to monstrous proportions, and reconfigures classical checked motifs to create optical illusions.

(A)

(B)

(A)

sion is facilitated by deconstructing ideals of beauty as well as form.

Kawakubo moves collars, fastenings and sleeves around the garment with surreal meticulousness; the darts, tackings, facings and haberdashery trimmings traditionally hidden within clothing surface as explicit design motifs, placing emphasis on parts of a garment that often remain unadorned. Kawakubo also extends this attention to the garment's back, probing the expansive surface that typically receives far less ornamentation than the chest, cuffs or neckline. This reversal of focus parallels a current trend in architecture to re-examine the values and functions of skyscrapers.[13] As architects rethink the role of a building's points of egress (comparable to the openings at a garment's collar and cuffs) lobbies are being shifted up to the middle floors of the structure. Moving their 'epicentres' away from the points of egress redistributes the buzz of human activity to the structure's physical centre rather than its periphery.

Kawakubo has a penchant for monochrome reds and the austerity of black (a colour that Kawakubo says comes in many different shades). Otherwise, her designs are cut out against a background of classic motifs that have been blown up to absurd dimensions, or bleached into near invisibility. Kawakubo interprets vertical planes of fabric as elaborate screening devices, using them to project optical illusions and monochrome façades. This approach is articulated more succinctly in the language of architecture than fashion: Kawakubo is exploring the relationship of the vertical surface to the section, rethinking the contours and structure of the garment as she abides by conventions of scale.

The architecture of the Pompidou Centre (1971–7) is in many

The designs in Junya Watanabe's autumn/winter 1998 collection were deconstructed back to their starting point. Rather than cutting and stitching lengths of fabric to create a garment, Watanabe merely looped fabric panels around the models and secured it in place with wire.

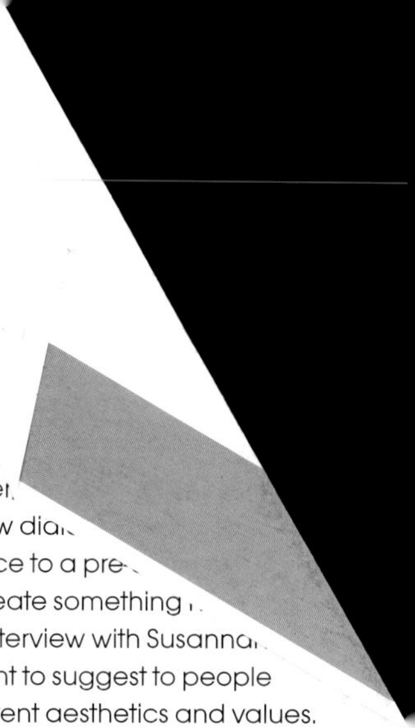

ways Kawakubo's muse, if not her sartorial equivalent. Although much of her work has resonance with Le Corbusier's Ronchamp Chapel (1954) (arguably the first exercise in architectural deconstruction) the design of the Pompidou Centre was central to the dawning of deconstruction fashion generally. Designed by Richard Rogers and Renzo Piano, the building became a beacon of the deconstructivist style, signalling a new technical and conceptual manifesto among fashion designers as well as architects. Its exposed structure was a deliberate attempt to alert the viewer to the mechanical and engineering aspects of architecture. Putting these traditionally hidden features on display rather than concealing them underlined the beauty and power of the entire building.

Architects have appropriated a multitude of concepts from Gilles Deleuze's text *The Fold*, bringing notions of smooth and striated space, affiliation, pliancy and folding into their practice. As Kawakubo blurs and folds (i.e. blends and intermixes) the highly figured with the seemingly formless, her work is an extension of these new architectural devices. The Deleuzean fold also generates a vision of seamless continuity, inspiring Kawakubo to experiment with folding the garment's back and the front into each other. By cleverly twisting the garment's panels, she simultaneously rotated the back panels into the front and vice versa, blurring the ornamented front with the (previously) disregarded back. This created complex, seamless, continuously flowing surfaces that appeared to bend, twist, warp or expand through space. The garment's structures had deeper resonance with Peter Eisenman's skyscraper projects for New York and Berlin than they did with fashion items. 'For Berlin...we took that section and then twisted or rotated it through its length to produce the final result,' Eisenman explained. 'For the second one – the New York tower – we took the Queen's grid, which was already rotated, and the Manhattan grid, and rotated one off the other.'[14]

Ever since she made her debut in Paris, her enigmatic and provocative collections have sent shock waves reverberating throughout the fashion world, and Kawakubo is still going strong. Her bold statements about body and dress were not intended to signal her departure from conventional fashion, but to define her own boundaries. In Paris, Kawakubo shows in a milieu where most of her contemporaries can be categorized according to their respective interests in retro styles, traditional classicism, couture or prêt-a-porter, a new dia service to a pre to create something an interview with Susanna 'I want to suggest to people different aesthetics and values. I want to question their being.'[15]

The nexus of making, wearing, dwelling and thinking about clothing questions assumptions about the lifespan of the garment, and wholly subverts the stability and regularity customarily associated with architecture. While clothing rarely has the same lifespan as a building, the impact of deconstruction points to meanings transmitted far beyond the life expectancy of a fashion trend. In the hands of Kawakubo and Margiela, the dialogue between fashion and architecture articulates innovations derived from construction techniques as well as theoretical constructs, providing a valuable tool for understanding the spaces between them.

Unconstruction

There is nothing more tangible in the analysis of space today than the elusive void. Its 'presence' is already widespread in art, design and architecture; now contemporary fashion designers are engaging with the enigmatic mythology of the void. Voids are complex and interstitial, enigmatic and seductive and the power of their nothingness is immense.

Standing in vivid contrast to the systematic examination of space, the void is a cipher for what cannot be contained or easily addressed, a universal metaphor for the formlessness that cannot be constructed. Its

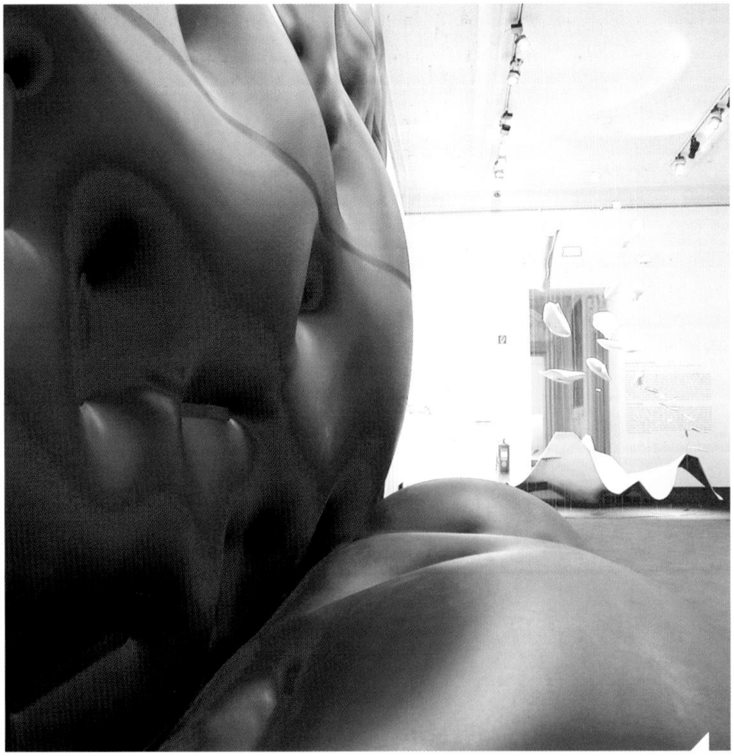

[A]

Dressing the Void

mode of unconstruction is characterized by materialities and concepts that are not permanently bound together, but understood as fluid juxtapositions, or promiscuous collaborations. The theoretical space the void occupies establishes a dialogue with cultural production, articulated in Mallarmé's mime of the imaginary, the sublime hymen of Derrida, the chaosmos of Joyce and Kristeva's uterine, semiotic space. Bataille's 'pure void' unmasked the precarious spaces of life as he deployed it to rationalize the inevitability of death.[16] For Deleuze, the void represents the rhizomatic chaos connecting all events and objects, a universal agent for transmuting the margins of thought into legitimate space rather than a vacuum.

The void has always existed but been systematically overlooked. Conspicuous in its absence, it has been systematically enclosed, confined and contained, its built existence tempered by flush walls, level surfaces and the recesses hidden within folds, pleats and linings. Voids of this order were created by default: although both fashion and architecture revolve around the deployment of form into space, their tangible shapes and structures serve as its antithesis, designed to create spaces that are lived in rather than uninhabited. Exposing the void seems to represent a move towards the transparency of materiality and methodology as well as concepts, a movement mirrored by conceptual fashion designers as they charge fashion with theoretical 'content'. Movements to make the theoretical principles of architecture more visible in the structures themselves has opened a dialogue with the informed public and generated popular interest in the symbolism of the void.

In fashion today, voids are being reclaimed as though they had been long lost or violently suppressed,

[A–B] For the *Latent Utopias* exhibition in Graz, veech.media.architecture created an interactive environment constructed from lightweight structural membranes. The prototype suggested that technological innovations would manipulate the forms to provide seating, walls and level surfaces as needed. This innovation is also being explored in fashion by designers researching the capacities of shape-shifting textiles that can expand and contract to accommodate the needs of the wearer.

(B)

but they have existed throughout fashion's long history. Bustles and crinolines add volume to skirts, effectively encircling the wearer with a void contained by fabric and frame. In the 1940s, Bernard Rudofsky criticized the surplus of pockets in twentieth-century men's dress for the excess voids they created between body and dress.[17] The inflatable dresses of 1960s space-age fashion consisted of air-filled voids, deployed to redefine the silhouette and imbue fashion with technical innovation. Michiko Koshino's blow-up couture updated this expression of the void for the 1990s. Koshino suspended the laws of gravity and inexplicably turned weight into lightness as she transmitted the feeling of translucence into the garment and onto the body of the wearer. Issey Miyake continues to turn inflatable plastics into clothing; chief designer Noaki Takizawa's spring/summer 2001 collection for Miyake rejected traditional circular hemlines, replacing them with inflatable tubes to give them a square shape.

Inflatable voids are also found in architecture, where transience and lightness are key considerations to the structure's design, reconfiguring the density and permanence required by traditional architecture. Inflatable architecture was developed in the 1960s, partly in rebellion to the straight lines, right angles and rigid modularity of modernists like Mies van der Rohe and Le Corbusier.

The British architectural innovators Archigram designed portable air-filled plastic buildings, replacing the hard surfaces of walls, ceilings and floors with pliable panels. Constructed like clothing, they were fused together by seams and their interiority conceived as a void for habitation. As structures they had more in common with fashion than architecture: they were portable, constructed from soft membranes, and designed and assembled in accordance with tailoring techniques. Created as individual pods rather than whole structures, their modularity related more to the system of separates common to fashion than to the architecture of the day. (In fact, their colourful motifs, materials and textures had more in common with the Suitaloon, Archigram's tent-like garment equipped with heating/cooling devices and communication transmitters, than with any of the firm's architectural designs.)

(A)

Dressing the Void

Stuart Veech, of the Viennese architectural practice veech.media.architecture, designed mobile and temporary structures that are given form by air-filled voids. Veech's pavilions take minutes to erect and shrink to one-tenth of their expanded size when deflated. 'These work especially well in exhibition design,' Veech explained, 'where the inflatable structures can create a portable exhibition space that can be instantly recreated in the different venues the exhibition travels to.'[18] Even when strengthened by steel lintels, the inflated membranes remain vulnerable and volatile, making them unviable as permanent outdoor structures. As they line a building's interior, their voids become the building's aesthetic epicentre. Used outside as a pavilion, the voids form the very core of the structure itself.

The habitable voids of William MacDonald and Sulan Kolatan's Raybould House (1997) also signal a new direction in architecture. The structure is based on the techniques used to design the athletic shoe, which they discovered as they explored the relationship between consumer fashion and the possibilities for hybridization with architecture. 'An analysis of the shoe', wrote Ellen Lupton, 'raises many new ideas of surface layering – they may be fused, sewn, constructed from silicone – and these may be used to influence materiality and construction in architecture.'[19] As MacDonald and Kolatan dissected the shoe, they discovered various voids and cavities resulting from the layering of the labile materials that create its flexible structure. The sinuous structure of Raybould House negotiates the fluidity between the body and the environment, re-navigating the boundaries between fashion and architecture.

A+B A search for dynamic design possibilities resulted in veech.media. architecture's choice of an inflatable form for the set of the Radio Night broadcast at the Technical Museum in Austria. As the pneumatic stage 'floated' seven meters above the audience it redefined the vaulted space of the museum, yet amplified the theme of flight already present in the gallery.

C Inflatable structures are also ideal for outdoor pavilions and travelling exhibitions.

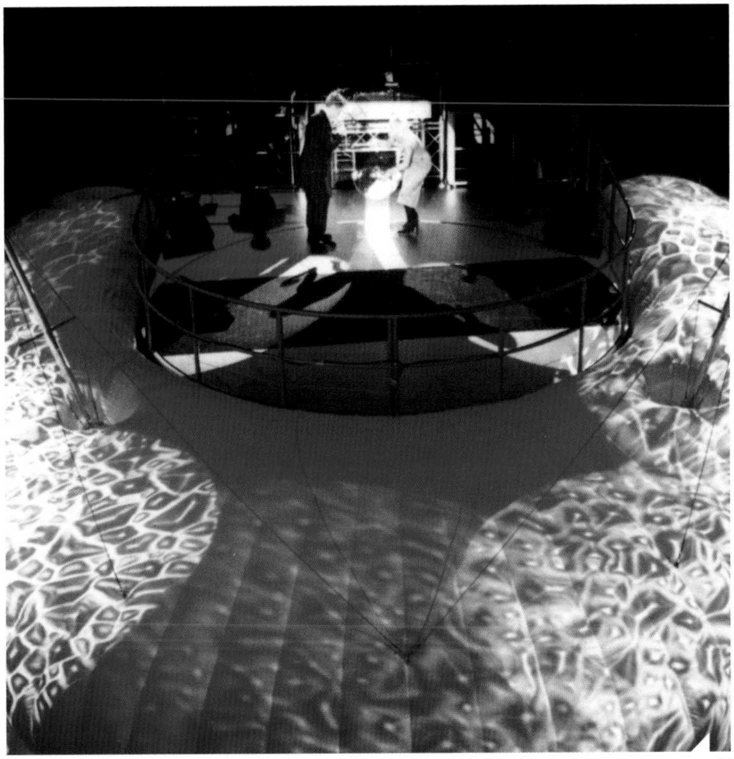

(B)

(C)

Identifying the void in architecture exposes a number of unexpected dimensions. While traditional architecture is actually a spatial enclosure that separates living space from the outdoors, architecture is a series of spatial enclosures within itself. Most of the structure is masked between internal walls and external skins, making us less aware of architecture as we become more familiar with the ornamentation imposed upon it. As architects open up linear spaces to reveal the supporting joists and ceiling structures, partitions are no longer erected around vertical pipes, airways and shafts. The ribs hidden behind supporting walls are exposed, disclosing contoured surfaces or perhaps the inherent curvature of a building, previously disguised within a structural void. Liberating these voids inverts the visual perception of architecture, mediating a new experience of the building for the individuals who inhabit it.

The void is imagined to be empty, unoccupied and without content, but it is rarely reductive to the point of non-meaning. But as an absent space, the 'presence' of the void redefines whole structures, generating a reality of form and a container for ideas. These polarities enable the void to assume the condition of an index, as the void itself does not separate the relationships between form and meaning to produce a set of arbitrary connections to the signified. The removal of arbitrary connections allows a possible non-presence to be contemplated in respect to form, and the void gauges the distances between them.

In his thesis on *ex nihilo* creation, Lacan paralleled the void to the kind of cultural production fashion and architecture characterize.[20] Using the ceramic vase as an example, Lacan treated it as a vehicle for containment, a material object that comes into existence as it forms the centre of the 'real'. The vase itself takes form *ex nihilo* from the void; as it is shaped by the potter, the emptiness of its interior arbitrates the shaping of the signifier by creating a void in the real. As Lacan considered different modalities surrounding and separating the void, the empty spaces apparent in wombs, caves, architecture and garments come to mind. Tempered

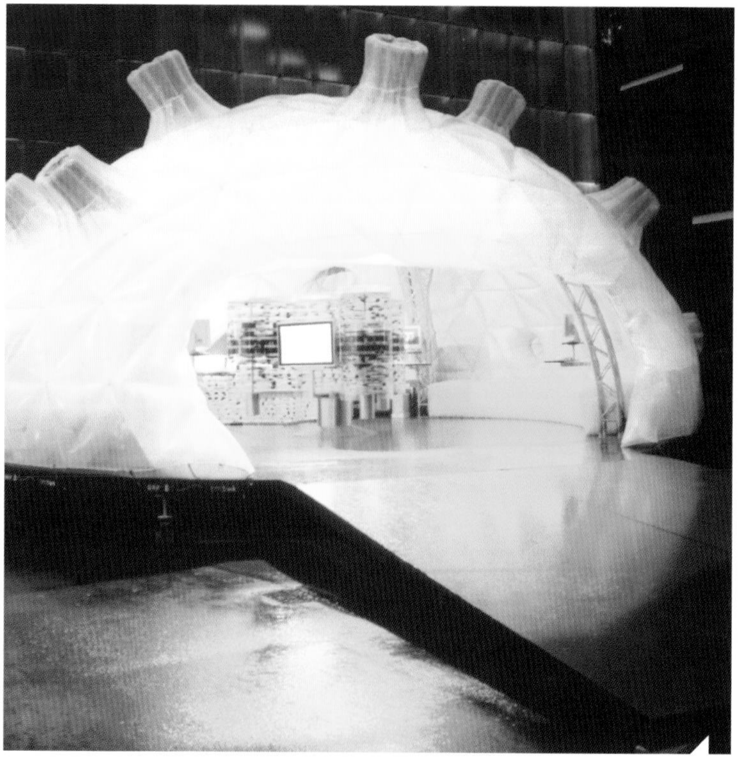

(A)

Dressing the Void

by physical form, the void is not a sacred space but a secularized object; by banishing any illusion of transcendence, its existence reveals the material characteristics of structure and shape. The void's existence in consciousness, Lacan concluded, can be understood as a lack or a negative, or as the opposite to what we perceive as 'being'. By 'existing' as a negative entity – or by its perception as 'nothing' – the void is empowered by the complex meanings condensed upon it, rather than the potential to produce certain meaning in itself. As Richard Patterson wrote: 'Synthesis of meaning will not be satisfactory for anyone, for any imaginary coherence with which we might temporarily embellish this incompleteness will be resisted by the persistent intrusion of that void – that nothingness.'[21]

The void's theoretical impact on material culture runs deep. The 1970s sparked environmental movements to recycle waste and create havens for 'nothingness', while political lobbyists called for the redistribution of governmental power and the transparency of information. By the late 1980s, architects were proposing solutions to urban congestion, setting aside open areas demarcated as voids or spaces. Rem Koolhaas, a leading proponent of the architectural void, proposed a new economy of space: Koolhaas's deconstruction architecture decentred the architectural signifier as he interprets space in terms of density and mass, reclaiming the void as an area of habitation. The architecture of Zaha Hadid designs voids as visual lures, which she considers to be an integral part of the building's surface. Just as human skin moves continuously from the body's surface into the cavities of the ear and nose, Hadid's surfaces

[A] Because an inflatable structure can be quickly installed and easily packed away, it was the ideal choice for veech.media.architecture's Sprachpavillon commission. The design facilitated communication and the exchange of information through its expression of flexibility and transparency.

[B] Michiko Koshino's inflatable dresses of the 1990s paralleled the rise of inflatable membranes in architecture. Koshino used compartments of air to create volume around the hips and expand the dresses' structure, in a design that could assume a variety of shapes.

(B)

appear to flow into the void – or trace their path out of it.

Similarly, a garment's interior can be conceived as a single surface that reveals a void as it folds into its interiority. As the garment's outer shell angles into hems, collars and cuffs, its inner surfaces become invisible to the wearer, and as such are conceived as amorphous areas extending throughout the garment's interior. Within the interior, a multitude of cavities, caverns and pockets are formed by the tacking, pleating and layering of the garment's construction. On the body of the wearer, a cycle of constant interchange between void and mass is enacted as each is continually dislodged by the fusion between body and dress. Body-conscious fabrics such as Lycra, Tactel, latex and nylon subtract the space of the void as they squeeze the body like a second skin, but fail to eliminate it altogether. Even though the process of displacement is initiated, the garment, like the Lacanian vase, cannot fully erase the presence of an interior void. Traces of it will always remain, forever imbued within the residues of space.

Whether a space of reverential silence, an abyss or an assenting place, the void is no longer perceived as a limiting phenomenon but one that provides sufficient content to convey meaning beyond its confines. In clothing, as in architecture, the very nothingness of the void can paradoxically support substantial concepts and solid physical structures. As designers like Yohji Yamamoto, Cristobal Balenciaga, Junya Watanabe and Rei Kawakubo explore the void within a broader cultural context, they highlight its capacity to simultaneously represent and evoke feelings of density and containment, or liberation and spaciousness.

In the process of probing and observing the void, Yohji Yamamoto has designed many crinoline styles, often making abstractions out of architecture. Historically, fashion has relied on volume and mass weight to counter the inherent flatness of fabric and shape the body in accordance with beauty ideals. From the fourteenth century onwards, skirts extended in width, circumference and volume. The bell-shaped underskirts known as farthingales are believed to have originated in Spain, evolving from stiff petticoats to geo-

Dressing the Void

metrical domes shaped by wires, metal bands, whalebone or cane that cocooned the wearer in negative space rather than tiers of starched linen. By the late sixteenth century, a lozenge-shaped hooped version was present in France, followed by the development of a bolster-like bustle tied around the hips. By the end of the seventeenth century a pannier hoop was developed, turning the lower half of the dress into a dome-shaped cage. It was attached to either hip, creating a core structure that was to later evolve into the space-consuming expanse of the crinoline.

Perhaps the most outstanding of Yamamoto's crinoline styles is the bridal dress and wedding hat ensemble for his autumn/winter 1998 collection. The dress was a simple, streamlined bodice that dipped into a monstrously oversized skirt some twelve metres in circumference. The dress was fitted with a matching hat too large to be worn; it was supported by bamboo poles and held over the model's head by four attendants as she moved down the catwalk. The prevalence of the crinoline in European dress reveals the persistence of such voids throughout previous eras. Yamamoto's dress is emblematically a container of time as well as symbolizing the sum total of all such voids in fashion's long history.

Yamamoto later referenced the hidden intimacies of the fashioned body in a subsequent wedding dress (spring/summer 1999), when he displaced its void by creating a random assortment of zipped compartments. When opened on the catwalk, they disclosed a pair of flat-heeled shoes, a wide-brimmed hat and a calico bouquet. The spirit of this approach suggested the practicalities of compartmentalizing the dress rather than accessorizing it, which Yamamoto achieved by reclaiming the space traditionally voided by generations of designers before him. The void in Yamamoto's dress was not displaced altogether, but reinterpreted as passages that link several systems.

Many of Cristobal Balenciaga's designs relied on volume, constructed with a series of voids that often relied on an organza lining and air to support his signature bold shapes. Many were so voluminous they obscured the body's outlines entirely. His 'Le Chou Noir' cape, for example, mimicked the organic folds of a cabbage. It consists of a long panel of silk sewn into a tube, wrapped around the torso, shoulders and head. One of his most superb expressions of volume was the wedding gown in his 1967 collection. Consisting

[A]Hussein Chalayan uses expandable fabrics such as Lycra and Tactel to create flexible designs that can be structured by the body. Body-conscious fabrics subtract the space of the void altogether, or stretch across its contours and create a void between them.

[B]Watanabe's origami garments are constructed from open weaves that fold and expand as they are fitted around the human form.

[C]Kawakubo inserted a series of voids between the body and the dress to create this distinctive silhouette.

(A)

(B)

(C)

of two pieces of fabric sewn together into a broad sweep, it was shaped by only three seams, one on each shoulder and one joining the two widths of fabric down the centre of the back. As the model moved down the catwalk, the dress assumed a cone shape around her.

Junya Watanabe's deconstructivist approach to fashion is legendary, his examination of the void, prolific. In one of his photographic campaigns Watanabe drew attention to the void by using pictures of wire-frame geometric models and images of lampshades. The interior area of the lampshade was photographed from below, revealing its empty core and the myriad voids located within the folds of its pleats. But as he begins to deconstruct the void itself, Watanabe's method of enquiry transmutes into unconstruction. To Watanabe, a garment, like a lampshade, consists of a labyrinth of nooks and crannies; he regards each of them as a void, and each is probed as a microcosm that evolves as the garment takes shape. As Watanabe 'unconstructs' the process, the puzzle is finally solved, allowing the wearer to 'know' each and every material facet of the garment.

Watanabe's origami dresses are hauntingly beautiful, constructed from honeycomb weaves that fold and pleat as they are fitted to the human form. In his autumn/winter 2000 collection, Watanabe's unconstruction methodology was deployed to extract the void from beneath the garment's surface, allowing it to spiral into density as it took the form of organic shapes and coils. By giving the void a sense of density an anti-void rationale arose, its sudden mass threatening to weigh the garments down or enable them to levitate as their striations swayed gently with the movement of the wearer.

Rei Kawakubo, Watanabe's professional mentor and business backer, has explored the void with intense fascination. Kawakubo never takes inspiration from retro styles or fashion trends, but describes her design ethos as starting 'from zero', eschewing geometric lines for more organically defined notions of the architectonic.[22] Kawakubo's work does have historical references, however. Her widespread use of black is appropriated for its 'power',

Dressing the Void

and as a colour it cannot be disassociated from the metaphoric associations ascribed to it by the Existentialists.[23] As an expression of nihilism, the Existentialists anchored the void to fashion decades ago, its blackness taken as the definitive signifier of the abyss, and the ultimate collapse of meaning.

'Body becomes dress becomes body,' proclaimed Kawakubo, as she tried to express her radical perception of clothes and their functions.[24] Her attempts to erase the boundaries between fabric and skin push the notions of the void to an extreme. Either Kawakubo strives to eliminate the void altogether, or like Watanabe, translates it into mass by tracing its shape around the surface of the body. In some cases Kawakubo has even indulged in literal expressions of the void, crafting dresses and woollen jumpers with deliberate gaping holes – for many designers these were the inspiration for the holey, unstitched garments designed today.

Kawakubo considers the void between body and clothing to be the benchmark from which the poetic, associative and metaphoric dimensions of her work emanate. Blurring the boundaries between dress and the body itself is typical of her; it has been central to her work for three decades. Kawakubo has routinely ignored the contours of the body, even wrapping lengthy swathes of fabric around the body to obscure its margins. Some of her early designs barely touched the body at all; she created monstrously oversized garments that moved with the body, but were constructed in a rigid shape that could stand independent of it. This was Kawakubo's poetic expression of the uncelebrated void between body and fabric, which she explored as a microcosm around the wearer.

Kawakubo's *Lumps* collection (spring/summer 1997) for Comme des Garçons, is in many respects a seminal work that outlined her examination of the void.

As Western fashion generally echoes the contours of the body, a system of cuts, pleats, ribs and rouching emphasize its shape, creating voids between body and cloth. Kawakubo's unique approach was to gaze into the void, physically and metaphorically, measure its depth and locate its bottom. As the voids took form, Kawakubo used goose-down padding or rounded foam inserts and inflatable panels to distort the model's figures to absurd degrees, swelling shoulder pads, expanding seams, disrupting the

A–B While Daniel Liebskind's Jewish Museum in Berlin houses the *memento mori* of Germany's lost Jewish population, the building itself is designed to foster a sense of personal loss that relates the individual to the collective narrative of the Holocaust

(A)

(B)

silhouette with inexplicable contours. Most of the models had bumps on their sides, humps on their backs, or long sausage shapes wrapped around their torsos. Some had their shoulders padded to the extent that their necks disappeared. As Kawakubo charged the void with a sense of density, the mass she created in the garments seemed to overwhelm the wearer. These were contrasted radically with balloon-like skirts constructed from waxed paper, imbued with such a sense of weightlessness that they appeared to levitate as they gently swayed with the movement of the wearer. Those in tune with Kawakubo's sensibilities regarded *Lumps* as her most powerful collection in years.

In Kawakubo's thinking, her work endows clothing with a sense of integrity it once lost, allowing space to be conquered by the garment rather than the designer. In liberating the void she reclaims a space of complete silence, giving it voice, expression and form, without announcing what the reclaimed space should be used for. Such spaces articulate questions, but, like Kawakubo, do not return solid answers.

Absence

Architecture, like beauty, can evolve from our desire to see life transmuted into art. The void created by death, staged artistically as the genre of tragedy, is represented in architecture in a poetic guise that gives romantic form to its terrible reality. In the hands of visionaries like Kawakubo and Koolhaas, the void is charged with renewal, but for many other practitioners, it symbolizes tragedy and loss. The genre of tragedy also constitutes a void: it summons lost cultural artefacts, forgotten ideologies and dead heroes; a void whose gravitational pull spawned a literary tradition and a genre of visual art and classical theatre.[25] Greek tragedy necessitated the death of the Hero; medieval tragedy rejoiced in the death of the Saviour.

The presence of the void, in the guise of classical tragedy, was essential to the development of the Western visual tradition, its legacy underpinning much of cultural production. Richard Patterson goes as far as suggesting that, 'the form of the tragic became the basis of aesthetic theory...narrative as a form

Dressing the Void

of recording or ritual, no longer held sway over the totalising imperatives of form'.[26] As the tragic created a visual metaphor of psychic transformation, it created a symbolic discourse that achieved psychic closure without offering any explanations. Benjamin, in his quest for the origins of German tragic drama, charted the movement of classical tragedy as it shifted from myth to Baroque history, noting that the tragic provided the basis for turning action into text.[27] In acknowledging a series of shifted meanings today, preconceptions of one true meaning of the tragic are erased and the metaphorical void can now be explored as a new, valid re-creation of meaning.

Throughout history, this basis was shared by both fashion and architecture alike, each discipline relying on the judicious construction of a visual language that translated memory into specific forms. Fashion's engagement with the tragic reflects these primary classical models and draws upon the art of representation, being the fundamental resource from which the designer, like the architect, can derive inspiration.

Few memorials exemplify this reversal better than Daniel Libeskind's Jewish Museum in Berlin (1999), which negates the traditional mode of collective memory by speaking directly to the individual. Voids often form the spatial epicentre of Daniel Libeskind's deconstructivist architecture. The Jewish Museum features many such areas, their emptiness designed to evoke the lost Jewish population of Germany. By refusing to portray death as frightening or sinister, a deeper connection between the void and its relationship to a cosmic order is articulated by metaphor as well as material space. The museum's voids are intended to be transcendent and immaterial – Libeskind describes them as 'the ineffable or the immeasurable' – despite their role in commemorating the tragic in civic space.[28]

Libeskind deploys the human as the tragic's essential signifier, despite the role of the architecture in communicating the tragedy of a nation.[29] Libeskind himself intended for the building to be read in terms of what it is not: the denial of collective memory inversely signifies it as an absence, triggering the reorientation that Freud described as the 'phantasy-life of the individual (wherein) real internal and external sensations are interpreted and represented to himself'.[30] Although the building is intended to evoke the

[A–B] Voids form the spatial epicentre of the Jewish Museum in Berlin as a metaphor for absence, tragedy and loss. The building's exterior also projects this metaphor through the series of gaps that appear randomly in its façade.

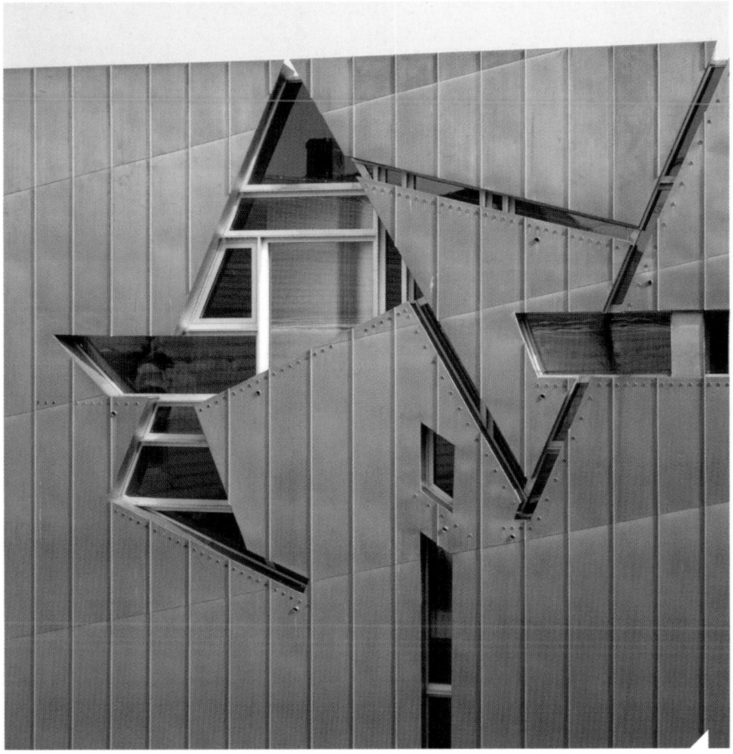

(A)

(B)

Jews who perished in Germany communally, its minimal architecture and the uniformity of its small-scale spaces evoke a deliberate sense of incompleteness, providing no moments of collective resolution in a large space.

The nothingness conveyed by these hypothetical voids is emblematic of dead persons, voicing their absence. Rather than charging the museum with a sense of *memento mori*, the mysterious intensity of solitude emphasizes individual loss, making the observer feel lucky to be alive. Museums dedicated to tragic themes often serve as both memorials to historic events and individual trauma. The combined effect is to interpret the tragic in modernist terms; as it is represented as sacraria, the onus is placed on the individual to relate the tragic to the collective narrative of the holocaust.[31]

The museum's figurative centre is interrupted by seven dense voids – discernible to the visitor only as inaccessible walled-off spaces – that signify the removal of the Jews from the continuum of German culture. The voids make sharp distinctions between the intended discursive path of the visitor and these areas of inaccessible emptiness, leading the average visitor to perceive the voids as mere obstacles to circumvent as they move through the museum. But the voids are intended to create a maze through which the visitors must move, esoterically generating apprehension and expectation: 'In architecture,' wrote Libeskind, 'the static nature of constructed space gains a dimension of perspective through experience and anticipation.'[32] Their presence has the effect of reorienting visitors towards the imaginary scenarios and narratives that fill these gaps, conveying the sense that something is out of balance, that the surrounding space remains unresolved.

The emptiness of these voids is intended to induce memory. But none of them prepares the visitor for the wholly devastating *Holocaust Void*, a monument which Libeskind conceived as a memorial chamber rather than an impenetrable structure. Positioned at one end of the museum, the void initially appears to be a bleak concrete tower rising to the full thirty-metre height of the museum. Access is permitted via a heavy door, designed to close automatically behind each visitor. The void offers no escape and no refuge; there are no uplifting images, poetic inscriptions or sculptural forms to soften the feeling of abject separation. Its effect is profound: like the void in Edgar Allan Poe's *A Descent into Maelstrom*, the visitor feels the terrifying undercurrent of an abysmal whirlpool, submerging them in a bottomless ocean of desolation. Unable to flee its unbearable confines, the visitor focuses on the stillness of the void, aware of the ever-growing remoteness of the world beyond it as the absence of sound resonates with its inconceivable silence.

One of Libeskind's most poignant metaphors for the building draws upon the dialogue between Moses and Aaron in Schoenberg's unfinished opera of the same name. According to Libeskind, 'Aaron is the voice of the people and Moses is a dissenter who despairs of ever communicating that which has no image.'[33] Words and their sum total can be understood to represent a nation, as the resounding dialogue between Aaron and the Israelites symbolizes the strength of their numbers. Yet Moses equates the incomprehensible concept of God with the single, unspoken word, which he eventually articulates in an isolated and unmusical manner, forever separated from the chorus. The single word is delivered at the close of the opera, its significance and impact eclipsing the weight of the dialogues sung previously.

Likening his buildings to 'frozen music', the primacy Libeskind gives to the individual note can be understood as the basis upon which to form a chorus. Symbolically isolating the note in any chord makes it clear that the sound of the individual can be detected throughout. Libeskind explains that, 'only when the means by which a building is built disappear does the "frozen musical" moment appear in architecture – allowing another story to emerge'. In recounting the tragic as a story to be told, Libeskind takes the museum beyond the shadow of tragic history and realigns it with the cultural space of art.

In fashion, the emptiness of death is connected to memorial rituals; rings, crucifixes, clothing, locks of hair and other vestiges of the deceased were charged with emotive content that gave them intense meaning.[34] Crucifixes, the most obvious signifiers of the tragic in the reliquary tradition, underline the relationship between memorial form and its relationship to the body. They symbolize the death and resurrection of Christ, providing an object for collective focus that contains the promise of transcendence, ultimately filling the void with the hope for triumph over tragedy.

Like the crucifix, the cathedral is a memorial to the suffering of Christ. As colossal poetic structures for symbolic contemplation, they are not unlike icons themselves; they provide an indisputable space within which the heroic embodiment of God's martyrdom can be recalled. The crucifix, as an icon, has been decontextualized to a significant degree in visual culture. As the crucifix is translated into architecture, it becomes an uncertain signifier capable of conveying abstract messages. Architects generally interpret it as a cruciform shape; in structures such as Tadao Ando's Church of the Light (1989), the cross is an opening – and therefore a space – charged with fresh symbolism.[35] The rituals and symbolism surrounding the cruciform as an architectural device approach narrative form, extending to art and fashion as they also deploy it to represent a spiritual and aesthetic memorial.

As architecture engages with the notion of memorial in a new era of discourse, it mirrors fashion's use of religious totems and reliquary icons to revive the collective pathos of the tragic. In dislocating the tragic from the realm of the body and committing it to collective experience, memorial architecture does not create space for the reflexive subject, or the rationale with which to form a sense of personal space. Monuments and memorials can designate a 'sad place', while fashion provides the possibility to explore human tragedy within the context of the body and create a poignant reflection tempered by the joy of wearing. That there is possibility to explore human tragedy and transcendence in fashion at all fuses fashion with optimism, as clothing is created to express the narrative of life and the promise of hope. Probed carefully, clothing's role in mediating the tragic provides a window on fashion's inner memories.

A collaboration between Alexander McQueen and Phillip Treacy created one such opening. The designer's vision of tragic angst was illustrated in a project inspired by the dark lustre of the black pearl. For McQueen, the black pearl denotes a sinister facet of beauty, which he accentuated by combining it with vestiges of the tragic. McQueen designed a full-length diaphanous shift, richly emblazoned with a baroque floral motif and mimicking classical drapery in cut. The bottom quarter of the dress consisted of a row of silken fringe, a trimming that has had associations with death and mourning since the classical era, when fringes at the ankles are believed to have been a naïve representation of a dress torn in grief.[36] Treacy's extravagant headdress featured a skull superimposed over a dagger, itself symbolic of warrior knights who revered the sword as a symbolic crucifix ceremonially.

The work of the Polish fashion designer Arkadius reveals a similar approach. Based in London, Arkadius uses images of art to mediate the tragic in dress, through his examination of the character, history, customs and conventions of religious iconography. Arkadius's work features crucifixes and images of the Madonna and child, the Virgin Mary, Catholic saints and reliquary motifs, which he chooses to invoke meaning, significance and a sense of wonder. Arkadius allows vestiges of the tragic to come closer to the observer, while providing a critical distance between individual tragedy and collective emotion. Religious icons, like the crucifix, are part of the ritual and attendant symbolism that represent the tragic as a collective practice in architecture as well as in visual culture.

Arkadius considers the deeper sacramental layers of sartorial significance. His use of religious imagery reveals that it is no longer necessarily symbolic of the Church. 'I see the crucifix as an architectural form', Arkadius explained, 'that becomes a metaphorical connection between the living community and a built form invested with the notion of tragedy.'[37] Arkadius's work embodies a sense of love and loss, using fashion's representational ability to connect the wearer with a sense of the sacred. As signifiers of collective memory, the iconography Arkadius employs continues to be associated with the social rather than with individual identity.

Such a modernist understanding of the tragic coexists with an infinite number of different readings. Although Arkadius's work encounters different worlds, it succeeds in uniting them in the realm of fashion. Using his descent into the tragic as a source of inspiration, Arkadius's work makes a metaphorical leap back to the present that reveals the extent to which the tragic in architecture, art and dress are deeply entwined. Arkadius eschews the historic references to dress evident in McQueen's expression in favour of the classical iconography that connects with an art-history tradition. Part of Arkadius's ethos is to interpret each individual garment as a collective structure that voices unity, reminding us that our traumas of identity and difference are collective as well as individual.

Arkadius's *Virgin Mary Wears the Trousers* collection (spring/summer 2002) gave the Madonna primacy over the Christ figure, exploring Mary's role as an icon of sexuality and power. Placing emphasis on Mary's beauty and femininity outlined them as markers of difference, charging her representation with the type of seductive lures ascribed to a female superhero. Powerful, invincible and heroic, Mary's strength and resistance made her invincible and uncompromising, dangerous and even deadly to male desire. Arkadius's representations of the Virgin were both curious and fetishistic; invested with a strong suggestion of fantasy and role play, the models appeared to renegotiate the boundaries between the 'tarts and vicars' of fetish ideals.

Arkadius's use of embroidery and appliqué crucifixes on the garments featured as texts to be decoded rather than as mere design motifs. Models stalked the catwalk in ecclesiastical stoles embroidered with gilt crucifixes or white cruciform shapes. One model draped a narrow gilded stole across her shoulders, which fell to her waist

[A]Arkadius's use of embroidery and appliqué crucifixes on garments transforms the iconography of religion into symbols of collective angst. The model's torso is encased in a resin cast that resembles an architectural surface more than a fashion garment.

[B]Arkadius built a framework around the model's upper body to pay a sartorial tribute to the Madonna.

(A)

(B)

and framed the cast of a torso and pelvis fitted to her upper body. Polished to a high gloss, the resin cast transformed the model's flesh into the animated statue of a naked saint. The cast encasing the body was more akin to an architectural skin than a fashion item, bringing the representation of the tragic into physical contact with the wearer. The flesh animating its contoured shape challenged the pious innocence ascribed to sainthood, combining the predetermined experience of movement and tactility with unsuppressed eroticism.

The 'Mary' showpiece, also from the *Virgin Mary Wears the Trousers* collection, renegotiated the boundaries of the body entirely by building a structural framework around the model's head, shoulders and torso. A tribute to the iconography of the Madonna, Mary resembled an icon of the Virgin, whose face and hands came to life as the model moved down the catwalk. As the icon's frame extended the contours of the body outwards, they symbolically expanded the body beyond its confines, illustrating the importance of scale as a memory device for both disciplines. The 'icon' was lengthened too, gaining a pair of legs – making the title 'Virgin Mary Wears the Trousers' a literal statement. The garment's extended structure enclosed the living body in a collective memorial, using tragedy to line the surface of the fabric to construct its form.

The bravado and fatalism evident in Arkadius's work is an expression of hope, rather than a fixation on the tragic. Arkadius's themes migrate between heroic deeds and malevolent fate, relating them to the melancholy of everyday life. Yet the inner subtleties of his work imbue fashion with the promise of transcendence, a notion memorial architecture lost as its narrative structure switched from the void to the heroic. By combining the lyrical and the intellectual, Arkadius voices the impossibility of achieving perfection and reclaiming beauty. In this sense, fashion makes a truly tragic statement. That the void exposes the possibility to explore human tragedy and transcendence in fashion and architecture at all charges the congruency between them with optimism, as clothing and architecture become expressive of the narrative of life and the long history of human existence.

Dressing the Void

[1]Peter Eisenman in conversation with Charles Jencks in 'The New Paradigm and Septmeber 11th', *Architectural Design*, 72(4).

[2]Fredric Jameson in Neil Leach (ed) (1999), *Architecture and Revolution*, London: Routledge, p72.

[3]Svetlana Boym (2001), The *Future of Nostalgia*, New York: Basic Books, p17.

[4]Hal Foster (1993), *Compulsive Beauty*, Cambridge, MA: MIT Press, p269.

[5]See Rebecca Arnold (1999), 'Heroin Chic', *Fashion Theory* 3(3), p279–95.

[6]See Claude Lévi-Strauss (1968 edition), *The Savage Mind*, Chicago, IL: University of Chicago Press.

[7]Alison Gill (1998), 'Deconstruction Fashion: The Making of Unfinished, Decomposing and Re-assembled Clothes', *Fashion Theory* 2(1), p27.

[8]Marc Augé (1995), *non-places*, London: Verso, p107.

[9]Quoted in Neil Leach (ed) (1997), *Rethinking Architecture*, London: Routledge, p317.

[10]Bernard Tschumi in Neil Leach (ed) (1999), *Architecture and Revolution*, London: Routledge, p146.

[11]These theorists wanted not simply to reverse, but to challenge from within the meanings offered by the binary oppositions through which structuralist thinkers of the post-war period had claimed to uncover hidden meaning in language. This paradigm is applied to reveal hidden meanings in fashion and architecture, as well as a range of other disciplines. Artists, film-makers, media theorists and theatre directors have subscribed to deconstruction as a theoretical tool and mode of methodology.

[12]Rebecca Arnold (2001), *Fashion, Desire and Anxiety*, London: I. B. Tauris & Co., p61.

[13]See Peter Eisenman and Elizabeth Grosz (2001), *Architecture from the Outside: Essays on Virtual and Real Space*, Cambridge, MA: MIT Press.

[14]Peter Eisenman in conversation with Charles Jencks, *Architectural Design*, 72(4).

[15]Susannah Frankel (2001), *Fashion Visionaries*, London: V&A Publications, p158.

[16]Michel Surya (2002), *Georges Bataille*, London: Verso, p3.

[17]See Bernard Rudofsky (1947), *Are Clothes Modern?*, Chicago, IL: Paul Theobald.

[18]From Veech's seminar at WINK, Barbican Centre, London, 25 June 2002.

[19]Ellen Lupton (2002), *Skin*, London: Laurence King, p61.

[20]See Jacques Lacan (1992 edition), *The Ethics of Psychoanalysis*, London: Routledge.

[21]Richard Patterson (2000), 'The Void That is Subject', *Architectural Design*, 70(5), p73.

[22]From an interview with Susannah Frankel, *Fashion Visionaries*, p158.

Notes

[23]Also referred to as 'Lettrists' or 'Situationists', French philosophers such as Jean-Paul Sartre, André Breton and Simone de Beauvoir were often characterized by the black clothing they wore.

[24]Rei Kawakubo was interviewed by Susannah Frankel in her book *Fashion Visionaries*, p154.

[25]Tragedy appeared at a critical period of transformation in Greek history. According to Aristotle it evolved from epic and the dithyramb, paralleling the rise of comedy from the practice of lampooning and Phallic songs.

[26]Richard Patterson (2000), 'The Metamorphosis of Tragedy', *Architectural Design* (70)5, p38.

[27]See Walter Benjamin (2003 edition) translated by John Osborne, *The Origin of German Tragic Drama*, London: Verso.

[28]Daniel Libeskind, 'The Walls Are Alive', *The Guardian*, 13 July 2002.

[29]Patterson, '*The Metamorphosis of Tragedy*', p73.

[30]Quoted in Robert Young (1994), *Mental Space*, London: Process Press, p80.

[31]In 'Sacraria, Tragedy and the Interior Narrative', Edward Winters defines sacraria as 'sacred spaces designed to house the spirit of the lost or the dead...humble objects invested with meaning by their association with the soul...' in *Architectural Design*, vol 70 no 5, p84.

[32+33]Libeskind, '*The Walls Are Alive*'.

[34]As Anne Hollander (1994) points out in *Sex and Suits* (New York: Kodanska, p19), 'clothes themselves might form a kind of family possession, each garment being transmissible to the next generation and never intended merely for one person'.

[35]Built in Osaka Prefecture, Japan.

[36]Chiara Caleo (2001), 'The Tanagra Larnakes: An Iconographic Analysis', *Anistoriton Journal of History, Archaeology, Art History*, 22 December 2001, p12.

[37]Arkadius was interviewed by the author.

Urban Nomads

Throughout the world, cities are enjoying a renaissance as they are reshaped and reinvented to reflect changes in society. Planners and architects are providing initiatives that make the relationship between the urban landscape and the city dweller as frictionless as possible. Initiatives to facilitate greater egress, air-condition interior spaces, designate comfort zones and give the urban environment an aesthetically pleasing façade are intended to create environments whose seductions and comforts lure prosperous residents and well-heeled tourists. And yet cities are also arenas for conflict; they stage confrontations between fluidity and stability, hinder movement and foster immobility. Pollution, homelessness, violent crime, overcrowding and constant transport delays are the realities of these unlikely Utopias. Recognizing that architecture alone cannot create an urban idyll, fashion is now addressing some of these shortcomings by finding solutions for a new type of city dweller: the urban nomad.

A+B Yeohlee coined the term 'urban nomad' as she made a response to needs of the fast-paced city-dweller of the 1990s. Her autumn 1997 collection highlighted the demand for a comfortable, multi-functional wardrobe for urbanites on the move.

(A)

(B)

Nomadism, through necessity, has become the new contemporary condition. As they travel from city to city, spend long hours at the office or continually commute across the metropolis they live in, urban dwellers are more likely to occupy several temporary habitats throughout the day for longer periods than the time spent at 'home'. The modern person's habitation is the body, assisted by technical devices and made comfortable through choice of clothing. As a new aesthetically driven dynamic of multi-functionality equips urbanites for their itinerant existence, fashion designers and architects alike are questioning the future role of 'bricks and mortar' structures, reviving the vision for mobile urbanization that Archigram pioneered decades earlier.

Fashion designers who work according to architectural principles are creating garments they conceive as 'dynamic structures' between the built environment and the immediate needs of the wearer. Interpreting fashion as moving forms that enclose and protect the urban nomad, designers are transforming the traditional two-dimensional plane of the façade wall into a three-dimensional spatial zone to be occupied, inhabited and trespassed. In relating the protective and sheltering functions of clothing to an urban system, the concepts behind these structures indicate that urban architecture may not be constrained by place forever. Although the construction and function of architecture has traditionally been static, the structurally based approach that fashion designers take merges principles of mobility and freedom with concepts of space and place.

As urban nomads confront the limitations of the built environment, the role of the architect as the problem solver of modern life is supplanted by the fashion designer. Some of the most progressive solutions have been conceived by fashion designers working in Europe, the United States and Japan, all of whom derive inspiration from concepts of space and principles of architecture. As this chapter continues to investigate the work of these key designers, the iconic garments and structures designed by Archigram are revisited to chart the origins of this genre. Yeohlee's progressive vision for fashion design encompasses many of the principles behind Archigram's oeuvre, designating garments as the key components of a larger spatial system. Likewise, Kosuke Tsumura envisages that clothing will eventually surpass housing altogether and function as the city dweller's final home, and he plans to equip the urban nomad with the means to colonize the public spaces of the city. C P Company are pioneering a fresh direction guided by radical new forms, shapes and materials deployed to redefine space, deriving inspiration from principles of architecture to move garments beyond conventional fashion. As these designers fuse functionality and utility to create some of the most high-performance fashions ever designed, they counter a world in transition by proposing solutions as visionary as the designs themselves.

Archigram

With their pioneering and challenging projections for urban architecture, the British group Archigram (deriving their name from architecture and telegram) spawned ideas that have influenced the vision of many leading architects. The group formed in 1960 through the alliance of the architects Warren Chalk, Peter Cook, Dennis Crompton, David Greene, Michael Webb and Ron Herron, all of whom questioned the tenets of architectural theory that had always championed the domus uncritically. The group's concepts took shape in projects they described as the group introduced 'Walking Cities', 'Instant Cities', 'Plug-in Cities' and 'Computer Cities', all of which have remained the icons of fluid architecture. Archigram conceived of urban dwellers who moved amidst newly discovered tactile, sculptural spaces in clothes, cars and housing, and would occupy the capsule apartments and living pods known as 'Gasket Homes' and 'Expandable Place Pads', or inhabit architectural skins like the 'Cushicle' and the 'Suitaloon'. Archigram were among the first to identify the changes that modern fashion would have to make, and designed wearable environments that foreshadowed the arrival of techno fashion.

Recognizing that clothing could adapt to needs of the modern urbanite more quickly than architecture – fashion is characterized by constant change and renewal, new paradigms of architecture take much longer to effect – Archigram pioneered a system of wearable structures. Archigram's Suitaloon, detailed in chapter 2, outfitted the wearer in clothing containing portable amenities. Likewise, the Cushicle, Archigram's inflatable body suit, contained compartments for food and fluids, a radio transmitter and a television monitor. The Cushicle and the Suitaloon were equipped to adapt to their surroundings and interact with them, responding directly to the environmental problems found in urban centres. Both garments provided the individual with a sense of refuge, enabling the wearer to regard their clothing as a source of shelter and security. Today these would most likely be interpreted as the 'technical devices' that Jennifer Craik suggests are able to 'articulate the relationship between a particular body and its lived milieu, the space occupied by bodies and constituted by bodily actions'.[1]

From their earliest projects onward, Archigram's utopian visions emphasized mobility and communication, focusing on systems of mobile architecture populated by communities or individuals. While historically clothing has generally been seen as an extension of the body, the garments Archigram envisaged were indistinguishable from the urban environment, incorporating a range of cultural influences that aligned them with other media. Pop art, music, science fiction and film inspired the garments' style and construction, while space travel was reflected in the garments' capacity to function as quasi-microcosms.

By appropriating techniques from fashion design, Archigram pioneered a smoother and more inter-effective relationship between architectural design, materials and the human form they house. The Cushicle and the Suitaloon collapsed existing interior/exterior and subject/object hierarchies and dualities evident in built structures, and formed a set of intelligent and interactive objects, surfaces and skins, with supple, responsive and interconnected interiors. As Archigram collapse the respective meanings of architecture and fashion, the unique environments they create maintain a continued dialogue that can progress and optimize each other.

Archigram's vision for a new urban environment defied the move towards the residential housing estates and tower blocks that characterized British urban life in the 1950s and 1960s. The group also eschewed the segregation of commerce, leisure, recreation and family life designated by rigorous zoning regulations that transformed urban streets into purely transitional spaces. Archigram converted flat street grids into dynamic three-dimensional webs of interaction where wearable environments, transport, public space and private dwellings all converged in a single, interactive system. Through expressing the interrelatedness of mobility, wearable structures and the lifestyle of urban dwellers, Archigram transported lived experience into architecture.

Over subsequent decades, the relevance of the group's vision has been proven. Archigram foresaw that urban life would extend beyond the city limits, although not necessarily into nature or suburbia. For many urbanites, the fast-paced lifestyle of constant travel, cellular communication and compact living that characterized the end of the twentieth century promises to escalate in this one. Each of Archigram's proposals seems to have served this emerging agenda, where, as David Greene states, 'nomadism is the dominant social force; where time, exchange and metamorphosis replace stasis; where consumption, lifestyle and transience become the programme; and where the public realm is an electronic surface enclosing the globe'.[2] Archigram interpreted architecture as an electronic interface that could communicate with clothing in a mutual system. Today, techno fashions, like the i-Wear prototypes developed by Starlab, also feature wireless communication devices that connect with each other and respond to sensors embedded in the built environment.[3]

The modular living pods featured in Archigram's Plug-in City were updated expressions of Le Corbusier's pronouncement that a house should be a 'machine for living in'. The pods were equipped with electronic communication devices and outfitted with floating hover-chairs and inflatable beds, all suggesting a kinetic lifestyle where the lived environment functioned as both a container and a vehicle. Richard Buckminster Fuller, an American architect and engineer, had envisioned similar pods in 1927, when he launched the Dymaxion project of interconnecting housing modules that presaged the prefabricated buildings and mobile homes constructed decades later. Fuller used to disconcert his contemporaries by asking them how much their buildings weighed – a significant question that would have been understood by Archigram. Archigram's mobile structures were often vast in scale; their Walking City was a colossal forty-storey mobile superstructure able to traverse the landscape on caterpillar-like legs that telescoped and extended as it moved over open terrain.

Archigram's vision of a highly mobile society connects with a continuous line of architectural discourse initiated by Mies van der Rohe and Le Corbusier, then continued through the avant-garde proposals propagated by the Congrès Internationaux d'Architecture Moderne and afterwards by Team X.[4] Archigram also drew upon a similar discourse advanced by the Situationists, an influential group of 1960s avant-garde radicals based in Paris who challenged the view that architecture should be essentially seen as inert, and devoid of political content. The Situationists rhetoric of content and form revealed the extent to which architecture exists within a political context, and is therefore always politicized by association. Some of their original discourses explored technology, social control and population dynamics, perhaps foreseeing the advent of techno-science, surveillance, urbanism and alienation. But while the Situationists routinely eschewed the exploding spectacle of consumer culture, Archigram's work celebrated it.

Guy Debord, a one-time leading member of the Situationists, has shaped many of the theses relating to urban life through his reflections on the impact of capitalist spectacle.[5] One of Debord's seminal texts 'Theory of Dérive', published in a 1956 issue of the Belgian surrealist journal *Naked Lips*, described modern architecture as 'a technique of transient passage through various ambiences'. As the essay closes, Debord concludes that, 'one day we will build cities for drifting'.[6] Archigram's nomadic cities aspired to realize this vision; their portable cities introduced a new global tribe of empowered nomads who could travel within roaming cityscapes, or traverse the urban landscape in the comfort of their own portable dwelling. While Debord conceived of drifting as a means of social surveillance, Archigram acknowledged its value as an emerging lifestyle.

Questions of mobility in architecture were also central to the concept of 'oblique' architecture pioneered by Claude Parent and Paul Virilio in the early 1960s. Together they investigated a new kind of architectural and urban order that rejected the traditional axes of the horizontal and the vertical, using oblique planes to create an 'architecture of disequilibrium'.[7] This allowed spaces to be constantly modified, and charged the built environment with a lateral model of the body in movement, generating a constant shift in readings of the urban site. Archigram paralleled this concept of a responsive environment, investing their designs with energy and flux rather than following traditional architectural rhetorics of beauty and sustainability.

Although not a single one of Archigram's designs was ever actually built, their ideas remain contemporary today. For many architects, the concept of urbanism presented by Archigram, the Situationists, Virilio and Parent remains a theory, but for fashion designers such as Yeohlee Teng, C P Company, Kosuke Tsumura, and Hussein Chalayan the margins between clothing, shelter, public space and urban egress are redefined in a variety of wearable structures discussed later in this chapter. The work of these designers reflects new architectural principles and changes in the urban environment, such as increased mobility, shifts in group dynamics, the growth and enlargement of transitional spaces, and the emergence of a modernist 'flâneur', the 'urban nomad'. The impact of contemporary architecture is especially visible in the garments equipping the urban nomads for their movements through city life, protecting them against noise, pollution and uncivil civilians. Archigram's future has finally arrived.

Final Home

In the hands of some designers, a coat can be interpreted as a glamour wrap, a padded cocoon, a biker's jacket, or even a strait-jacket. To Kosuke Tsumura, the coat is the body's final home; a 'minimum dwelling' station that provides the wearer with the means to face the daily dramas of modern life. 'Living in a big city, you could do without housing. Your clothing could function as your housing,' Tsumura explained, describing his functionalistic designs as a 'mobile home' and a 'clothing solution' for the problems faced by everyday urban life.[8] Tsumura's futuristic vision of the cityscape is one that collapses the boundaries between indoor living, street life, forays into nature and enjoying outdoor performances and sports events.

For Tsumura, the true meaning of fashion evolves around the lived experience that garments undergo on the body, which ultimately means that their role is premised on activity. Likening an immobile garment to an uninhabited building, Tsumura wants his designs to be 'lived in', differentiated from the sublime images of fashion that typically present garments as delicate, refined and static.

Tsumura began producing his Final Home label in 1993, after leaving his job at Issey Miyake, where he had worked for ten years. His manifesto was to create a comprehensive shoes/coats/accessories collection to meet the needs of an itinerant society. Today, Tsumura is a highly respected designer who has presented several outstanding collections at Fashion Weeks in London and in Paris for several seasons, his Final Home label now synonymous with the concepts of survival, protection, functionality and recycling. Tsumura's design ingenuity has secured Final Home's presence at numerous architectural and design exhibitions around the world, including the architecture biennale in Venice, as well as multimedia collaborations with artists and architects.

(A)

Urban Nomads

The Final Home collection was exhibited in the Japanese pavilion at the Seventh Venice Architectural Biennale. The entire pavilion and the garden around it were whitewashed, and the floor, on several levels, was lined with white gravel or had sections excised to create voids. Tsumura's project, titled 'Mother', was commissioned by the curators, Arata Isozaki and Kazuko Koike, and presented within the rubric of an exhibition titled 'City of Girls'. The theme of the exhibition revolved around the premise that the preferences of Japan's population of teenage girls – who, incidentally have assumed an iconic status in Japanese society – is predictive of the cultural and environmental sensibilities of the twenty-first century. What they wear, how they want to live and where they want to hang out seems to forecast the vision taking Japan forward – a concept that does not fit neatly into Western grids of comprehension. But for the architects behind the exhibition, the teenage girl also symbolizes a figure not yet fully indoctrinated by tradition or convention, voicing an optimistic future for a new mode of urban life.

Mother was based on a cocoon-like range of suits and jackets designed without any distinct form or shape of their own. Installed to hang from the pavilion's ceiling, it resembled an amorphous overcoat, yet provided a mobile shelter. The distinction of clothing and housing was muted; as heavy-duty clothing it assumes both roles, yet it is formless and dispossessed. Its stretchable, expandable dimensions can be worn by one individual or two, made to enfold a mother carrying her child. Tsumura's inspiration behind Mother was to conceive of a single garment as an intimate clothing structure for mother and child, collapsing the

*The Final Home Jacket is a waterproof nylon sheath fitted with enough pockets to equip the urban nomad for almost any eventuality. The jacket is intended to highlight the role of clothing as the body's ultimate shelter - literally its 'final home'.

distinction between clothing and shelter as it assumes both roles. Tsumura's message voices a move to protect the young from noise and pollution, fitting Mother with a hood and belly that can be completely zipped up and closed off from its surroundings. Tsumura equates embodied sensation with the capacity to dwell in the phenomenological sense, which he interprets as an essentially architectural experience.

Poetically, Mother represented a range of architectural tropes. In the guise of a maternal protector, she represents the continuation of life, evoking architecture's role of nurturing and protecting, essentially providing structures that facilitate and sustain human life. But the structure also constituted a void, denoting the absence of the bodies intended to inhabit them. Striking a poignant chord, Mother also constituted a memorial or a monument; not necessarily commemorating a loss of life, but perhaps of beauty or even nature. The materials and formal characteristics of Mother's construction, along with the aesthetic sensibilities invested by Tsumura, connected her to the other Final Home garments in a system that mirrored the macro- and micro-structures of architecture.

Stylistically, Mother is atypical of Tsumura's design, but conceptually her message of mobility, protection and rootlessness mirrors the ethos that underpins most of the designer's work. Tsumura's signature garment, the 'Final Home Jacket', could function as his mission statement. Tsumura first assigned the name 'Final Home' to this particular garment and later appropriated it as his the name for his label, deliberately equating the jacket to the idea that clothing constitutes the ultimate shelter. The jacket is a multi-functional, transparent, nylon sheath, equipped with forty-four zipped pockets creating folds and geometries that redefine conventional body shapes and fabric cuts. The pockets function as compartments, providing the wearer with plenty of space to store belongings. Pockets hidden inside the jacket can be lined with warm materials for extra insulation, or cushion the wearers when they sit or recline. The transparency of the outer pockets enables the wearer to customize the surface of the jacket, filling them with pictures, postcards or artwork to create different surfaces. Tsumura also suggests that some of the pockets be stocked with survival rations and a medical kit, equipping the jacket with the potential to provide first-aid assistance in medical emergencies. Each jacket features a label sewn on the sleeve for the wearer to write in their blood type and vital statistics in case of emergency, literally providing the means to wear your life on your sleeve.

When Final Home was launched in 1994 it aimed to create a new wardrobe that incorporated the principles of mobility and autonomy. Tsumura's message seems to be that, as urban nomads, we should be fully equipped with clothing that can transform into a protective shell equipped with extra warmth and enough supplies to enable us to spend a night away from home. Final Home's multi-pocketed systems signify organization as much as they do storage and mobility. Filling them with groceries, garments or work-related instruments displaces these objects into the domain of the body, eliminating the need for backpacks, shopping bags, luggage and even tool kits. Although the provision of individual compartments may initially seem like an ideal solution, the bulk of the filled pockets could inhibit the wearer's movement, bringing the ergonomics of the jacket into question.

Equipped with such resolute properties, the jacket can be structured by the owner rather than merely worn as a garment. The emphasis placed on its inherent potential for shelter and mobility symbolically equips it with the means to resist a regimented lifestyle. The jacket's utilitarian image suggests an aesthetic crisis as much as a social one, effectively projecting an anti-fashion message as it rejects the clichéd notions of wearing everyday clothes for an ordinary life. Through

(A)

his commitment to functionality, Tsumura is also introducing a subtle counter-cultural narrative that disconnects his label from the luxury and artificiality associated with high-fashion brands. This differs from the counter-cultural dynamics of political and sexual resistance projected by radicals such as Vivienne Westwood, John Galliano, Jean Paul Gaultier and Katherine Hamnett, who were attempting to invert gender norms or explore taboo practices. Tsumura's dialogue with urban modes of mobility, egress and individuality does not have the same radical connotations, but projects an oppositional message even so.

Final Home's production ethos resembles an industrial manufacturing process more than fashion design. Tsumura develops new products through experimentation and collaboration with companies in other industries who share a similar approach towards urban mobility. Tsumura later embarked on a project he called 'ReHome', creating a line of products designed to extend his ethos to a variety of lifestyle scenarios. Tsumura predicted that the urban dweller, to keep up with a fast-paced cosmopolitan lifestyle, would look for accelerated mobility to manoeuvre through the chaos of daily life more quickly. He provided for this eventuality with a line of 'Skate Furniture', producing an ellipse-shaped bag tailored to contain a skateboard and function as a chair cushion. Other components in the lifestyle range include cardboard sofas and pocket sofa covers, providing the urban nomad with the means of domesticating the street or cityscape.

Part of Final Home's manufacturing policy is intended to promote the transformation of waste into high design, and its garments' capacity to survive an extended life

^The message behind the Final Home label is principally mobility and autonomy, but comfort plays a role too. This cardboard sofa is an innovative design that transforms into a temporary seat, making flat-packed furniture the ultimate accessory for Final Home fashionistas.

cycle of reuse attests to the ingenuity of their designs and their high-quality materials. Tsumura is aligning his collection with a growing international consciousness towards waste, designed to reform the transitory values of consumer society and the norms of disposability and obsolescence. Tsumura juxtaposes the incompatible agendas of sustainability and consumerism, inverting the notion that once the fashion 'moment' has passed, the garment is rendered obsolete. This move equates fashion's transience with the ageing process associated with buildings, which continue to function even after their architectural styles have been surpassed. As such, Tsumura's garments signify a changing order of temporal values, perhaps erasing the conditions that generate the fashion moment to begin with.

Tsumura's studio and workshop participate in a Japanese system of recycling known as the 'waste business', where textile floss is made from scraps and re-spun into cleaning materials or protective clothing. Tsumura is committed to sending surplus materials, outmoded stock and former display garments to disaster areas through international aid organizations, a pledge he encourages other designers and fashion consumers to also make. The Final Home coats are even sold with a written message instructing the wearer how they can participate: *This is recyclable. After enjoying it as a fashion item, please wash it thoroughly and bring it to one of our outlets. We will donate it to organizations such as NGO for the benefit of refugees or disaster victims. For further details, please read the message card enclosed in the bag*. But although the aesthetics of the recyclable products in Tsumura's collection are based on a concept of eco-design, once they disintegrate into unwearability, the problem of disposing of the base materials still remains.

Ecological issues have had a strong impact on the types of textiles being developed today. Now the entire life cycle of the fabric must be accounted for, from the raw material through to each stage of textile development and its disposal. Because it can take synthetic materials hundreds of years to biodegrade, manufacturers are producing fabrics from recycled materials found outside the fabric industry. Even building materials are being used for fashion. Lightweight metals, reinforced plastics, glass fibres and industrial mesh introduce a vocabulary of forms and materials more common to a building site than a design studio. While the use of these reclaimed materials is more characteristic of architecture than clothing, new technologized processes make it possible to create ranges of hi-tech fabrics. Tsumura's bonded seams, transparent materials and waterproof fabrics echo the materials of buildings, revealing the garment's construction process without adopting the ruptured look characteristic of fashions inspired by the aesthetics of deconstruction and reconstruction discussed in chapter 3.

Just as architects are identifying how new urban paradigms will unfold in the twenty-first century, Tsumura reacts by assimilating similar principles in his garments. His Final Home collections surpass the notion of fashion as mere clothing, creating a highly individual system that fulfils many of the same functions of a home or dwelling. As Tsumura's collections respond to the demand for mobility, shelter and autonomy, they forge a dialogue with architectural concerns that echoes the need for social and ecological changes. While the designs of Final Home provide practical clothing appropriate for an urban outing, they also provide a vision of survival in a world where mother nature and the built environment collide.

C P Company

The spirit of the modern nomadic age, according to C P Company's designer Moreno Ferrari, comes from primal urges to build shelters and stake out our own territory. 'A man carries certain forms, colours and sensations deep inside himself,' Ferrari said, explaining his mission to capture such impulses in his chic range of transformable garments for

(A)

(B)

Urban Nomads

the modern nomad.[9] Primal instincts aside, C P Company's collections create a distinctive urban utility and practicality that updates clothing for use in the civilized world.

Living in an era characterized by unprecedented mobility impacts on our expectations and demands of clothing, as urban fashions evolve parallel to our need for independence and refuge amidst the cityscapes we traverse or on our travels between them. Within this milieu, C P Company have identified the 'DUE' (Dynamic, Urban, Educated) man, a new breed of body-conscious male consumer who appreciates the comfort of casual clothing, and the efficiency of multi-purpose, high-performance design. As C P Company combined their simplified tailoring technique with advanced technological design, they devised a series of transformable fashions designed to assume the form of furniture, tents or garments, depending on the needs of the wearer. Giving garments the potential to transcend their medium embodies the human fascination with extensions of themselves. Just as the car is an extension of our inherent mobility and the telephone an extended mouthpiece, transformable fashions reflect a garment's ability to provide shelter, amplifying its architectural properties.

Architecture emerged as early humans confronted nature to the full extent that technical skill would allow, attempting to banish the elements as much as possible from the human domain, with architecture negotiating space for survival. Identifying how clothing evolved from the need to simultaneously maintain interior and exterior spaces, C P Company's design ethos explores the principles of architecture and fashion to shape

As C P Company create fashion for the modern nomad they succeed in blurring the boundaries between fashion, furniture and architecture. Their overcoats and parkas transform into inflatable mattresses and one-person tents that can create a temporary environment almost instantly.

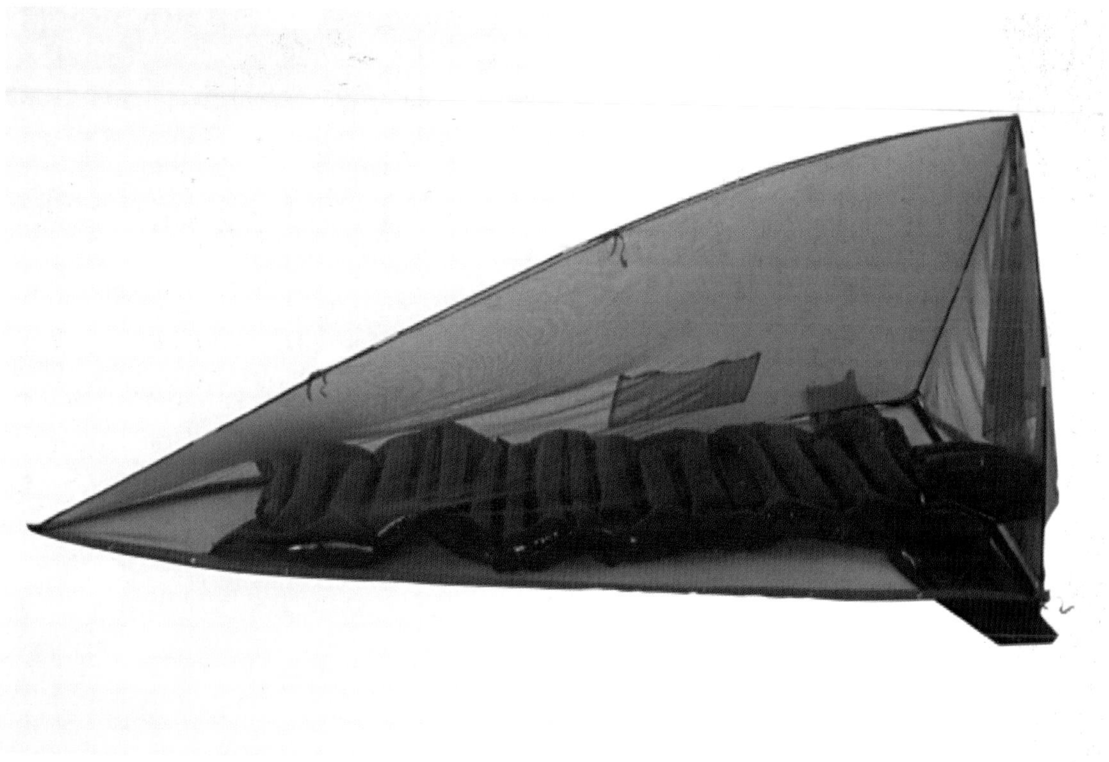

(C)

and define space according to human needs. C P Company also strive to create the possibility for humans to embrace nature rather than differentiating themselves from it, providing the means for humans to coexist with the natural environment through the protection and warmth of individual shelters.

Central to C P Company's philosophy is that we live in world in transition, where the urban domain continually bridges and interweaves the zones between nature and culture. They designed four distinct ranges that address the needs of those navigating the urban sphere: *Outerwear, Urban Protection, Transformables* and *C P Relax* (spring/summer 2001). The ranges are characterized by streamlined tailoring that eliminates the labels and exterior logos common to most high-performance clothing. The garments include only a bright blue loop on the front seaming that identifies them with C P Company as they rely on their characteristic innovation to create their design hallmark.

The *Transformables* range features three unique items that inflate, turning into an airbed, a cushion and an armchair. Dubbed the 'Caban', the 'Gilet' and the 'Parka' respectively, their inflatable components are made in blue-tinted transparent polyurethane, or an opaque earth-coloured PVC reinforced by a carbon coating. Their outer layers comprise a thin nylon mesh that protects them within a waterproof and tear-resistant cover. Each piece is made with magnetic buttons instead of snaps, and comes equipped with an air compressor to inflate it. They are laser cut and unlined, and made with simple detailing like Velcro tabs, expandable pockets, hoods and funnel necks. The range expresses mobility and multi-functionalism at its best, in clothes that can enhance individuality, provide comfort and bring a sense of utility and novelty to the wardrobe. The precise details and functionalism of the collection imbue the garments with design features that take the fusion of clothing and furniture far beyond the practice of hanging a jacket on the back of chair in an attempt to reserve it.

In our mobile society, we relate to interchanges, departures and arrivals more than we do the traditional idea of 'home'. To many urban dwellers, the stable site of dwelling is now considered to be a

Urban Nomads

myth, a view C P Company's designers reinforce with their portable abodes. The most innovative of these is the Caban, an overcoat that transforms into both an inflated mattress and an aerodynamic one-man tent, fitted with a torch to illuminate its interior in darkness. In the urban realm, the Caban provides a perfect mini-environment for sleeping or finding solitude – a great means of coping with long plane delays and the lack of privacy in public areas, or for designating private space in an outdoor spot. Other C P Company garments provide a similar function: the 'Foldaway Hammock' jacket from the Urban Protection range stretches into a sleek hammock comfortable enough to sleep in. Likewise, the 'Amaca', a dark-green hooded cape, also transforms into a hammock, supported by industrial-strength straps attached to its hood and bottom hem. Flexible, hybrid structures like these mimic the system of 'open architecture' that Daniel Libeskind calls for in the regeneration of Berlin, in his vision of a fluid architecture that can adapt and evolve according to urban life.

The Gilet is a polyurethane waistcoat that transforms into a cushion. Once inflated, the garment's back panel is strong enough to comfortably support full body weight, and durable enough to rest on almost any surface. The waistcoat's front panels remain attached to the back, inflated to flank either side of the main cushion to provide armrests. The Parka is made from an airtight polyurethane material that inflates into a one-person armchair. The compressor pumps up the shoulders and collar to form the chair's backrest, while the sleeves become armrests poised above a rear panel that morphs into a seat cushion. The wearer can be seated in comfort while camping out in ticket lines, watching sports games, or relaxing on the beach.

The notion of fashion as furniture brings to mind the relatively recent drive towards 'furniturisation'; a trend to regard everyday forms as objects of desire.[10] Domestic objects like chairs and tables are no longer valued for their characteristic utility, but for the design features that elevate them to the status of cultural artefacts. Architectural elements like panels, ledges, plinths and partitions are valued for their dual application as built-in furniture, shelving or screens, ascribing an idealized utility to functional form. This is also symbolic of the trend to downsize or minimalize living spaces, providing an antidote to the shopping culture that floods the home with an avalanche of products. In the context of fashion, C P Company's *Transformables* range presents a seamless unity between human activities and their corresponding objects, although they require a degree of technical skill beyond the point of purchase. This is especially evident in the 'Move' parka, a multi-pocketed jacket designed for their autumn/winter 2000–1 collection. The parka contains the components of a lightweight scooter within its built-in backpack, assembled on the street by the wearer to give the parka real mobility.

By injecting their transformable ethos into a culture already saturated with furniturization, C P Company are establishing a market for a range of other designs to be recognized. If garments can become furniture and tents, it is logical to assume that they also hold the potential to transform into large structures, or perhaps even permanent dwellings. The pioneering work of the artist Lucy Orta (discussed in chapter 7) produces wearable dwellings made up of individual sections or units that can be interconnected to make a number of individual dwellings or combined as a single construction. The 'Basic House' designed by the Spanish architect, Martín Ruiz de Azúa, is a structure so lightweight it can be folded and carried in the wearer's pocket. Opened up and expanded by body heat or solar heat, it extends into a cube-shaped shelter that can provide a temporary dwelling for several people. For Ruiz de Azúa it represents 'a life of transit without material ties', satisfying the need for shelter without engaging in the complex system of value and utility triggered by transformable garments.[11]

The *Urban Protection* range features communication technology developed by Sony, which is integrated into the garments. Ferrari's design team adapted pre-existing communication technology with newly developed fabric technologies to create new information interfaces in clothing. Like the wireless technology of i-Wear discussed earlier, the range's integrated devices symbolize fashion's foray into the interactive environments created within modern architecture. Sony's sound technology is adapted for two models in the range, converting them to mini music environments: 'Yo' and 'Life' are parkas equipped with integrated Sony Discmans to provide the wearer with a respite from city noises or create a relaxation zone.

C P Company's 'Global Positioning Jacket' interfaces with an Etrex navigation system that enables the wearer to communicate with a ground control base that can track their movements by satellite and advise alternative travel routes. The jacket extends the reach of surveillance capabilities without relying on optical devices to do so, making it possible for the wearer to contact databases and retrieve information from systems beyond their immediate environment. As well as gauging travel directions, portable technology of this type could potentially be used to navigate the wearer around alarmed routes and restricted-access areas, as the wearer tracks the environment rather than gets tracked by it. The Global Positioning Jacket is significant because, like the surveillance equipment discussed in chapter 1, it equips the wearer with the technology that facilitates surveying the environment and the activities of others, both near and remote.

Fabric technology is often the starting point of C P Company's designs, engineering textiles strong enough to be weatherproof and durable. Dynalfil, a high-performance polyester bonded to nylon mesh, was developed by C P Company to be rip- and abrasion-proof, oil-proof, wind- and waterproof. Steel threads are woven into the structure of the fabrics to create a reinforced grid, making it tear resistant. The spring/summer 1999 collection featured jackets made from Carboguard, a protective fabric developed to filter out magnetic and radioactive waves polluting the urban environment. They cocoon the wearer within a nickel-plated shell, providing fashionable protection against the health risks attributed to ambient radiation.

Transformable garments are the simplest and most minimal fashion statement of all. Though their design may seem complex, the principles behind them bring utility and functionality to fashion, refining and maximizing the wardrobe beyond its wearable potential. While the emerging trend for transformable clothing commissions designs from the most elevated corners of the fashion universe, transformables also make it apparent that we live in a culture dependent on these technologies and others to create a sense of equilibrium. For visionary designers like C P Company, their continued experimentation with space and construction provides a rich source of innovation, enabling them to transcend established boundaries and challenge conventions in fashion.

Yeohlee

Yeohlee Teng is a fashion designer who has forecast, rather than followed, recent cultural and theoretical developments redefining the social organization of urban society. Through her conceptual approach and her concise examination of the human form, Yeohlee's work generates a critical discourse on clothing and space, the body and anthropometrics. Her intense analysis of modern life has inspired her to experiment with new forms and fabrics that achieve the concise form and utility of an engineering blueprint. Yet as Yeohlee conceives of clothing as a component within a larger spatial system, she consciously refutes the abstractions of architecture to produce structures and spaces for use by the human body alone. Yeohlee's methodology is not just negation, subtraction and purity: she reduces the creative process to the basic concepts of volume, function and proportion to arrive at an architecture of the body itself.

Yeohlee's garments are arrestingly beautiful, modern and breathtaking in their simplicity. That they possess a subtle spirituality is undeniable; many of her signature pieces are at once ecclesiastical in their flowing sleeves, sweeping capes and dramatic hoods, but undeniably futuristic in their clean, simple lines, technologized fabrics and muted colours. It would be hard to overlook the transcendental properties of the garments themselves, which soothe the boundary between ethereal anonymity and maverick identity. Yet beyond their

[A+B] Yeohlee's expressions of urban chic are breathtaking in their simplicity. Yeohlee advocates an economy of design that juxtaposes clean lines and pure forms with utility and streamlined functionality.

[C] As Yeohlee explores principles of revealing and concealing, she highlights the body's role as a superstructure.

(A)

(B)

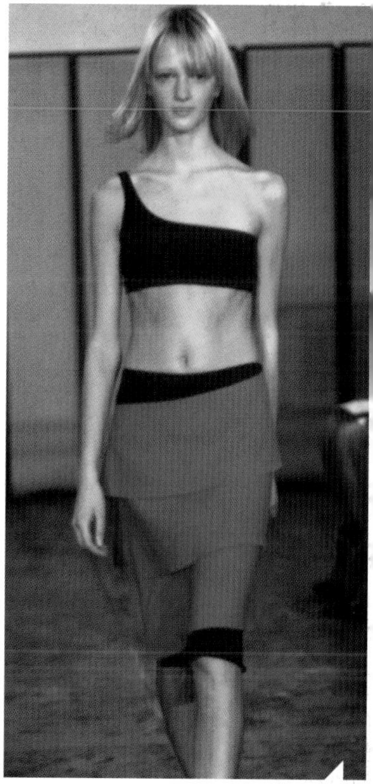

(C)

intrinsic beauty, Yeohlee's clothes have a distinctive utility unique to high fashion. 'She represents herself as an anti-fashion designer, a clothing architect who is more concerned with comfort and maintenance that with glamour and display; she describes her clothes as "shelters",' wrote John Seabrook, who profiled Yeohlee's visionary approach in a feature for *The New Yorker*.[12]

As Yeohlee's clothes present a wider vision of fashion they also create a new context in which to discern the meanings inherent in codes of dress. 'The nature of fashion is information. I think that what we choose to wear is impacted by things around us,' she said.[13] Yeohlee's work evolved in response to changes in the city infrastructure, shifts in the social fabric and the evolution of the urban dweller. The term 'Urban Nomad' was coined by Yeohlee herself to describe the impact of urban signifiers on fashion construction, culminating in her *Urban Nomads* collection (autumn/winter 1997). Since then, Yeohlee's collections have effectively charted the disappearance of the traditional woman of fashion, as her wardrobe now dictates multi-purpose garments and maximum functionality, providing her with high-calibre elegance and even a sense of refuge.

'There is an aspect of clothing as portable architecture,' Yeohlee said, 'and our clothes, which are modular, are also our shelters, which is the main function of buildings. Depending how extreme you want to be, you could say that clothes are your ultimate home. There has always been a dialogue between the two disciplines. It is a constant in our lives. I think it is a very practical step for designers to explore the possibilities and potentials the two yield.' More fundamental than architecture, Yeohlee's clothing achieves a synergy between garment and wearer, expressed in an intimacy rarely found in conventional architecture. In many respects her works remain unfinished, completed by the presence of the wearer within them and their relationship with architectural structures. 'Both architecture and fashion are concerned with appreciation of material, the ability to organise information and how humans function within their environments,' Yeohlee said. 'In many respects the environment they are worn in determines clothing's

(A)

(B)

Urban Nomads

function,' said Yeohlee, pointing out the impact that the built environment can have on finished garments.

From the end of the 1990s onward, Yeohlee's practice evolved to meet the needs of a twenty-first-century *flâneuse*, who traverses the urban realm with the same rationale as their nineteenth-century predecessor. Yeohlee's *flâneuse* is typically ultra-modern: a corporate professional, a gallery director, a renowned architect, a publishing executive. Her following includes Susan Sontag, Patti Smith and Oprah Winfrey; many other women in the public eye also number among her regular clients. Yeohlee imbues her collections with a subtle note of austerity, aware that for many women her designs represent the type of empowerment they assert within these male-oriented domains. Yeohlee combines the old with the new; tailored femininity with contemporary fashion, old perspectives on urban space with a new type of rambling.

'I like the nomadic nature of our lives right now,' she explained, 'and making clothes that enhance that nomadic existence is interesting.' Yeohlee's *Urban Nomads* collection engaged with the crazy acceleration of global travel and the aesthetics of transitional zones like Renzo Piano's Kansai International Airport in Osaka. 'I was taken with how very curvy the building is. I was looking at the interiors and noticed that the other travellers were in a mess as they traversed the space. They looked very interesting and textural, but Kansai looked so modern that it made the travellers look so dated. I did a collection around how I thought people should look in that space,' she said.

Yeohlee's process and methodology extend beyond the garment and the wardrobe, into the living sphere of the wearer's every-

[A]Techno textiles often feature in Yeohlee's work, where their properties of durability and versatility suit the demands of the urban lifestyle. The garments achieve the comfort level typical of casual wear, while their streamlined styling gives the garments a formal feel.

[B]Yeohlee employs architectural principles to structure garments like these through a system of tiers.

day world. Yeohlee explores this vision of human life through the micro-shelter provided by a garment and the macro-shelter of architecture and technologized spaces. Intrigued by the prototype A3XX aeroplane that can transport up to six hundred people, Yeohlee considered how travelling in such a huge crush of people would impact upon the urban nomad. 'I would like to travel wearing the most efficient outfit possible. I would want my outfit to define my space, making a clear and concise statement about my relationship with my surroundings,' she said.

Such juxtapositions are almost Situationist in scope, as they align with the critique against the pervasive expansion of consumer spectacle invading and restructuring the spaces of travel, leisure and private life. While defining oneself against such spaces may initially appear to be an expression of individual isolation, it is an act of resistance against the passive consumption of capitalist spectacle. Garments like Yeohlee's recognize the individual need for privacy, refuge and agency as urban space is increasingly appropriated for the masses. Interpreted as mini-environments, Yeohlee's designs propose alternative structures that designate the intimate, individual spaces of everyday life within the sites of mass consumption. 'I think about clothing first as a shelter, then as a modular system in which one dwells even more intimately than in architecture,' she explained.

The principle of modularity is central to Yeohlee's thinking. Her minimalism scales the wardrobe down to layered, interchangeable components that facilitate individual expression. While Yeohlee's garments are not modular in the sense that they transform into completely different garments, many of her separates maximize the utility of each garment through subtle tailoring that can offer a single design several looks. Skirts are gently contoured into a faintly crinoline-like silhouette by a back panel that can also be extended over the head to cocoon the wearer in a futuristic shawl. Capes can be fitted close to the body like a tailored coat, yet expand to shroud the wearer in a dramatic mantle. Designs like these conform to the principles of the modular systems promoted by Archigram, enabling styles to be reconfigured by interchanging the modules. Ultimately Archigram envisaged a modular system that enabled any one piece to be replaced without affecting the rest of the system, or modules to be rearranged in a new style. The range of clothing combinations Yeohlee offers each season is infinite – a single collection features several core designs that can function as separates or be combined to create a series of different looks, none of which are restricted to being the 'right way'.

By structuring garments in terms of modules and layering, Yeohlee coordinates dress for climate control and environmental changes. The use of high-performance fabrics, like Teflon, polyurethane, nylon and polyester, create breathable water-repellent surfaces that empower the wearer to negotiate environmental conditions in clothes succinctly tailored to create a formal feel and still meet the needs of the everyday casual. Yeohlee routinely avoids applying the phrase 'special occasion' to any of her designs. Her clothing is intended to achieve maximum utility for the wearer throughout the day rather being confined to the categories of daywear or eveningwear. In this respect, her garments draw upon principles more common to menswear or even sportswear, combining the means of formal expression with the comfort and practicality of sportswear.

Yeohlee's approach is not to echo lines of contemporary edifices in the cut of fabric, but to fully assimilate visual and intellectual principles of architecture into fashion, interpreting the two disciplines in terms of congruity of ideas.

'Fashion and architecture operate along the same principles,' Yeohlee said, often referencing her approach to buildings designed by

(A)

(B)

the architect Ken Yeang. Like Yeang's structures, Yeohlee conceives of sinuous panels supported by the body, as a façade is extended across the architectural framework. The tiered construction of her garments also mirrors the bioclimatic circulation of heat around the body, insulating the wearer in cushions of air.

In a landmark presentation of the two genres, Yeohlee exhibited a selection of her garments together with Yeang's work at the Aedes Gallery in Berlin. The exhibition revealed their mutual vision for environments defined by spatial awareness, working with and against the human form to create spaces whose meaning does not depend on an associated discourse or a predetermined landscape. Both Yeang and Yeohlee share a similar Chinese heritage and a Malaysian upbringing; Yeohlee moved to New York several decades ago, while Yeang remained to establish his architect's practice in Kuala Lumpur. Yeohlee draws inspiration from the cultural connections between native Malay traditions and Islamic shrouding, while Yeang's work (he has been commissioned to design buildings throughout the world) often references Malaysia's tropical landscape in his 'ecological corridors' and 'vegetated landscapes'. Yeang is famous for his lateral approach to architecture. His 'groundscrapers' and 'subscrapers' are designed to integrate humans with the urban landscape rather than distance them from it in high-rises.[14]

Both Yeohlee and Yeang map the boundaries of the body by creating climatic ecosystems around it. Yeang's bioclimatic skyscrapers constitute microclimates. The buildings are layered with a system of adjustable panels that can vary positions as the seasons change. Yeang's Shanghai Armoury Tower, for

Yeohlee's outerwear consists of a soft layering system that alternately retains and circulates body heat throughout the garment. This enables the wearer to navigate between seasonal weather temperatures and the 'fifth season' of climate-controlled interiors.

example, is equipped with a double-skin façade that circles the building's exterior while creating an inner void. In summer, windows can be opened within the inner skin to facilitate circulation of cool air rather than drawing in the temperate air from outside. In spring and autumn, natural ventilation is controlled by adjustable louvres fitted between the façade's skins, while in winter, a minimal supply of air is allowed into the building solely to circulate the retained the heat trapped inside the building.

As Yeang layers his buildings in different materials for better adaptation to climate, Yeohlee's stratum of clothing is determined by the use of tiers rather than conventional layering, which is a more efficient way of circulating air and body heat. The hollow spaces captured in the clothing's folds vary from open edges to thin vacuums, giving the garment's walls and centre spaces the same related values apparent in Yeang's architecture. The layers in Yeohlee's environments are structured so that each is contingent on the other. Their ability to trap and circulate warmth around the body is facilitated by the entire system of tiers rather than the properties of an individual layer. Studied together, their designs suggest symbiosis of the aesthetics of fashion and architecture, although Yeohlee's simplicity makes a sharp contrast to Yeang's complex architectural designs.

Noting how Yeohlee's soft layering created textile environments that enabled the wearer to navigate both weather patterns and climate-controlled interiors, Richard Martin credited Yeohlee with developing a 'fifth season' of fashion. In his essay, 'Yeohlee: Energy and Economy, Measure and Magic', Martin wrote: 'While Yeohlee conforms to fashion's seasonal calendar of showings and store delivery of merchandise, her clothing...often surpasses the seasons, allowing wearers to function in the "fifth season". The year-round wardrobe offers another economy from what was turn-of-the-twentieth-century's apportioning of the year and closet space into four separate parts.'[15] Yeohlee's strategy has the effect of extending the mid-season periods, creating a breathable, balanced garment that facilitates both ventilation and heat retention.

Yeohlee's frugal approach to material eschews the extravagant waste of fabric common to the practice of many twentieth-century designers. In some respects Yeohlee's spare approach can be attributed to her precise conservation of energy and material. She sustains a design economy that husbands every available resource, maintaining an attitude of reverence and respect for the integrity of the fabric. From her days as a fashion student onward, Yeohlee created her designs from a single length of fabric, crafting the garment, its belt, ties, collar, cuffs, waistband and lapels without leaving a single scrap of fabric behind. This sort of economy is achieved in the mass production of garment multiples by laser cutters programmed according to computerized calculations. For Yeohlee, this process is instinctive, directed entirely by the eye and cut out by hand. Yeohlee refines the norm of conventional cuts by conceiving unconventional shortcuts, such as combining the bust dart and side seam by contouring them into one.

As Yeohlee relates the human shape to fabric and scale, she engineers a fluid structure around it with the same considerations an architect would have for a building project. But her expression of functionality is a far cry from the shapeless unisex garments that usually characterize functional clothing. Yeohlee's understanding of the body's contours cuts the fabric to define a feminine shape in her garments, mirroring the architect's approach to integrating a building into a landscape. Like an architect, Yeohlee plots the sweep and sizing of her garments with mathematical precision to master proportions that will remain to scale as they are reconfigured to conventional sizes. 'A jacket is made out of numbers,' she said, emphasizing that a garment is calculated as well as designed. 'For a fashion designer, there are traditional approaches, like sketching pictorial references on paper or draping muslin on a mannequin. I use geometry to plot something two dimensionally and make a flat pattern that will have three-dimensional proportions. Knowing these measurements is like making a witch's brew: you throw numbers into the pot and come up with a formula. To determine the sweep of the garment you have to calculate the stride. Once you attribute that to the scale of people the whole equation is demystified.'

The dynamic nature of fashion dictates that garments are perpetually in motion. Although both fashion and architecture are concerned with ergonomics, a designer has to equip clothing with kinaesthetic properties rarely applied to architectural structures. In Yeohlee's case, each garment presents a challenge to conventional fashion thinking as she gives it the ability to first move on the body and then move through space itself. Yeohlee is not tyrannized by conventional cutting and simplified lines, but balances their construction against the geometry of the body and its range of natural movement. 'First I look at the minimum requirements. A garment has to go over the head or provide access for the arms. In a sense those are my only constraints. Like an architect, I consider where they would enter, exit and congregate. Egress is therefore an essential consideration for both disciplines', Yeohlee explained. 'Whether or not a button-fronted shirt is chosen instead of a turtleneck has to do with egress. How we get in is important to consumers because of time – our most precious commodity,' she explained. 'Unless it can function as a garment, it has failed.'

Women and men, as inhabitants of architecture, are regarded with the same equity in its genderless spaces and uniform proportions. Yeohlee's work draws upon these democratic tenets to focus on the features that men and women share rather than emphasizing the differences between them. While Yeohlee offers her clients eight sizes to choose from, she actually produces only six by sizing a women's 'medium' to fit as a man's 'small', and a women's 'large' to fit as a man's 'medium'. Occasionally her collections include a one-size-fits-all range of dresses, borrowing a principle from the architect's paradigm of standard doorframes and consistent ceiling heights, designed to facilitate egress to both the shortest and the tallest in a uniform proportion.

A+B+C Yeohlee seldom relies on appliqués, motifs or surface decoration to embellish her work, as her treatment of materials often creates subdued patterns or subtle textures. In these designs, Yeohlee highlights geometric shapes in the garments' construction by choosing fabrics in contrasting colours.

(A)

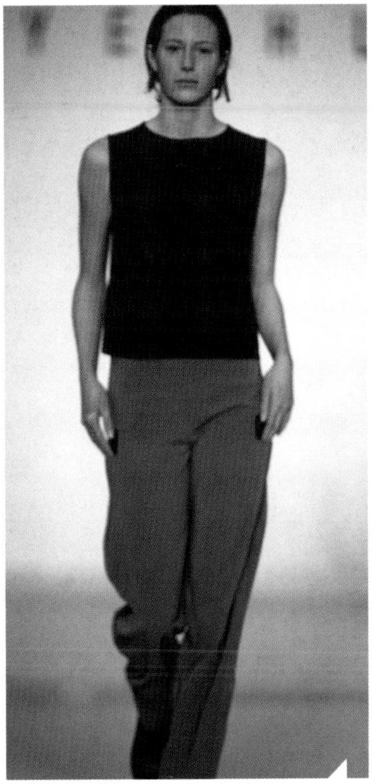
(B)

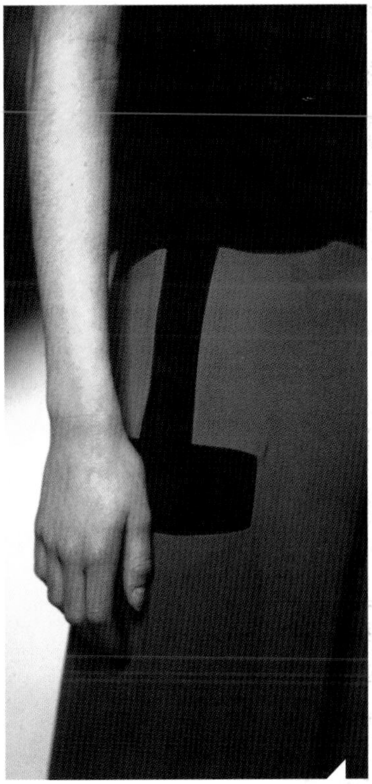
(C)

Critics of such concisely aestheticized work allege that puritanical approaches divest fashion of fantasy, an element many designers consider to be at the very epicentre of their work. In Yeohlee's work, her critical examination of the principles of clothing steers her away from ornamentation, much like Alexander Rodchenko's vision of Constructivism consciously rejected decorative elements to integrate technique and organization with fashion design. Yeohlee's work echoes the space-age geometry of Paco Rabanne and André Courrèges, bringing to mind the sci-fi sets and costumes of Kubrick's 2001. Though Yeohlee may not be inspired by fantasy per se, her garments anticipate a future lifestyle that is already a part of contemporary visual culture. Susan Sidlauskas featured Yeohlee's designs in *Intimate Architecture: Contemporary Clothing Design* at the Massachusetts Institute of Technology's Hayden Gallery, of which she wrote: 'Despite the fastidious, economical use of fabric and facility with drapery, both of which harken back to old couture, her juxtapositions and simplicity are modern.'[16]

Richard Martin also recognized Yeohlee's work as three-dimensional art, describing the spirituality evident in her spare approach to the essentials of form. In many cultures throughout the world, textiles encapsulate spiritual principles, representing the convergence of the tangible and the intangible. Yeohlee's oeuvre is a journey through simplicity as much as it is through minimalism. 'Basically I am a simple person. I like simple solutions, so the minimalism comes from that. Simplicity captures truth and elegance and encompasses a lot of intellectual values,' she said. 'An essential part of minimalism is knowing where to stop – I think that is really important'.

Having stripped fashion bare and systematically rebuilt it to compensate for the shortcomings of the urban world, Yeohlee's visionary approach enables her to confront the problems of twenty-first-century living head on. By exploring architecture's potential to identify and solve the dilemmas of the modern human, she fuses fashion with principles of self-sufficiency, security and shelter, giving fashion the potential to create completely new roles, and function within systems outside of its own.

[1]Jennifer Craik (1994), *The Face of Fashion*, London: Routledge, p4.

[2]Quoted in Michael Sorkin, 'Amazing Archigram', *Metropolis Magazine*, April 1998.

[3]Starlab was a scientific research laboratory based in Brussels. Starlab placed fashion on the cutting edge of both marginal science and advanced technology by pioneering techno fashions.

[4]Sourced via the The CIAM Collection, Frances Loeb Library, Harvard Design School.

[5]As expressed in Debord's film, *Society of the Spectacle*, and related writings.

[6]Guy Debord, 'Theory of Dérive', in K Knabb (1989) (ed), *The Situationist International Anthology*, Berkeley, CA: Bureau of Public Secrets, p50.

[7]See Pamela Johnston (1996), *The Function of the Oblique: The Architecture of Claude Parent and Paul Virilio 1963–1969*, London: AA Publishing.

[8]Quoted in Andrew Bolton (2002), *The Supermodern Wardrobe*, London: V&A Publishing, p71.

[9]Quoted in C P Company's spring/summer 2001 press release.

[10]The term was coined by the design historian Reyner Banham, writing in the exhibition catalogue for 'Modern Chairs: 1918–70', shown at London's Whitechapel Gallery in the summer of 1970.

[11]Quoted from a press statement released on 18 June 2002 by the Royal Institute of British Architects in conjunction with the *Basic House* exhibition.

[12]John Seabrook (2002), 'Nursing Chic', *The New Yorker*, 18 March 2002.

[13]Yeohlee Teng was interviewed by the author.

[14]See Ivor Richards (2001), *Groundscrapers and Subscrapers* of *Hamzah & Yeang*, Bognor Regis, England: Wiley-Academy.

[15]Richard Martin (1998), 'Yeohlee: Energy and Economy, Measure and Magic', *Fashion Theory*, 2(3), p287–93.

[16]Susan Sidlauskas (1982), *Intimate Architecture: Contemporary Clothing Design*, Cambridge, MA: The MIT Committee on the Visual Arts.

Notes

New College Nottingham
Learning Centres

Designing, Dwelling, Thinking: Hussein Chalayan

Hussein Chalayan's clothes are minimal in look but maximal in thought; his fascination with architecture, spatial dynamics, urban identity and aerodynamics are expressed in garments based on concepts, architectural systems and theories of the body. Chalayan's sense of the visual is ultimately true to his grasp of the practical and cultural needs resolved by clothing. Like Yeohlee and Kosuke Tsumura, Chalayan is one of the few fashion practitioners who can be recognized as a 'designer' rather than a 'stylist'. Many of the creatives working in the fashion industry merely resurrect older modes of dress or reinvent the basic garments found within the traditional fashion canon. Chalayan moves forward with completely new forms, shapes and materials conceived to define space, reflecting the construction principles and notions of contemporary architecture more than conventional fashion.

[A]As Hussein Chalayan imbues clothing with the aerodynamic properties of aeroplanes and land vehicles they acquire surprising shapes and unconventional surfaces. The 'Fin' top (spring/summer 2000) combines the silhouette of classic cars with aeroplane wings.

[B]The 'Glass Dress' (spring/summer 2001) contours the body in a sleek surface that neither bends nor folds like traditional fabrics.

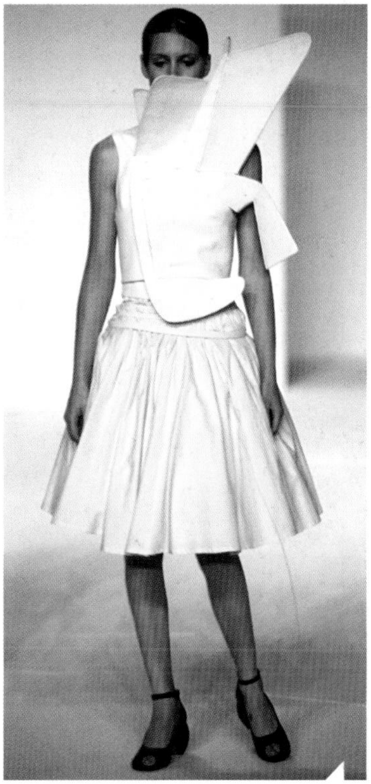

(A)

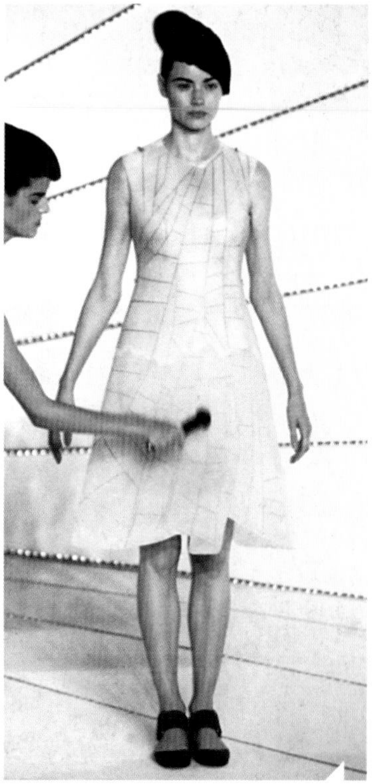

(B)

Chalayan rose to fashion fame soon after he received his BA degree from Central Saint Martin's School of Art in London in 1993. His final-year collection, *The Tangent Flows*, is the now infamous series of buried garments that had been exhumed just before the show and presented with an illustrated text that explained the process. The ritual of burial and resurrection gave the garments a dimension that referenced life, death and urban decay, in a process that transported the garments from the world of fashion to the bounty of nature. The work attracted the attention of the London boutique Brown's, who featured the collection in their window display. Since then, Chalayan has collaborated with architects, artists, textile engineers and set designers, won awards and produced collections for other established fashion labels.[1]

Despite his British education and long-term residency in London, Chalayan is true to his Turkish Cypriot origins, only recently coming to terms with being labelled as a British designer. 'I'm grateful that I have a bi-cultural background,' he said. 'I was exposed to more things. You have more to respond to and you question things more.' The idea of 'national' style is problematic for the fashion world, where designers of diverse nationalities show in the fashion capitals. While his work overlaps with the genre that Yeohlee also explores in New York, Chalayan seems to have more in common with Issey Miyake and Rei Kawakubo who show in Paris than any British designer showing in London. Fellow Turks Rifat Ozbek and Nicole Farhi are also acclaimed for their collections, but their work bears no similarity to Chalayan's at all.

Despite becoming an overnight success in the fashion world and receiving world-wide recognition for his ground-breaking designs, the first decade of Chalayan's career was haunted by financial turmoil. Chalayan elected to voluntarily liquidate his business in 2001 and began looking for new assets in order to continue. His label was restored by a licensing deal with the Italian manufacturing company Gibo, who manufacture clothing for many leading designers. Chalayan's arrangement with Gibo has resolved a long-standing saga of production problems – with Gibo comes an assurance that each collection will be delivered on time. With Gibo's backing in place, Chalayan later struck a deal with the

(A)

(B)

Designing, Dwelling, Thinking: Hussein Chalayan

classically inclined British luxury retailer Asprey & Garrard, who appointed Chalayan as creative director of fashion for their clothes and accessories line. With Chalayan's new role at Asprey & Garrard comes the challenge to transform his fascination with architecture, aerodynamics and geo-spatial politics into a collection described as 'lighter, more classical' in scope than his own label. However 'light' the collection may appear, the garments will require an audience with the confidence to carry off clothing still heavy with the thought process that created it.

The genius of Chalayan's work lies in his ability to explore principles that are visual and intellectual, charting the spectral orientations of urban societies through tangibles like clothing, buildings, aeroplanes and furniture; and through abstractions such as beauty, philosophy and feeling. While Chalayan accepts the practical reasons for clothing, he does not regard them as the starting point in the design process. 'My work is about ideas, really. My starting-point isn't always the woman. It's the idea,' Chalayan said, regarding fashion as a vehicle for the concepts he explores and the structures he envisages.[2] Chalayan does not relate his works to the canon of iconic fashion or the notion of design classicism, nor does he view them as expressions of the time we live in. 'They are more about timeless objects,' he explains, refusing to limit them to fashion-oriented interpretations or assign them to a specific era. Chalayan takes clothing far beyond the modernist fashions of the early twentieth century that echoed the architectural lines of buildings in the cut of dress.

Chalayan briefly considered becoming an architect before deciding to study fashion, and his affinity with the built environment

[A] Chalayan views the body as a mobile structure that can be equipped with technological devices and architectonic constructions. Here, the model's face is shielded by visor-like transparent panels.

[B] Exploring the idea of a global ethnicity or a generic bone structure, Chalayan created a cantilevered device that would appear to contort the wearer's facial features.

continues. 'I work in a cross-disciplinary way with people in other fields who contribute to what I am doing. I am interested in forms generally, not just in clothing but in other things too,' he said. Chalayan has collaborated with architects on a number of collections, and even lectured to the architecture and interior-design students at the Royal College of Art in London. 'One thing to keep in mind,' Chalayan said, 'is that when fashion looks modular and structured, people automatically call it architectural when it isn't. It takes a lot of structuring to make a dress truly architectural. Architecture can be designed in a fluid and unstructured way that doesn't look architectural, but it is still architecture.'[3] As Chalayan's adherence to architectural principles becomes more pronounced, his work represents a congruity of ideas that indicate fashion and architecture are coming closer together than ever before.

Dynamic Structures

While outwardly Chalayan interprets clothing as individual structures, he is mentally withdrawn into a quest to discern their meaning within the collective structures of society and material culture. Chalayan's vision is to fully integrate clothing with their surroundings, rendering a comprehensive understanding of different environments and the diverse factors that create them.

Chalayan maintains that city dwellers, irrespective of their nationalities, often have more in common with each other than they do with any of their fellow citizens in the provinces. The concept of fashion as urban armour appeals to urbanites around the globe, and, like Chalayan, a range of designers and architects throughout the world are looking to fashion to find solutions for modern life. In Holland, Hella Jongerius designed the *Mobile Dreaming* series of suits that function as a coat/blanket/sleeping bag, enabling the wearers to rest comfortably as they travel across the city. In Stockholm, the architect Jennie Pineus created the 'Cocoon Chair' and the 'Cocoon Mask' to provide a simple and accessible antidote to the stressful intensity of public spaces and transitional areas.

Her designs engulf the wearer's head in a beehive-shaped microcosm, or envelop the entire body in a womb-like enclosure. Based in New York, Toshiko Mori, also an architect, designed a *Woven Inhabitation* that proposes a solution for temporary urban shelters that can be quickly assembled in the wake of an urban crisis.

In garments, Chalayan has identified their potential to function as components of a modular environmental system, in which they conform to the architectural principles of shelter, protection and social structuring, yet maintain the mobility, flexibility and individuality that architecture lacks. As Chalayan charges process with the same equity he invests in form, he blurs the boundaries between the 'real' and the intangible, creating an intellectual forum as fluid as the concepts it represents.

Chalayan's long-standing fascination with aerodynamics manifested in his autumn 1995 collection, when he designed a series of flight-path prints. His 'Aeroplane' Dresses and 'Kite' Dresses were created through the use of architectural proportions to direct the spatial relationship between the fabric and the body, while Chalayan reflected on the relative meanings of speed, flight and the gravity of the body. The dynamics of the Kite Dress amplified its interplay with its surroundings by encoding 'messages' from the body, the built environment and the spatial zone above it as it flew, returned to earth and rejoined the physicality of its wearer. 'Everything around us either relates to the body or to the environment,' Chalayan explained. 'I think of modular systems where clothes are like small parts of an interior, the interiors are part of architecture, which is then a part of an urban environment. I think of fluid space where they are all a part of each other, just in different scales and proportions.'

For his *before minus now* collection (spring/summer 2000) Chalayan returned to his

(A)

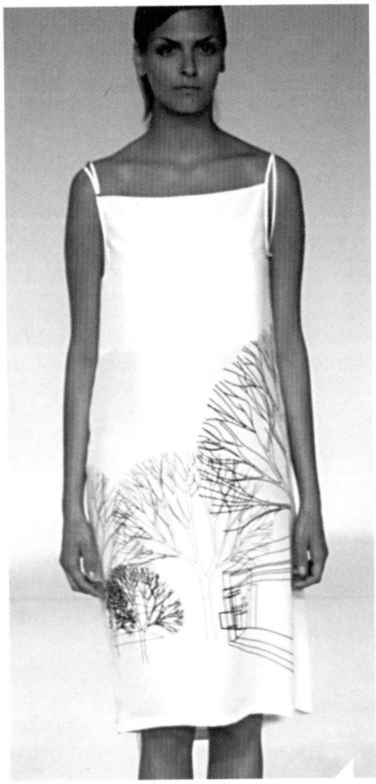

(B)

architectural theme, designing a series of dresses in collaboration with b consultants, the London-based firm of visionary architects. The dresses featured wire-frame architectural prints against static white backgrounds, generated by a computer programme designed to facilitate drawing a range of three-dimensional perspectives inside an architectural landscape. The renderings' geometric dimensions suppress the depiction of real space and create a reality independent of the shapes and textures found in the organic world. Such absolute symmetry and concise angles create the illusion of a realm that has been carefully ordered and controlled; yet the architectonic expressions correspond to physical registrations of surfaces, smart systems and programmatic mappings.

Juxtaposed against the organic curves of the body, these representations of inhabitable spaces reinforce the truism that the body inhabits its clothes. As abstractions, the images can simulate either dystopia or Utopia, providing a representation of a refuge or a token of resistance. Each garment was designed to present a challenge to conventional fashion thinking. Chalayan was not tyrannized by conventional cutting and simplified lines, but applies mathematical principles to the garments themselves, balancing their construction against the geometry of the body.

In Chalayan's hands, all garments and built structures manifest as externalizations of the body, shaped and proportioned to contain an individual or designated to house groups of people. In the *Echoform* collection (autumn/winter 1999) Chalayan created thought-provoking designs like leather dresses inspired by car interiors to represent

[A] Chalayan created this pattern from the flight patterns recorded by aviation tracking technology.

[B] This motif was designed as a wire frame architectural drawing, then transferred onto the fabric.

[C] Chalayan attached a padded headdress to this dress, recalling the design of aeroplane interiors.

[D-E] Chalayan reinterprets chairs as wearable designs as his work explores the idea of a nomadic existence.

(C)

(D)

(E)

'externalising speed and putting it back on the body', and mimicked airplane interiors by attaching padded headrests to dresses to evoke thoughts on speed, spatiality and well-being. 'We subconsciously amplify the structure of our bodies when we build something – a building or a machine,' Chalayan explained. 'If you look at car interiors, they are like a negative of the (reclining) body. I wanted to re-project that projection back on to the body and see what I came up with.'[4] Chalayan's examination of speed connects his work to a range of discourses that intepret the body in terms that makes human as analogous to a machine as possible. He imbues the dresses with technologies that represent the interactivity, productivity and uniformity akin to the machine-like principles of control and efficiency. References to these hi-tech systems in fashion fuse its body-conscious ideals with a belief in automation, speed and accuracy as the means of achieving it.

The *Geotrophics* collection (spring/summer 1999) adapted chairs to be wearable extensions of the human form. Chalayan's 'Chair Dresses' represented the idea of a nomadic existence, which, like the vision of Archigram, would be facilitated by living within completely transportable environments. With a determination to express 'how the meaning of a nation evolves through conflict or natural boundaries', Chalayan explored the meaning of geographical places and politicized spaces that cannot easily be defined architecturally.[5] Acknowledging the body's role as a locus for the construction of identity, he highlighted how its appropriation by national regimes would orient and indoctrinate it according to the space it 'belongs' to. In his symbolic effort to equip the wearer with a portable homeland, Chalayan reinstates a sense of individual identity in defiance of the myth that a homeland is designated by geographical borders alone.

The relationship between space and identity was later expanded in the ground-breaking *After Words* (autumn/winter 2000) collection (previously discussed in chapter 3), and demonstrated for the audience of the fashion show. Chalayan chose to stage the fashion show at Sadler's Wells theatre in London, relying upon the architectonics of the theatre and the stark design of the set to boost the collection's message.

(A)

Designing, Dwelling, Thinking: Hussein Chalayan

Chalayan designed a bare, white backdrop flanked by asymmetrical planes on three sides, featuring 1950s-style furniture that the models transformed into clothing in the show's finale, either by wearing it or carrying it off the stage. Some of the garments in the collection were equipped with pockets and compartments that could hold essential belongings, or fuse with other items of clothing so that they could be put on more quickly. 'A part of the idea was camouflage, so that things could be left in an obvious place and still be there when people came home again. That was part of the concept behind the dresses, that they were something valuable disguised as chair covers that no one would take,' Chalayan explained.

The space occupied by clothing is central to Chalayan's vision: clothing defines the intimate zone around the body, architecture a much larger one. In *After Words*, Chalayan expressed how either could become a danger zone and a refuge, a means of transportation for what could be carried and a camouflage for things left behind. Symbolically, the models were able to transport items from a 'threatening' environment to a safe place, re-establishing the safety and familiarity associated with them in different surroundings. It is significant that they transported the garments by bringing them into contact with the body, rescuing them as one would carry a child to safety.

The show was based on the idea of having to evacuate home during the time of war, hiding possessions when a raid was impending, and using the agency of clothing as the means to carry them away. The show's finale recalled the 1974 Turkish military intervention that displaced both Turkish and Greek Cypriots from their homes. 'You hear these stories of

(B)

A+B The *After Words* collection culminated in an expression of the transmutability of fashion design, as textiles that initially appeared to be chair covers transformed into sophisticated dresses. The collection introduced the concept of urban camouflage, where functional objects can be disguised as clothing and worn on the body, or garments adapted to conceal other structures.

how people would sneak back home when they weren't supposed to and take away what belonged to them. In some respects that's what was recreated on the stage, more poetically,' he said.

The collection was intended to express displacement and expatriation, but the objects made for the collection were also recognized for their design genius. Each piece of furniture featured on stage belonged to the collection; they had been systematically designed to transform into dresses and skirts, complete with pieces of luggage to pack away the clothes taken off.

The collection's congruency with architecture became even more apparent as rumours spread that Chalayan was launching a furniture and home-accessories line. While Chalayan has no immediate plans to do so, many fashion designers routinely produce ranges of soft furnishing, tableware and decorative objects. Architects also design lines of furniture or even lighting for the environments they design. Their presence in living spaces establishes a point of congruency where the two disciplines meet on equal ground; while interior design is neither architecture nor fashion, both disciplines employ it as a means of subdividing and conquering space just as Chalayan did. Dressing the body and dressing the interior are part of the same process, ornamenting and understanding proportions, matching textiles and colours. Architecture, fashion and interior design exist symbiotically in the same system – none would be possible without the other.

Chalayan's furniture was deployed as extensions of the theme he was representing through the fashion. For architects who produce furniture, the designs are generally intended to compliment their own architectural projects, unifying the aesthetics of the building and the functional objects within it in a single, harmonious whole. Although home and work environments are typically separate spaces, they are also integrated aspects of the built environment. For fashion designers, an interior-accessories range is a lifestyle statement that amplifies the message behind the label. They 'fashion' the interior in an expression of personal style that can be worn off the body, yet frame the body stylistically within its milieu. The inhabitants explore and define their identities through the interior as they interpret their meanings

Designing, Dwelling, Thinking: Hussein Chalayan

for themselves, creating images that speak both to the individual who has created it and to the world at large.

Freedom and Mobility

As Chalayan continues to establish a dialogue between the body and the environment, he is pioneering fashions that integrate wireless technology, electrical circuitry and automated commands directly into the structure of the garment. Mirroring the 'intelligent' systems controlling and regulating the functions of modern buildings, the 'Remote Control Dress' (spring/summer 2000), was a hi-tech triumph that married fashion to architecture and architecture to technology. 'The dress expressed the body's relationship to a lot of invisible and intangible things – gravity, weather, flight, radio waves, speed, etc,' Chalayan said. 'Part of it is to make the invisible tangible, showing that the invisible can transform something and say something about the relationship of the object – the dress in this case – between the person wearing it and the environment around it.' Chalayan established a new affinity between the human body and its surroundings, mediated by clothing designed to transmit information between the wearer and the built environment around them.

The Remote Control Dress, like those in the Aeroplane series, was designed by means of the composite technology used by aircraft engineers, mirroring the systems that enable remote-control airplanes to fly. Crafted from a combination of glass fibre and resin, the dress was moulded into two smooth, glossy, pink-coloured front and back panels that fasten together by metal clips. Each panel is encased within grooves of two millimetres in width that run throughout the length of the dress. These seams create the only textural differences in the dress, revealing interior panels made in translucent plastic, accentuated by lighting concealed within the solar-plexus panel and the left side elevating panel. The cast plastic surface of the panels resembles contemporary armour; the fine details of its lines and poetic gestures of its pale pink contours illustrate Chalayan's maxim that clothes are a second skin – albeit one that echoes the attributes of the fashioned body more than the organic body.

The plastic shell used in the dress's construction is created via a range of new hi-tech fabrics and new technologized processes that make it possible to adapt industrial materials for use as garments. Lightweight metals, reinforced plastics, glass fibres and industrial mesh are now crafted into shapes

[A+B] Following the transformation of the chair covers into garments, the models were able to transform the furniture designed for the *After Words* collection into pieces of luggage. As they carried them off the catwalk, they revealed fashion's potential to create a mobile environment.

(A)

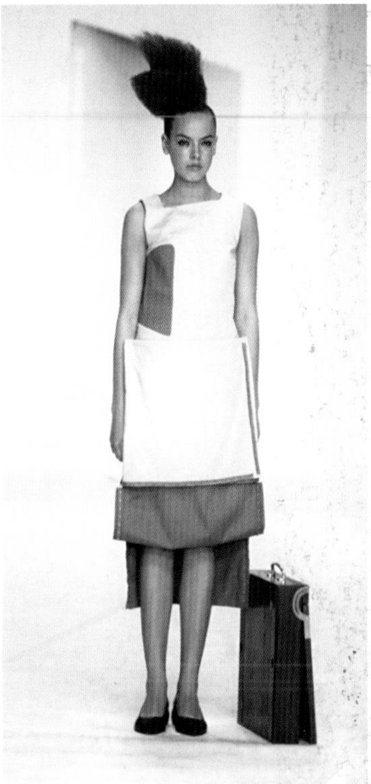

(B)

more characteristic of architecture than clothing – in fact, the dress's moulded shape, resilient materials and waterproofing all mirror the built environment more than conventional fashion. In recent years, Chalayan has focused more and more on the use of new materials, while also continuing to use traditional fabrics.

As the façade-like structure of the dress forms an exoskeleton around the body, it imbues it with elements of body consciousness. The dress's contours mimic the curves of the fashioned female body, arcing dramatically inward at the waist and outward in the hip region, echoing the silhouette of the corset and the crinoline. This gives the dress a defined hourglass shape that incorporates principles of corsetry in its design, emphasizing a conventionally feminine shape, while creating a solid structure that simultaneously masks undesirable body proportions.

In aesthetic terms, the Remote Control Dress has been variously described as 'arrestingly modern', 'beautiful' and 'breathtaking in its simplicity'. The dress possesses a subtle sensuality that is remarkably futuristic in its clean, simple lines, shining surface and lustrous colour. It would be hard to overlook the transcendental properties of the structure itself, negotiating a fine line between machine-like homogeneity and ultra-modern style.

Wireless systems of this type were first appropriated from architectural blueprints and adapted for garments by the now-defunct research organization Starlab. In researching their i-Wear prototypes, Starlab developed clothes that could be programmed to anticipate and respond to the wearer's needs by communicating wirelessly with remote systems. Although their prototypes featured state-of-the-art technology that provided the wearer with a broad range of functions, they never progressed to a finished model before the projects were terminated in 2001. Chalayan's Remote Control Dress, though less technologically sophisticated, was the first wireless device to be presented as a fully functioning fashion garment, with the capacity to interact with sensors embedded in the architectural structures surrounding it.[6]

Recognizing that the built environment is no longer inert, Chalayan began to explore the technological and material innovations that are giving architecture an

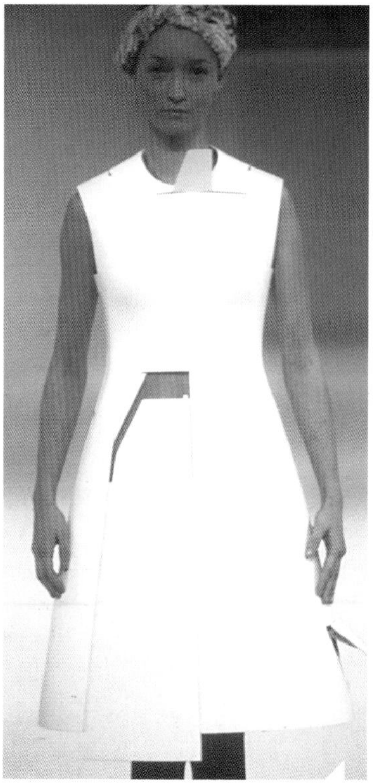

(A)

(B)

Designing, Dwelling, Thinking: Hussein Chalayan

intelligence of its own. Buildings are learning to respond and adapt to their environments through 'smart' systems that detect and adapt to changing weather conditions or security alerts. Buildings are becoming living organisms, probing their surroundings to collect information for the structures and systems they house.

The Remote Control Dress is a ground-breaking achievement on many levels, not least because it reveals the role that technology plays in the congruency between fashion and architecture. Rather than isolating the wearer from tactile experience, the dress employs technology to enhance the individual's relationship to the material world. While this initial prototype makes only basic responses to the activities around them, it holds the potential to become increasingly sophisticated over time. The dress was conceived as an interactive machine that roams the city and engages with buildings as well as with the public; by doing so it stimulates a relationship with public space by injecting personal experience into what can be a harsh, anonymous environment. Subsequent models of the Remote Control Dress will be improved and adapted as the garment is slowly transformed by the experiences of its wearers.

The Remote Control Dress was not designed specifically to explore the relationship between technology and the body, but to examine how the form of the garment could evolve around the body in a spatial relationship to its environment. 'If you alter the way the body comes across in the space around it, then the body alters everything in the space that affects it,' Chalayan explained. 'The dress can also be transformed invisibly by the environment. The idea was a technological force between the environment and the person.'

[A]'The Remote Control Dress' is an icon of techno fashion, encasing the wearer in technological systems that communicate with other technologies distant in time and space.

[B]The rigid structure of Chalayan's resin dresses moulds the body into an hourglass silhouette, but features flexible panels that accommodate the wearer's movements.

Extending the function of dress beyond clothing is a recurrent theme in Chalayan's work, and the Remote Control Dress demonstrates that a garment itself can be constructed to interact with other humans as well as computerized systems distant in time and space.

The interoperation and integration of clothing into 'intelligent environments' is a major forum for both architecture and science, since pioneering wireless technology is the key to expanding existing networks and paving the way for a range of new systems. The relay systems embedded in intelligent buildings include speech-recognition technologies, advanced sensors, infrared data transmission and new types of interfaces. Such electronic systems can be embedded invisibly almost everywhere, so that sensors can exchange information about the stimuli they are programmed to detect. These systems could even connect the wearer to larger bodies of people, businesses and governments through the agency of wireless communication technologies. In a more visionary context, the Remote Control Dress also heralds a new axis of fashion and architecture, one that signals the integration of the constructor and the constructed as they coalesce in a mutual system.

The dress confronts one of the most profound issues raised by new technologies: that human identities could potentially take on the characteristics of machines or architecture. Though the wearer can access external symptoms via the remote-control mechanism, inherent in the dress is a sinister reversal: the potential for those systems to control the wear, or maintain constant surveillance over the wearer's activities. The interface of flesh and technology is both thrilling and terrifying, if technology holds the potential to override the body's commands and take control of it before the wearer is able to escape. Confining the body this way is tantamount to caging it behind panoptical walls. With architectural systems now lining the surface of the body itself, their presence in built environments could become redundant.

As the dress moves through the urban landscape in this new, technologized guise, the wearer assembles and organizes information according to its engagement with remote sensors. The wearer, encased within the dress's shell, also distances herself from the observer, effectively constructing a barricade between self and voyeur. In the thinking of Benjamin, this heightened sense of observation and remote interaction would signify the return of the flâneur, resurrected from nineteenth-century Paris and reoriented within an ever-changing matrix of urban consumption. The system that the dress belongs to expands capitalist relations of production into areas beyond production: the restructuring of urban life by invisible modes rather than spectacle.

The dress's engagement with surveillance places emphasis on visibility; a concept essential to the consumption of fashion but often underestimated in interpretations of it. Clothes, being the form in which the fashioned body is made visible, give the wearer a public identity while fostering the construction of the self. The gaze of visual technologies makes the experience more intimate and more exotic, amplifying the function of clothing as both boundary and margin in the ever-widening gap between public and private personae.

As an architectural structure the dress is loaded with symbolic value: it is a hallmark of scientific progress, a tool of communication, a shelter for the human form and metaphor of the body. For fashion, it achieves innovations never thought possible, and amplifies the potential that fashion has to interact and communicate with other systems. As the dress interacts with its immediate environment, or performs manoeuvres originating from a remote command centre, it enables the body to extend its range of movements and control beyond arm's reach. The dress makes it clear that the fashioned mechanization of the body and the integration of clothing into a larger technological system produces a whole new range of practices, possibilities and aesthetics that eliminate many of the boundaries separating the fashioned body from the architecture surrounding it.

Designing, Dwelling, Thinking: Hussein Chalayan

[1]Chalayan produced the *Temporary Interference* collection with British fashion label Jigsaw's sponsorship, designed knitwear collections for TSE in New York, created a capsule collection for the British retail chain Top Shop and became the creative director of fashion for British jewellery company Asprey & Garrard.

[2]Quoted in an interview with Susan Irvine (2001), 'Deconstructing Hussein', *The Telegraph*, 5 December 2001.

[3]Hussein Chalayan was interviewed by the author.

[4]Quoted in Irvine, 'Deconstructing Hussein'.

[5]Quoted in Irvine, 'Deconstructing Hussein'.

[6]For further reading see chapter 5 in Quinn (2002), *Techno Fashion*, Oxford: Berg.

Notes

Fashioning Architecture and Art

Many exchanges are taking place between art, fashion and architecture. Their fascination for one another seems to spiral around their mutual desire to see life transmuted into art. Artists succumb to fashion's inexplicable allure as they attempt to reproduce its fetishistic command of fantasy and desire; architecture, longing to transcend modes of production and abstractions of mechanization, looks towards art to reiterate its forms in fluid, labile gestures validated by philosophical principles; and fashion, forever dependent on other forms for its imagery, structure and identity, pushes forward into the cultural landscape in pursuit of the accomplished forms mastered by art and architecture.

^The artist Do-Ho Suh draws upon tailoring techniques to create large-scale architectural structures. His work explores the sculptural characteristics of rooms and entire houses, using fashion techniques to expand his idea of 'clothing as space'.

(A)

(A)

Fashioning Architecture and Art

Imagination, memory and emotion, traditionally the preserve of the fine arts, are finding their way into architecture and fashion. No longer just spaces for living, working or wearing, architecture and fashion seem to engage on an equal footing with the philosophical, historical and formal principles once reserved for art practice alone. At the heart of this debate is reflected contemporary society's ever-changing relationship to material culture, where contemporary techniques and environments have become interactive, and the division between functionalism and representation is breaking down. As buildings and garments are acknowledged as legitimate reflections of society's traumas and aspirations, they begin to acquire the poetic voice of painting and sculpture.

Installation artists use fashion principles to understand how identities can be created, dissolved and formulated anew; their work is rooted in the everyday and the ordinary, proposing a rhetoric of communication through social space. And just as art has become a site for understanding the self, so have architecture and fashion. Architects use the built environment to alter our relationships to each other and to ourselves, exploring the impact of materials, colour, tactility and trophes of memory to create places which are at once real and imagined. Such sensual devices are also common to fashion, where, likewise, they highlight the gulf between private experience and public content.

Beyond the colour palettes, painterly textures and sculptural sensibilities expressed in clothing, the sections that follow in this chapter explore a varied spectrum of art forms that investigate the material relationship between fashion, art and architecture, as well as the conceptu-

^Lucy Orta designs garments as both wearable shelters and poetic expressions of social issues. Orta's work is three-dimensional and often sculptural in form. She often transfers two-dimensional drawings and motifs onto the fabrics to voice messages of solidarity.

al framework underpinning them. These projects span installation art, relational aesthetics, fashion photography and art theory, moving with considerable ease between genres. Much of this art draws inspiration from the city, exploring the space between the public sphere of architecture and the individualized experiences contained with fashion's folds.

Fashion and Art

While historians and academics may challenge fashion's claim to be a legitimate art form or a valid discipline of the arts, no one can deny the profound impact it has had on the arts, as well as architecture, photography, cinema and other types of design. In recent years, fashion has gained recognition and critical acclaim in the art world, and also serves the artistic expression of architects. Yet, the vast stranglehold of commercial fashion is so mainstream that the most creative expressions are often suffocated by commercial tastes. Once showcased in galleries, museums and art installations, fashion's design innovations are elevated beyond their surface values.

Architects also give fashion a platform to express itself in a sculptural guise. Bernard Tschumi called on Pia Myrvold's fashion expertise to create the textile sculptures that he showcased at La Villette, and Lucy Orta collaborated with an architectural practice to redesign one of the London College of Fashion's public spaces as an expression of textile structures. Joep van Lieshout has collaborated with Rem Koolhaas on the Grand Palais project in Lille, to express his artistic signature in an architectural style described as 'modular hedonism'. In a work that took direct inspiration from iconic architecture, Yeohlee unravelled the famous Guggenheim spiral designed by Frank Lloyd Wright in 1959 to create a series of assymetrical spirals around the body. Zaha Hadid's set designs and performance costumes for the Metapolis Ballet charged architectural principles with expressive movement.

These alliances are by no means a contemporary phenomenon. Since the late nineteenth century, architectural visionaries such as Gottfried Semper, Sigfried Giedion and Walter Gropius drew comparisons between the economy of dress and the practices of architecture, alternately denouncing fashion's ornamentation and praising its design principles. That dress could be considered a metaphor for modern architecture at all points to the subtextual parallels between dress reform and the critical discourse of modern architecture. Semper viewed a building's shell as an example of clothing, associating and directly linking the German words 'dress' (gewand) and 'wall' (wand). Likening textiles to built surfaces, which he regarded as modes of veiling rather than purely tectonic structures, Semper argued that the evolution of architecture resulted from technological changes rather than from the pursuit of idealistic forms.[1] Georg Simmel, the first intense analyst of fashion and architecture, regarded society as a whole to gewand, tracing the threads of it weave and the embroideries of its surface to the manifestations of modern life.[2]

Adolf Loos also claimed that a building's robust outer shell should be wholly differentiated from its intimate, inner spaces.[3] Dismissing the type of ornamentation associated with feminine dress as 'something that must be overcome', Loos advocated a paradigm of architecture based on men's fashion, extolling the subdued understatement of a tailored suit as the ideal façade for modern aesthetics.[4]

The relationship between art, fashion and architecture in the early avant-garde was inextricably linked to the beginnings of modernism. Nineteenth-century dress reformers advocated a new utility of dress, which they summarily equated with beauty. British dress reformers collaborated with Pre-Raphaelite artists (and later with those of the Arts and Crafts movement) to produce modern fashions. The resulting styles paralleled discourses of emancipation with those of beauty and aesthetics. Many of the radical transforma-

Fashioning Architecture and Art

tions achieved in dress from this time onward were labelled 'art dresses'; the representations they produced were not evocative of art, rather, they presented an image of modernity that cited fashion reforms as a central principle of modern life. As architectural discourse engaged with dress reform, the architecturally inspired fashions of Art Nouveau also had visual links to interior design and craft traditions. This axis also voiced resistance to hegemonic styles and classical aesthetics, manifesting an anti-fashion critique that still exists in contemporary clothing.

Architects also played a major role in dress reform. At the turn of the last century, Henry van de Velde designed reform dresses (his wife, Maria Sèthe, modelled his designs and also published them as texts), and along with the painter Alfred Mohrbutter, was one of its leading proponents in Germany. Van de Velde also forged links with Joseph Hoffman's Vienna Werkstätt movement, who continued the Arts and Crafts rationale initiated by William Morris. Hoffman integrated dress styles, interior decoration and architectural design in a common aesthetic. The dress designs created by Hoffman and his students influenced Poiret in Paris, who presented them in a fashion show at his Paris salon. Exhibitions of 'art dresses' designed by Anna Muthesius, Else Oppler and Lilli Behrens were organized in Leipzig, Berlin, Cologne and Paris. Anna Muthesius was the wife of Hermann Muthesius, and always collaborated with him on the interior design schemes of his architectural projects.[5] Lilli Behrens was married to Peter Behrens, who designed dresses as well as maintaining an architect's practice, which at this time also employed Le Corbusier.

The Utopian architectural visions of the Russian Constructivists and the pioneering designs of the Bauhaus led to structural decisions inspired by the contrasting lines and machine aesthetics of modern buildings.[6] Using blueprints and graphs, they measured the garment's proportions geometrically, and employed the grid (which had already been appropriated from industrial design by the avant-garde artists) as a pattern and a basis of motif. To the Russian avant-garde of the 1920s, post-revolutionary expressions of fashion were manifestations of a new model for an aesthetical and political paradigm of reform. A conceptual context for rethinking the built environment underpinned their aesthetic decisions and construction principles. These were shared by the artists and architects working alongside them, who also positioned dress within their visual and spatial systems.

Alexander Rodchenko, along with Lyubov Popova, Vladimir Tatlin and Varvara Stepanova, consciously rejected traditionalist modes of art, calling for a shift away from isolated studio-based practices.[7] As an alternative, they advocated a new 'Productivist' art form that incorporated principles of post-revolutionary style, architectural design and abstract art. The new movement was to unfold as a framework for the construction of homes, furniture, art forms, textiles and fashion. Stepanova and Popova, together with Alexandra Exter dramatically updated the craft traditions and folk arts of the Russian provinces, reinterpreting their motifs in radical colour schemes, stark geometrical shapes and austere silhouettes.

Of the Productivist comrades who explored the potentials of clothing, Stepanova was the only one trained as a fashion designer. Stepanova designed everyday garments as well as theatrical costumes, combining an industrial aesthetic with graphic gestures of geometry and painterly abstractions. The overalls she designed for Rodchenko featured rectangular panels of colour to define its collar, pockets and belt. The garment's streamlined cut and utilitarian design echoed the functionality of the architectural movement of the time, designating the overalls as a pragmatic shelter with the efficiency of a machine.

Popova's inspiration for dress took shape in uncompromising silhouettes and vivid, abstract motifs. Her 'First Proletariat Dress' mirrored the abstractions of her painting technique, many of them forming a body of work she titled 'Painterly Architectonics'. Moving away from painting and into sculptural form, Popova designed theatrical costumes that amplified the garments' surfaces while expanding their shapes into sculptural statements intended to be viewed from every angle. Her costumes and sets for 'The Magnanimous Cuckold' interrelated garments, set design and props into a single spatial gesture. Exter's theatrical costumes were also architectural in their shape and in their construction principles, intended to articulate transparency and mobility that would take garments out of stasis. Her costumes for the film *Aelita* were a fusion of fragile form and dramatic, planar projections that charged the wearer with a visual and kinetic potency. Based in Paris, Sonia Delaunay also designed theatrical costumes for films, plays and private performances which she presented as sculptural versions of her 'simultaneous' paintings. Delaunay borrowed the colours of fauvism for her designs, creating an aesthetic characterized by strong colour, which she expressed in fabrics, jewellery and colour schemes for cars and whole buildings.

The fusion of Constructivist artists, fashion designers and architects evolved set design from a painted backdrop to a three-dimensional built environment. The Constructivists experimented with theatre design to develop industrial and architectural prototypes, waiting for the impoverished post-war economy to recover so that large-scale works could be carried out. The set designs created during this time took minimalism and functionalism to an extreme; theatrical sets were so spare they were virtually skeletal, relying on the dynamics of body and costume to dress them. Ramps, stairs, raised platforms and bridged walkways animated the actors in a style of movement known as Biomechanics. This method was devised to gauge the efficiency of body and space in the mechanized age by creating a system that eliminated unproductive motion and superfluous architectural elements. The costumes and the set design integrated and interrelated the lines and colours of the costumes; as the actors moved through the space they also created patterns, motifs and vibrant juxtapositions of colour.[8]

Chaptersix

Fashioning
Architecture
and Art

(A)

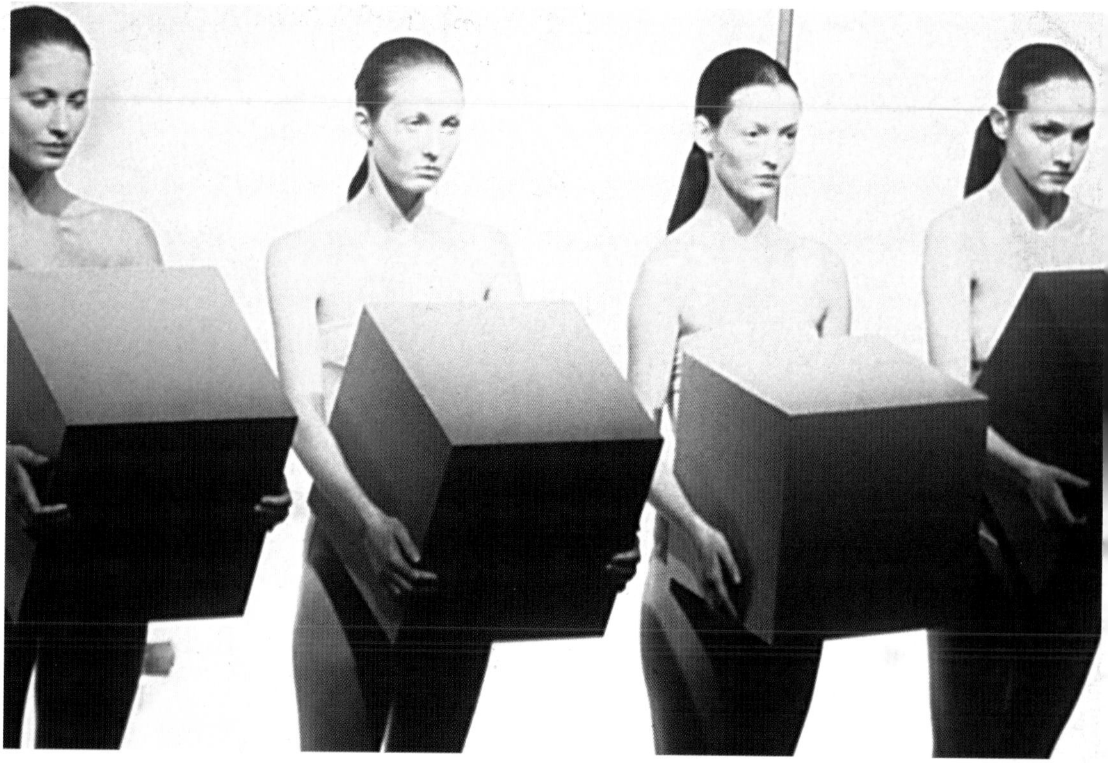

(B)

[A]Yeohlee's 'Guggenheim' dress was inspired by the museum's Frank Lloyd Wright spiral. The dress is constructed as a system of tiers that mimics the winding ramp of the gallery as they trace the outline of the body's contours.

[B]The 'pixellated' designs Chalayan created for his *Panoramic* collection recalled the geometric costumes that Oskar Schlemmer created for the stage workshop he led at the Bauhaus. Schlemmer represented the body in a system of wearable blocks he described as 'ambulant architecture'.

Oskar Schlemmer's multidisciplinary approach to set design created a dynamic synthesis of the arts in the stage workshop he headed at the Bauhaus in the 1920s.[9] Schlemmer regarded the movement of forms through space as linear pathways, which he recorded graphically in illustrations and line drawings of costumes and clothing. By contrast, he gave the two-dimensional geometry of his graphic studies spatial depth by designing outfits shaped by layers of padding or concentric metal arcs. In the conceptual drawings he made to illustrate his courses on figure drawings, Schlemmer portrayed the body as a scheme of blocks he called 'ambulant architecture'. This translated materially as wearable hoops, cubes and batons that symbolized architectural extensions of the body's organic framework. The performers charged Schlemmer's extraordinary costumes with dynamism that projected the body beyond its usual contours in shows that achieved a complete fusion of costumes, music, movement and set design. The dance was intended to fuse the physical geometry of the dancer with the planar geometry of the set surrounding it.[10]

The Triadic Ballet, probably Schlemmer's most acclaimed performance, expressed the full range of the spatial theories and kinaesthetic gestures he regarded as interventions in space. Schlemmer choreographed the movements of three dancers he dressed in blue, yellow and red respectively. The costumes included masks intended to conceal traces of individual identity or expressions of emotion, employing principles of anthropocentric design that injected a sense of Dadaist abstraction into the decorative and functionalistic rationale behind the clothing. Hussein Chalayan also expressed a surrealist theatre of geometric forms and distorted images in his *Panoramic* collection (autumn/winter 1999).

Panoramic culminated in the idea of infinity, which was expressed in an environment intended to eradicate the perimeters dividing the built environment and cultural landscapes. The models were distorted into generic shapes and unified by architectural proportions; cones were fixed to the top of the head to elongate the body's shape, while faces and bodies were swathed in black to create a non-distinct cultural/ethnic identity.

Fashioning
Architecture
and Art

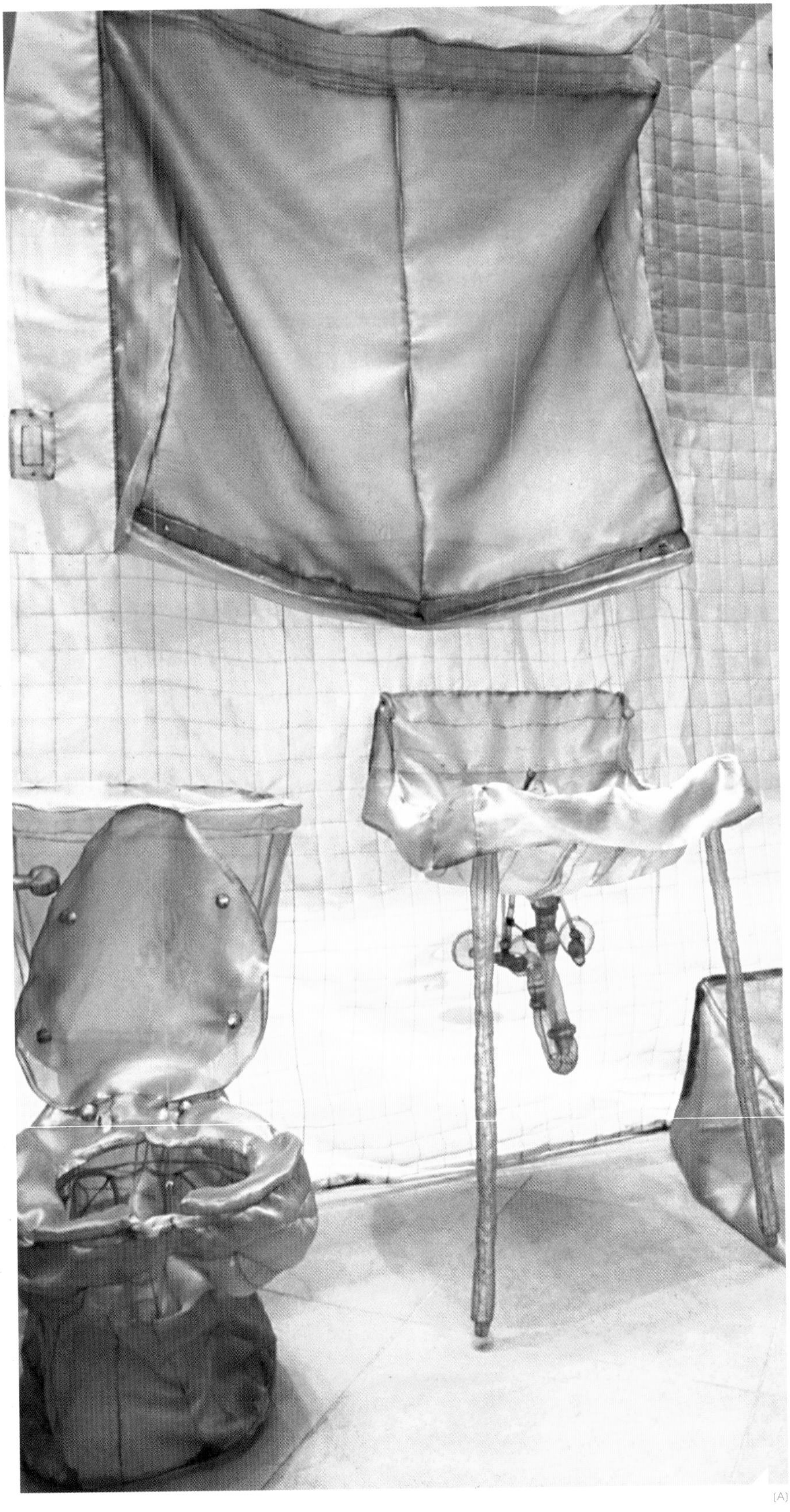

(A)

[A]Do-Ho Suh recreated the interior of his New York apartment through textile 'skins' that captured every detail.

[B]Artist Maria Friberg transformed the fashioned body into an architectural signature as well as an artwork when she used this model to mimic a building support.

[C]Paulina Wallenberg Olsson's bulletproof ballgown makes a statement about elegance, danger, protection and vulnerability.

(B)

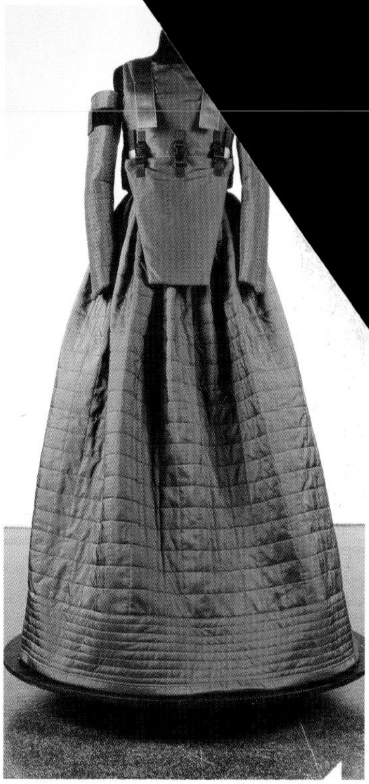

(C)

Chalayan broke the images of the environment down to its most basic graphic symbols: pixels. Body and clothing were then merged into a digital landscape, which was re-created in enlarged cube-shaped pixels carried by a column of models clad in sombre bodysuits as they processed slowly down the catwalk. The overall effect was that of experiencing spatial geometry created by bodies and cloth, interchanging the basis of fashion's relationship to the body and its surroundings.

Both Andy Warhol and Joseph Beuys produced garment-based works. Beuys related an apocryphal account of his wartime military service in his 'Felt Suit' (1970), intended to relate the story of being rescued by Tartars when his fighter airplane was gunned down over the USSR. The Tartars rubbed fat into his frozen body and wrapped him in felt to counter his hypothermia, leading Beuys to later interpret felt artistically as a protective, supernatural material. Felt Suit is shown as an uninhabited shell that expresses the idea of contemporary armour made of humble cloth, and the concept of charging the space made to house the body with security and transcendence. As Warhol printed clothing with the labels and logos of a range of everyday products he made a commentary on the exclusive labels circulating in fashion culture, disputing the idea that fashion 'multiples' could be any more rarefied than other mass-produced goods. Warhol revealed the degree to which fetishism defined articles of fashion, imbuing them with significance beyond their everyday function as clothing.

The possibility of discovering a new artistic identity through fashion has prompted numerous contemporary artists to deconstruct and reconstruct fashionable designs. A variety of artists ranging from Salvador Dali and Henri Matisse to Beverly Semmes and Barbara Krueger have regarded dress as a blank canvas upon which to voice messages protesting the inherent limitations of the body, or explore its ability to act as a metaphor for society and sexuality. Fabrice Hybert, Tobias Rehberger and Rosemarie Trockel have created works using fashion as a means to investigate the forms, strategies and motivations underlying artistic production. Paulina Wallenberg Olsson's evening gown is crafted from bulletproof fabric, using fashion to

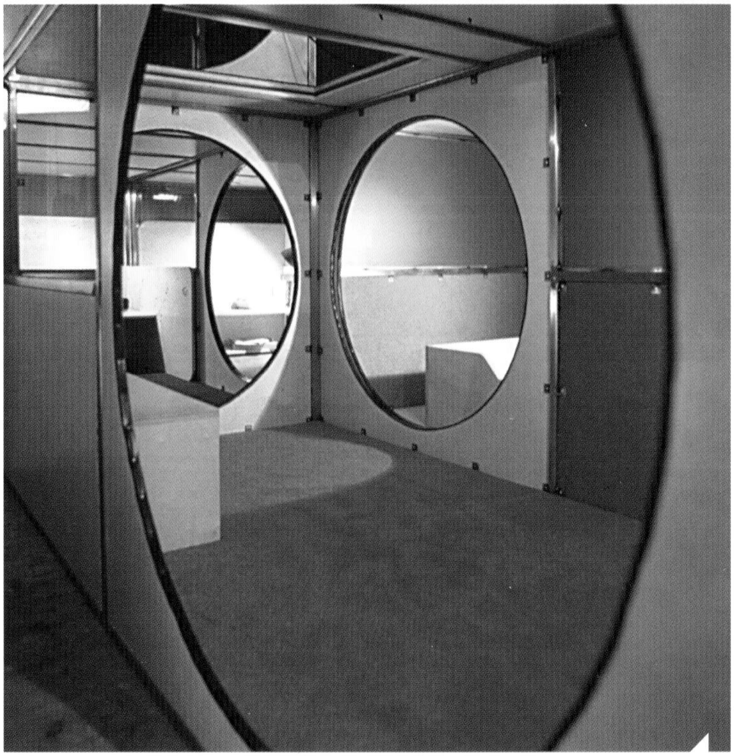

(A)

sculpture a sense of fortification and protect… …her than feminine frivolity. … Christo & Jeanne-… …riberg 'dress' bu… …mmis-sions; Fribe… …g fashion imc… …çades, Christo & Jea… …y wrap-ping landscape… …itectural landmarks in fabric.

For Korean a…ist Do-Ho Suh, dressmaking is like architecture. He expands the spatial confines of clothing to produce habitable structures, such as rooms, buildings and houses made from fabric. 'When you expand this idea of clothing as space, it becomes an inhabitable structure, a building, a house made of fabric,' he explained.[11] Do-Ho Suh has re-created the interiors of his various living spaces in translucent nylon, combining the casting techniques of Rachael Whiteread with the nomadic principles behind Rirkrit Tiravanija's reconstructions of his private domains. Do-Ho Suh's work also recalls the architectural wrapping of Christo & Jeanne-Claude; as they occupy the interior rather than the outside, they appear to be ghostly negatives of their work.

Fashion and art came together spectacularly in the designs of Rei Kawakubo, who from the outset of her career deliberately distanced herself from the hype surrounding fashion by working according to principles more akin to art and architecture. While Kawakubo's examination of the void detailed in chapter 3 in terms of its fashion significance, she also explores the void artistically as an expression of cosmonology. This connects her work with artists such as Anish Kapoor, whose transcendental sculptural forms also explore the void. Much of Kapoor's practice explores the concept of the void through works cut deeply into stone,

^Andrea Zittel's 'Cellular Compartments' integrate principles of architecture and interior design in specialized environments that can be easily transported from place to place. Her work connects with Chalayan's concept of nomadic environments and Yeohlee's *Urban Nomads*.

often coating the interior surfaces with rich pigments and transforming the void into a dark, charged space.

Kawakubo has clearly articulated her alliance with the art world by gaining support from art-world 'celebrities', who she photographed wearing her clothes. The painter Enzo Cucchi, New York art dealer Leo Castelli and the actor John Malkovich were photographed in grave monochrome in her promotional images, which have also featured Francesco Clemente, Julian Schnabel, Robert Rauschenberg and Willem de Kooning. Other artists, such as Cindy Sherman, have contributed to Kawakubo's fashion promotions by directing the creative process. Sherman styled and directed a series of uncompromising shoots for Comme des Garçons that remained true to her signature chameleon sensibilities.

In a similar strategy, Prada commissioned Andreas Gursky to direct a photo campaign of the brand's collection of coloured underwear. The images were executed with the same eye for revealing the monumental in unlikely places that Gursky previously brought to his images of buildings such as the Shanghai Stock Exchange (1990).

Whereas Kawakubo tends to broker connections with individual artists, several mainstream fashion designers have turned to institutional sponsorship to forge links with the art world. Giorgio Armani, preparing to float his company on the stock market in 2001, was awarded a retrospective of his work that occupied the whole of the spiral at the Guggenheim Museum. Traditionally know for its radical exhibitions of twentieth-century art, the museum's unexpected exhibition of mainstream fashion – however elegant and expensive the clothing may be – seemed at odds with the museum's exhibition programme and perhaps even its core remit. The Guggenheim has not denied rumours that it benefited from US$15 million in sponsorship from Armani, or confirmed that applying Armani's endowment towards an exhibition of its own fashion collections rather than contemporary art is acceptable to its public.

Gucci's art sponsorship has been more subtle. Gucci financed the exhibition of Richard Serra's architectural, tilting steel ellipses held at the Venice Biennale in 2001. Presumably, their motivation was to identify the brand with Serra's heavyweight art-world credibility than to place their own work centre stage.

Architecture features prominently in the status games of fashion. Armani paralleled Prada's much publicized associations with leading architects by commissioning Tadao Ando to renovate a derelict chocolate factory in Milan. The site has been transformed into an exhibition, performance and entertainment space that Armani describes as a 'theatre'. The building's interior is demarcated by an indoor avenue of stark concrete columns, dramatically opening into a cavernous reception area in which Ando has re-created the feeling of Serra's monumental spirals in concrete. Colossal doors give way to the performance-cum-catwalk space, adjacent to a long dining hall, its low windows framing a reflecting pool in the courtyard beyond.

The emphasis placed on theatre and performance suggests that the fashion show is an art event in itself, unrelated to the banalities of presenting Armani's collections to buyers and agents, with the real business of buying and selling taking place elsewhere. Ando's concrete corridors are intended to erase the functional purposes of what would otherwise be considered a fashion space, attempting to create a paragon of art, architecture and fashion design.

Commercial fashion has entered the same phase of industrial consolidation that the motor industry underwent when Chrysler, Ford, Jaguar and Mercedes started to divide the automobile world between them. It is no longer the individual designer who predominates, but the multi-national conglomerates who buy out almost every profitable

(A)

Fashioning Architecture and Art

designer brand, creating a gradual shift in the balance of power as the industry becomes increasingly formulaic. Ultimately, the garment factories need to manufacture more designs to keep their production costs from rising; the operation becomes more cost-effective for the conglomerates as they deliver more brands to the same factories and receive substantial discounts based on the sheer volume of work they commission.

Elite brands rely upon their status as couturiers to justify their high prices and appeal to an exclusive customer base. But as they fold into corporate homogeneity or float on the stock exchange, this exclusive status will slowly begin to erode – unless they can find a means of distancing themselves from mass production. Art, and to a certain extent architecture, with their long histories of highly individualized creation, provide the antithesis to perceptions of mass production. Fashion's simultaneous alliance with iconic architecture and attempts to reinvent itself as an art form are not coincidental, but tactical manoeuvres spearheaded by marketing and PR objectives. As these strategies parallel the artistic elements of fashion design with their architectural destinations, the trinity of fashion, architecture and art mutates into a complex axis of commercialism.

Commercially minded designers such as Armani and Prada have always paid lip service to couture principles yet mass-produced as many garments as their markets demanded. While some designers liken this strategy of commercialism to the production of multiples characteristic of fine-art practice, such associations between fashion and art are unconvincing. When artists such as Beuys and Warhol initiated

[A] Described previously in the Dynamic Structures section, Toshiko Mori's 'Woven Habitation' makes an artistic response as well as providing a practical solution for temporary dwellings.

[B] Woven Habitation incorporates many of the principles of Lucy Orta's temporary urban shelters.

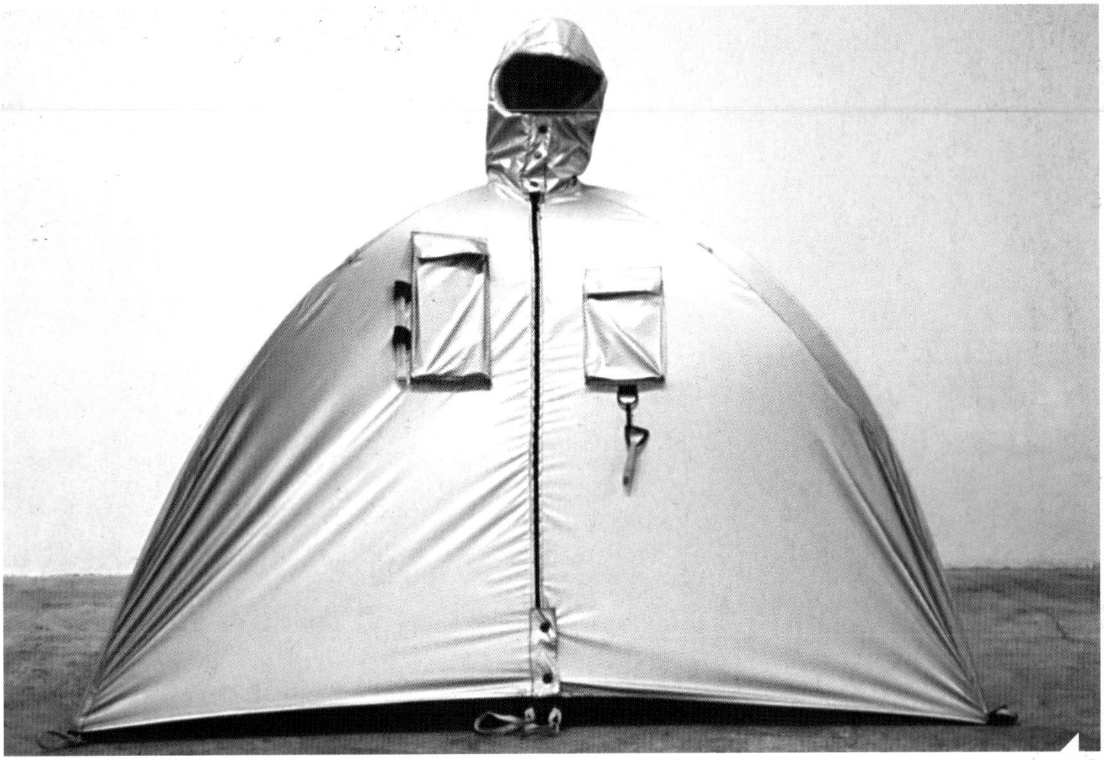

(B)

the concept of multiples in the late 1960s, they copied some of their original works in limited editions that could be sold inexpensively and circulated more widely among the general public than one-of-a-kind works. They also believed that such widespread production would be more potent than the hype surrounding a single art object. Although fashion has the ability to communicate a range of messages and codes, retail distribution is intended to saturate certain markets in order to strengthen the brand rather than promote any particular design ethos behind it.

Art as a Modernist Metaphor

> 'All architects I know want to be artists and all artists I know want to be architects, it's a virus.'
> Dan Graham[12]

The modern union of textile traditions, home furnishings and architecture were given a historical context by Semper's claim that the home environment was first established in primitive textile structures – arguably in the same type of fabrics worn on the body. Today, such basic spaces still exist as micro-environments within the larger structures of architectural design and fashion space, but continue to bring to mind the idea of containing and decorating space through textile arts and other craft traditions. The concept of a 'capsule' is an apt description of such environments, a term that recurs with frequency in the vocabulary of modernism.

Capsules represent an integrated aesthetic of interior design and architectural structure, which have been continually re-fashioned since Le Corbusier introduced his concept of home 'as a machine for living in'. According to Ulrich Lehmann, 'There is a temptation within modernity...to flee the realm of the artistic and become occupied exclusively with all things ephemeral. One is drawn toward the quest for social and cultural expressions that are in closest contact with the present...'[13] In modernist projects, these environments were almost always designed to shape the behaviour and motivations of the inhabitants, communicating a mode of efficient living for urbanites as well as those outside the city. Archigram's Suitaloons, the Final Home Jacket and C P Company's *Transformables* range reveal that these sensibilities have been present in fashion and architecture for at least several decades.

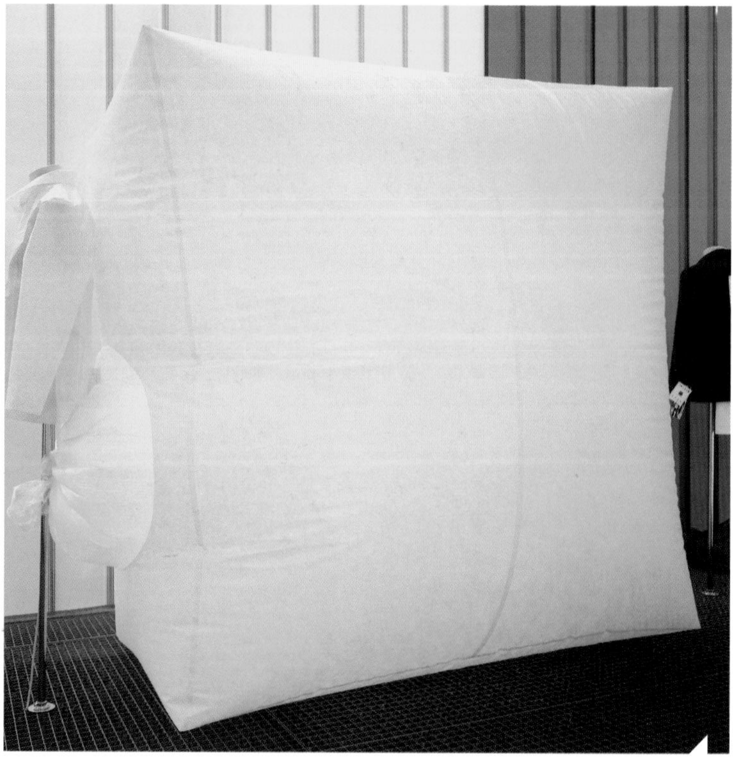

(A)

Fashioning
Architecture
and Art

Few inventions have transformed the modern interior like the capsule. They are typically highly specialized environments, created to support an expanding population or sustain the needs of individuals moving from place to place. Most were designed to collapse, taking up minimal space. As the nomadic tent gave way to the horse-drawn carriage, mobile environments were built to afford a sense of safety and comfort to their passengers. Railway cars, boat cabins, airplane cabins and even spaceships are designed to attract individuals as much as they are to transport them. While they encapsulate many of the characteristics of a dwelling, they are in many ways the antithesis of the built environment, existing as metaphors for travel and rootlessness. The multifunctional efficiency of such capsules is intended to eliminate the possibility of dark, dirty corners, implying that the structure and the space surrounding it has been purified. This reflects the architectural tenets of modernity, described by Mark Wigley as 'that of utility perfected, function without excess, the smooth object cleansed of all representational texture'.[14]

In recent years, a movement premised on the concept of inhabiting capsules or 'containerised' spaces has begun to gain momentum in contemporary art. Artists such as Joep van Lieshout, Jurgen Bey, Andrea Zittel, Dré Wappenar, Alica Framis and Lee Boroson are designing self-contained units for living, working or communing, with a remit to facilitate communality and social interaction. These are mobile environments that take shape architecturally as hermetically sealed dream domes, simplified domestic spaces, inflatable structures and tent-like pavilions, or assume

[A]Jurgen Bey's 'S.L.A.K.' pieces represent wearable architecture, drawing on the snail's ability to take refuge within its shell.

[B]Andrea Zittel expands this idea in her 'Living Unit' to include household objects in structures that are fully mobile but not wearable.

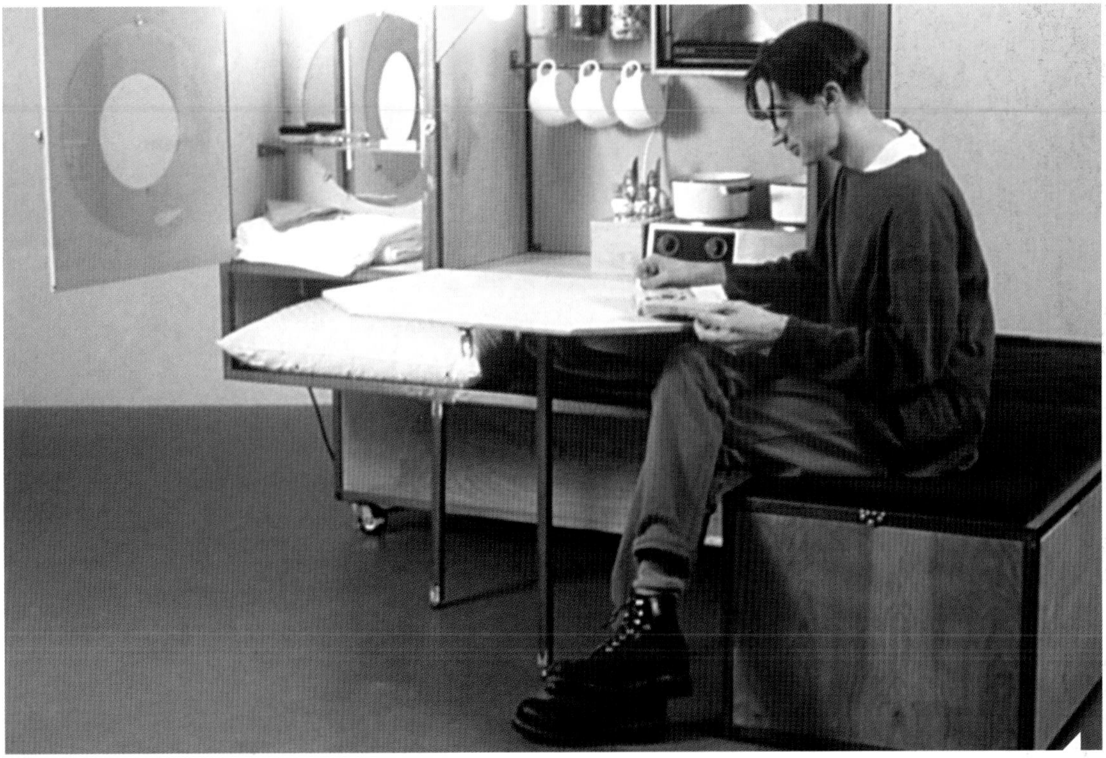

(B)

fashion characteristics as environmental suits and wearable structures. Intended to be sculptural in form and interactive in scope, these works effectively disenfranchise interior spaces from their architectural confines and use them as vehicles for relational aesthetics. These projects are often devised as points on a vast network of digitally connected sites; they are global in scope, irrespective of their physical location. Although some of these artists explore the extent to which clothing and shelter can be rolled into one, their work is distinct from Orta's. These artists do not directly address the need for refuge or inclusion, nor intend to effect social change. The commentaries they make on dividing space highlight the important role of interior environments, critiquing the shortcomings of modernist architecture.

These works are circulating in exhibitions at galleries and museums around the world and receiving critical acclaim as they successfully reactivate interest in art and culture beyond the walls of the museum. They reveal many of the dualities, dichotomies and contradictions present in social space, addressing themes as diverse as migration, necessity and luxury, communication and the aesthetics of social housing. In a sense, they are artistic extensions of urban redevelopment projects, although they are established independently of them. They function in a space between the public sphere of architecture and a more isolated desire to create an autarkic space.

Such forums pervade public spaces where the role of architecture and fashion is central to the development of social interactions, but they also impact on private domains. None of the objects included within the capsules are chosen arbitrarily; each is considered for its impact and significance on the inhabitants. However minute, they form part of a sequence of spatial links that extends beyond the confines of the container, yet also relates to the smallest instruments of the system.

These environments represent an ambiguity of scale and orientation. While their presence is intended to communicate with the public, the space they enclose is small and private. Although they are created to house the social body in a poetic guise, they mediate an intense connection with the body as their scale reduces the proportions typical of permanent habitations. Their proportions enfold the human body more closely than those of the built environment do, just as Chalayan, in his *Echoform* collection, identified this spatial relationship and represented it in garments that mimicked car interiors, making commentaries on their potential to function as vehicles and confined environments.

As artistic works the containers highlight emergent sites and explore the overlaps between architecture, urban planning and transitional systems to realize a fully self-sufficient and mobile social space. They relate to the self-contained environments of i-Wear discussed in chapter 5, sharing a goal to integrate communication devices and information technology within a mobile environment. Many of the works contain networks to facilitate the technological transport of data, or facilitate communication in more lo-tech modes. Like i-Wear, they literally draw these systems closer to the wearer, paralleling the complex relationship between fashion and technology. As living spaces, the containers function as metaphors of the built environment, yet they are fully mobile. Their capacity to create shelter surpasses i-Wear, yet they do not constitute wearable architecture or a built environment in the lasting sense. Architecturally, they point to the importance of transcending the confines of place; as mobile vehicles they can extend the spatial framework of the urban environment, or invert the designated function of spaces within a gallery or museum.

The containerization of living spaces forms part of Dutch artist Joep van Lieshout's project to realize a fully self-sufficient, mobile social space. Working together with a team of artists known collectively as Atelier van Lieshout, the mobile units van Lieshout designs are intended to literally transport art spectators beyond the museum walls to emphasize accessibility, portability and everyday integration of the arts. Using industrial materials or simple building forms, the Atelier creates environments that often resemble portacabins in their construction. Their aesthetic locates the vision of the engineer as much as it does the artist, architect or designer, lending itself to industrial compositions that appear to be machine-like. With titles such as 'Ambulatory Bar', 'Office Unit' and 'Reception Unit', their functions and target audiences seem obvious, but are far from clear-cut. The Atelier's 'Autocrat' from 1997 explores the

^A Andrea Zittel's 'Trail Trailer Units' compress space to maximize functionalism. The units are prototypes of mobile domestic spaces that consolidate living needs within a single mobile unit.

(A)

notion of self-sufficiency in its attempt to provide every necessity that an individual would need in a single capsule, but reveals a dysfunctional microcosm instead. Each exhibition challenges the spectator's views and preconceptions about a range of cultural issues or social principles.

'Spitaal', constructed by Atelier van Lieshout in 1998, is both impressive and menacing for its surgical representations of body modification. A fully functioning hospital situated in a shipping container, Spitaal presented the spectator with a clinical atmosphere in which to gauge their views on body aesthetics. The work was presented at a time when debates about fashion's role in promoting unrealistic stereotypes were attracting criticism and condemnation. Spitaal revealed the dangerous extremes of elective surgery, suggesting that the obsessive quest for physical perfection was tempered more by individual vanity than by fashion propaganda.

The soft capsules created by Jurgen Bey, also a Dutch artist, are the structural and theoretical opposite of van Lieshout's work. Bey's 'S.L.A.K.', an acronym for 'Suits Light Architecture Ken', brings to mind Bachelard's analogies of snail-shell dwellings, as 'slak' is also the Dutch word for snail. Bey intends for the work's meanings to change and mutate as they migrate from place to place, stating that the work represents 'an architectonic, psychological and aesthetic tour de force'.[15]

Andrea Zittel is an American artist who seeks to resurrect modernist sensibilities. Zittel's works suggests that the Utopian vision of modernist designers and architects remain unfulfilled; she embarks on a quest for the ultimate living system. Zittel is striving to realize the promise of individualism, while also, paradoxically, creating idyllic environments that encapsulate the inhabitant in a world of fully functional living units, microcosms that simultaneously compress space and maximize functionalism. Her works are prototypes of mobile, simplistic domestic spaces devised to 'liberate the user from an overwhelming barrage of decisions and responsibilities, by consolidating all living needs into a small, organized living unit'.[16]

Zittel's 'Living Unit' is a four-square-metre structure containing all the amenities of an ordinary home. The unit occupies the space of a

Fashioning Architecture and Art

large wardrobe, displacing the clothing to accommodate the necessities of modern survival. Living Unit can be described as a mobile kitchen/bathroom/bedroom equipped with a cooker, mattress, mirror, kitchen utensils and toiletries. Zittel's 'A–Z Escape Vehicle' (1996) is a collection of customizable mini mobile homes made for a single occupant. Each of them features a metallic surface crafted into an ovoid shape of approximately thirty cubic metres in volume. Zittel customized these for the occupant – her own vehicle is filled with coloured lights, a waterfall, a couch padded in blue velvet and a bar. A more recent work, 'Deserted Islands' consists of ten capsules made of fibreglass and wood. These are flotation tanks; beyond habitation, they are intended to revitalize and regenerate the occupant.

Dré Wapenaar is a sculptor based in Rotterdam who takes his practice into the architectural realm by maintaining that art should be lived in. Wapenaar designs mobile pavilions that function as a travelling platform where artists and the public can develop and exchange ideas. Wapenaar's 'Tree Tents', designed in 1998, signalled a turning point in his work as he elected to move beyond his sculpture practice and create what he describes as 'meeting points for people'.[17] Wapenaar's work is intended to signal a shift from the 'I' to the 'We', making the Tree Tents atypical of his work. Because the tents hang from the sides of trees, access is limited to only a few individuals. Wapenaar regards them as hanging sculptures that operate as both sculpture and practical living spaces. Womb-like in their soft interiors, they designate a sense of escape, an entrance to a parallel world in nature.

Wapenaar's 'Family Tent' is emblematic of his practice today. Echoing Orta's interventions, the tents are also intended to create forums. Tents are more or less universal in shape and immediately recognizable, communicating mobility, shelter and exchange wherever they are erected. While they were intended to facilitate family familiarity, sometimes spectators were hesitant to enter. Wapenaar countered the spectator's reluctance in his next work 'Coffee Stand' by employing another tactic to lure visitors into the tent. '(If) people won't enter the tent just for aesthetic reasons,' he explained, 'they will go inside in the first place to drink a cup of coffee.'[18]

Lee Boroson constructs environments out of parachute fabric. Boroson's 'Pleasure Grounds' features rows of round, flat forms inflated by small compressors that occupy the floor under a canopy of billowing white silk. Each form is connected by electrical cable to larger cloud-like structures filling the space overhead. According to *The New Yorker's* review of Boroson's work, Pleasure Grounds resembles 'a cross between Robert Irwin's recent installations at Dia and the cartoony, pneumatic architecture of Dr. Seuss'.[19] They are tents for interior environments, subverting principles of architecture as they resonate ephemerality and portability throughout the galleries where they are installed. By creating a psychological and metaphoric landscape, the spectator can explore a spatial environment that is unrelated to the proportions of the human form; containerized but distinct from the characteristics that define capsules.

Alicia Framis works together with individuals from different disciplines, collaborating with fashion designers and architects out of a desire to move her practice beyond the domain of the visual arts. In her projects she searches for a new form as well as a new function for art. Framis's latest body of work focuses on the functional aspects of urban architecture. Investigating the distinctive boundaries that articulate different types of inhabitable space, she creates architectural models that merge diverse aspects of social life together. Her 'Remix Buildings' photographs combine existing and seemingly opposing structures to give the interiors they contain new architectural meanings. Framis restructures the contemporary European interior to make it seem more interactive and less isolated. The theme of urban isolation has played an important role in her work for a number of years, manifesting in a critique of urban development and planning.

This new genre reflects the changing nature of contemporary art production and re-examines the ideological and practical conditions in which art is exhibited today. Although these artists do not aim to provide Utopian solutions, their work reveals the potency of the interior in bridging the world of art and the urban place. The work of these artists unfolds in situ as they directly address spatial narratives, expanding the notions of what art can be, and questions whether a gallery context is necessary at all. By offering alternative sites for social interaction, these artists adapt existing systems to create new alliances for interdisciplinary platforms.

[1]See *The Four Elements of Architecture and Other Writings*, translated by Harry Mallgrave and Wolfgang Herrmann (1989), Cambridge: Cambridge University Press.

[2]See Ulrich Lehmann's account of Georg Simmel: 'Simmel and the Rationale of Fashion in Modernity' in *Tigersprung* (2000), Cambridge, MA: MIT Press.

[3]Adolf Loos's 1898 essay, 'Das Prinzip der Bekleidung', has been translated as 'The Principle of Cladding' by Jane Newman and John Smith (1987) in *Spoken into the Void: Collected Essays 1897–1900*, Cambridge, MA: MIT Press, p66–69.

[4]Quoted in Mark Wigley (1995), *White Walls*, Cambridge, MA: MIT Press, p9, from Loos's essay 'Ornament and Crime' of 1908.

[5]See Eckart Muthesius (1979), *Hermann Muthesius, 1861–1927*, London: Architectural Association.

[6]See Susan Sidlauskas (1982), *Intimate Architecture: Contemporary Clothing Design*, Cambridge, MA: The MIT Committee on the Visual Arts.

[7]See Victor Margolin (1998), *The Struggle for Utopia: Rodchenko, Lissitsky and Moholy-Nagy, 1917–1946*, Chicago, IL: University of Chicago Press.

[8]See Judith Clark (1998), 'Kinetic Beauty: the Theatre of the 1920s', *Addressing the Century*, London: Hayward Gallery Publishing.

[9]See Oskar Schlemmer, Laszlo Moholy-Nagy, Farkas Molnar, Walter Gropius and Arthur Wessinger (ed) (1996 edition), *The Theater of the Bauhaus*, Baltimore, MD: Johns Hopkins University Press.

[10]See Karin von Maur (1988), *Oskar Schlemmer*, Stuttgart State Gallery's 100th anniversary exhibition catalogue, Stuttgart: Staatsgalerie/ Editions Cantz.

[11]Lisa Corrin (2002), 'The Perfect Home: A Conversation with Do-Ho Suh' in *Do-Ho Suh*, the Serpentine Gallery's exhibition catalogue, p37.

[12]Quoted in *Material Intelligence* press release, Entwistle Gallery, London, 28 March 2003.

[13]Ulrich Lehmann (2000), *Tigersprung*, Cambridge, MA: MIT Press, p57.

[14]Mark Wigley (1995), *White Walls*, Cambridge, MA: MIT Press, p3.

[15]Quoted in *Frame Magazine*, Jan/Feb 2002, p48.

[16]From a letter to Linda Weintraub written by Andrea Zittel, 1994.

[17+18]www.sputnik.ac.

[19]Quoted in *The New Yorker*, 20 September 1999.

Notes

Intimate Architecture: Lucy Orta's Social Structures

Many people just pass by the cardboard boxes and blanketed figures without a second glance, but not Lucy Orta. Refuting the premise that clothing and shelter should remain separate entities, Orta forges an unexpected alliance between fashion, architecture and art to transform our perception of urban outcasts and give them visibility in the public sphere. 'Art can react in many forms,' Orta explained. 'It can challenge our feelings about our selves and our bodies, and change our beliefs in the social structures and values around us. My work breaks down barriers between clothing and architecture to remove many of the limitations they represent, with the intention of eventually leading to some sort of transformation.'[1]

^All of Lucy Orta's works are artistic expressions created to promote awareness of social issues. They eliminate many of the boundaries between fashion and architecture as they become metaphors for shelter, dress, mobility and social space.

(A)

Intimate Architecture: Lucy Orta's Social Structures

There are reportedly five hundred million homeless people around the world, and the garment-cum-shelters Orta creates provide a potent response to the practical problems of every one of them. Through a series of installations, exhibitions and social interventions that put her garments to practical use, Orta has consistently addressed the social conditions that condemn individuals to an existence on the margins of society. The plight of disaster victims, political refugees, the elderly, the invisible poor and the socially disenfranchised are brought unequivocally into the foreground. The categorical denominations between them are seldom self-referential; they are designated according to the identities conferred onto those who fall outside the social order. Orta's work does not view the space beyond this order as marginal but interprets it as a frontier for a new set of urban connections. Her direct, unmediated engagement with urban space reflects the Situationist stratagem of détournement, dérive and psychogeography, as she rethinks the interface between space and society.[2]

Although Orta's shelters are made to be worn, they are no ordinary garments. Orta's point of departure from conventional fashion was her use of clothing to produce and define urban space, conceptually as well as materially. Recognizing fashion's potential to delineate degrees of separateness and individuality, Orta decided to expand its capacity to designate separate spheres and collective worlds for temporary habitation. While fashion is traditionally regarded as a statement of style over content and image over substance, Orta's work serves as its visual antithesis; she interprets clothing as a social commentary and injects it with a message of collective resistance. 'My work is designed to provoke some sort of conscious awareness of certain issues in society,' she said. 'But they function on many different levels: on a poetical level, on a metaphoric level, and on the level of social awareness.' Using art as her medium, Orta charts the axis between buildings and garments, reclaiming both of them as sculptural, tactile and spatial expressions of society. By moving beyond their ability to provide protection, she amplifies their inherent power to communicate, negotiate social bonds and unite members of a community. Orta's work centres around the ephemeral nature of these social bonds, tracing their networks within the systems of habitation that create community and a sense of belonging. Orta's work is a reminder that the security and social inclusion so often taken for granted is tenuous and, like fashion itself, disconcertingly transitory.

In considering the role of the marginalized, Orta has identified an archetypal creation of contemporary society, an urban wanderer whose role reflects the transiency of the city. Uncertain and directionless, their rambles through the urban landscape parallel the patterns of the nineteenth-century *flâneur* but constitute his exact opposite. The homeless wanderer is regarded as 'other' – perhaps a figure rather than a persona – who represents the abnegation of the consumer-oriented values so inextricably linked to the urban landscape. 'They go to shopping streets and commercial spaces to find the social interactions they need,' Orta said. 'It is in social space that the disenfranchised want to become visible and receive sustenance, participating in the urban fabric whether they are permitted a role in it or not.'

Orta's affinity with the homeless was sparked by a series of workshops she initiated at a Salvation Army shelter in Paris, where she worked with the homeless to facilitate renewed expressions of personality. This resulted in a series of catwalk shows (arguably the very first presentation of the reconstruction fashion aesthetic) that presented a collection made out of old and discarded garments as a commentary on the need to reclaim wasted material and abandoned spaces.[3] By 1994, these sentiments had become encapsulated in Orta's signature wardrobe of protective shelters. These evolved into a series of interchangeable garments that linked wearers together by detachable cords to represent the collective body. Orta's work operates like a scalpel in social consciousness, peeling back the skin of indifference to expose the ruptures soothed by unawareness and indifference.

Refuge Wear continues to engage fashion with disciplines ranging from architecture and art to social regeneration and ideological activism. Orta began to conduct practical workshops and community activities that focus on individual identity, perceptions of the body and impressions of home.

Orta's community-oriented projects led her to identify the value of collective action and collaborative efforts. Although *Refuge Wear* pieces provided emergency housing for the dispossessed, they did not necessarily provide the solace and security of a community. As Orta expanded both the conceptual and physical frameworks of *Refuge Wear*, she conceived of *Nexus Architecture*, a series of wearable garments that zip together to unite several people in a literal and symbolic link. *Nexus Architecture* is a manifestation of the philosophy underpinning the artist's entire practice, poetically acknowledging the interdependency of all members of society while hinting at the protection and psychological refuge provided by a physical enclosure. Orta acknowledges that individuals or small tribes of homeless people often form communities of their own – cardboard cities are often the most tangible example of these – but recognizes that they seldom empower the homeless with the means to move beyond them. In linking these groups to larger society, they can maintain their existing bonds with each other and use them as a basis to improve their situation.

The concept of establishing a social network is developed more elaborately in Orta's *Modular Architecture* project, a forum she established to clothe, shelter and protect the wearers while joining them together to form a single, linked environment. Resembling flexible architectural components in their design, they merge the solidarity afforded by *Nexus Architecture* with the utility of *Refuge Wear*. Individuals can attach links to share and circulate body heat, or use the system of pockets and zips to create a single survival shelter by fully integrating four individual pieces. The pockets

Intimate Architecture: Lucy Orta's Social Structures

also function as containers for storing food, water and supplies, with their shared design facilitating the circulation of resources. The garments-cum-habitats can be removed and assembled in the manner of modular architecture, reconnecting the inhabitants to a secure sense of belonging. 'The physical link weaves the social link,' Orta explained. 'There is a sense that these communities include – and are constructed by – individual, intimate spaces that are united in a homogenous whole.'

To alienate an individual from architectural structures is to render them homeless; for their dress to disintegrate into rags is tantamount to social invisibility. Orta's designs relate the story of the tension between movement and stillness, between the visible and the invisible. Orta describes the plight of the urban homeless today as 'tangible invisibility' but finds them ever present; she follows their traces as they 'literally melt and disappear into the margins and framework of the city', combating this act of social disappearance by rendering the invisible visible once more. Combining the vocabularies of art, fashion and architecture, Orta harnesses the visual power they project: 'From a design perspective, seeing a suit that can transform into a tent-like structure is visually very interesting. It brings awareness to the person inside it. As an artist I define the visual aspects of the work to transmit a message from the wearer to onlookers or passers-by. Whether or not they have "noticed" the homeless before, they can no longer ignore them when they wear the pieces I designed.' Orta inscribes the fabrics with texts, symbols and images that mimic tattoos, packaging or urban graffiti. 'There is an on-going dialogue in my work between the principles of design, social awareness and concepts of visibility. It brings issues into view.'

Although the construction of enclosures is central to Orta's work, she operates beyond the confines and conventions of urban space to liberate the homeless from the disorientation of the street. In doing so, Orta operates in opposition to the political mandates that reassign the homeless to alternative sites of difference and 'other' by merging public place, private space, architectural form and intimate apparel into a structure that can be inflected and interpreted in personal terms. The social and cultural conditions of location inform much of Orta's output, emphasizing the individual's right to occupy public space rather than attempting to reintegrate them with the authoritarian structure that may have been the source of their alienation. For many homeless, it is the traumas suffered in institutions or domestic environments that has led to their existence outside them. Rather than condemning them to the confinement of the hostels and shelters they avoid, Orta reclaims spaces that address the individual's need to be accepted and nurtured on their own terms. But Orta is not merely producing a sense of individual space, she is producing an environment for living – albeit a transitory one. Paradoxically, Orta brought the invisible into sight by giving them space in which to feel secure, a space they can consider to be 'home'.

Rather than interpreting home as a stable base or fixed point of origin, Orta represents it existentially as the act of dwelling, which she defines as a phenomenon of 'being' in space rather than mediated specifically by place. Her thinking connects with that of scholars and philosophers from a wide range of disciplines, who evaluate geographical space as a social construction. Like the social sculptures Joseph Beuys created to effect social change, Orta liberates the idea of home from the confines of geographic place by utilizing the human's fundamental capacity to adapt to changes. As home is reconceived as a shared environment, the notion that it can be denied to outsiders is voided.

Martin Heidegger traced the concept of home back through its Old English and High German roots to equate 'building as dwelling, that is, as being on the earth', and concluded that habitation was indistinguishable from human existence.[4] Ironically, Heidegger's reflections on the built environment linked people to their corporeality, revealing that human existence is in itself a type of habitation. He regarded the occupation of bodily space to be driven by its compulsion to dwell on earth, and imbued with emotional attachments and meanings that extend far beyond the occupation of territory. Derrida interpreted such attachments as desire; identifying the idea of places and dwellings so universally longed for as the very locus of desire. When strong emotions manifest themselves in architecture, the dynamics of desire establish it as place and give it meaning.

To dwell is to be protected from the elements, but it is also a mode of belonging. Being is as much an experience of the senses as it is a physicality; it is an encounter that unfolds through the meaning of touch and the exchange of glances. The visionary Russian Formalist Victor Shklovsky, who also interpreted the home in terms of sensation, wrote: 'habitualisation devours work, clothes, furniture...and art exists that one may recover the sensation of life; it exists to make one feel things'.[5] Physical bonds in turn generate social ones, and Shklovsky's work recalls the intimacy of home that is denied those who dwell outside of it. Orta interprets the spaces between the senses and the physicality of the body as an essential habitation, giving primacy to the feeling of 'being' and belonging over bricks and mortar. As her interventions, workshops and exhibitions reveal, Orta's work speaks volumes about the intimacy of personal relationships.

Situations of crisis and conflict erase the conventions of belonging and territorial affinities. What remains is the integrity of the body and its relationship to other humans, which Orta interprets as the literal and symbolic links that connect individuals to each other within a larger body of space. Such places reflect the complex interactions between individuals and the spaces they occupy. Recalling the polemics of Georg Simmel, one of the first academics to equate fashion and architecture, Orta explained: 'Since to inhabit a space means to consider it part of one's body, clothes are fully entitled to become architectural dwellings, temporary shelters affording protection against cold and storms in the stopping-places on the long journey of human existence.'

Intimate Architecture: Lucy Orta's Social Structures

Orta connects the design process to issues much wider than the individual. The twentieth century was characterized by migration on an unprecedented scale, and readings of its cultural history chart the disappearance of space as the frequent shifts of individuals and whole populations resisted the habitualization of everyday dwelling. Although twenty-first-century Europe is determined to collapse borders, the continual flow of asylum seekers and other refugees is greeted with confinement and exclusion rather than acceptance and integration. Although Orta does not deliberately charge her work with political content, it manifests a critique of the political and social policies that marginalize 'outsiders' and house them in conditions of confinement, ghettoization and deprivation. By extending her work to the plight of refugees, Orta also highlights the instability of 'home' as privacy, intimacy and security collapse. Home is also a site for the construction of the unstable and the unfamiliar.

In her struggle against exclusion, Orta continues to combine architecture, body art, fashion, social dynamics, ideological activism and even political agendas. Her work results from the collective force that fashion and architecture mediate, in many respects documenting the dynamics between them. Orta's structures capture the essence of fashion and architecture, deploying the principles of both in her organization of space. Orta starts at the level of the body, providing protection for the marginalized human, mimicking the primeval textile shelters from which architecture evolved. While her work shows how architecture continues to be fashioned by its dependence on the human form, it also illustrates the extent to which their interdependence can constitute the critical difference between life and death. Yet, as Orta's structures delineate space around the body, they also imbue it with essential mobility, proposing a new paradigm of movable, modular architecture that could redefine future environments.

Orta's principal projects operate as spatial scenarios, works of art, architectural prototypes and interactive platforms. Their titles speak for themselves: *Refuge Wear, Body Architecture, Nexus Architecture, The Connector Mobile Village, Modular Architecture, Citizen Platform* and *Commune Communicate*. As these designs are considered in the sections that follow, the process of transformation they initiate unfolds against a vision that collapses the distinctions between media. 'The prototypes I have built are not designed to solve the growing problems our society is facing. However, they have brought to light certain problems and have opened up a debate which I hope will include as many people as possible.' While Orta's work is not intended to provide a solution, it provokes an effective response.

Urban Camouflage

From the outset, Orta's mission has been one of listening and participation; a formula she applies to every aspect of her work. Identifying the fear that many homeless people experience about living in a home or a shelter led Orta to consider how the street could be appropriated as an extension of the household. Sensing the individual's need to define an area of personal space within the urban matrix, Orta conceived *Refuge Wear* as a space where the individual can seek solace as well as shelter. In this respect, each structure is also designed to designate a literal refuge, a place of seclusion, comfort and hope as well as a vehicle for survival.

Refuge Wear takes form at the level of the individual, linking and combining material, space and social action to bridge individual differences. Orta regards each piece as a carefully conceived prototype designed with the potential to be produced industrially to aid those in need of temporary and immediate clothing and shelter in crisis situations. Universal in scope and understanding, each piece of *Refuge Wear* confronts harsh realities on the very terrains where they exist – instigating a poetic redistribution of resources from the affluent to the dispossessed.

Refuge Wear are essentially textile structures, instantly transformed from garments into corporal architecture using a system of pockets, zips and Velcro fasteners to stretch natural materials and technical weaves over lightweight carbon armatures that anchor it to the ground. Their walls are constructed from high-performance fabrics or techno textiles that surround the body with a breathable membrane that functions like a second skin. The first garment in the *Refuge Wear* series was the 'Habitent', a water- and windproof jacket incorporating a collapsible framework that provides the wearer with an efficient system of dress and shelter.

Parallels can be drawn between Orta's work and the art of the late Brazilian artists Lygia Clark and Hélio Oiticica, who examined the mutability of the body through its relationship to signifiers outside it. They created architectural structures similar to capes and banners for 'habitation' in order to connect individuals through the intermediary of touch. *The Parangolés*, Oiticica's best-known work, were fabricated from textiles and plastics, in structures Oiticica conceived as clothes-cum-dwellings. The *Parangolés* were also commentaries on the individual's role in a collective experience as, 'a participant, transforming his own body into a support, in a ludic experience that becomes an expressive act'.[6] Like Heidegger, Clark and Oiticica structured their work according to a concept of body existence as dwelling or habitation, but specifically referenced the theory of 'anthropagy' proposed by Oswald de Andrade. As an amplification of the body's structure, the *Parangolés* were also intended to represent architecture as the first manifestation of human existence on earth.

Each individual piece of *Refuge Wear* was designed as a personal environment that could be varied in accordance with weather conditions, social needs, necessity or urgency. The pockets were made to contain utilitarian supplies: water, food, medicine, clothing, portable stoves and documents. Further *Refuge Wear* prototypes were fabricated as personal environments in response to social conditions and could convert according to need, necessity or urgency. In the case of refugees, for example, *Refuge Wear* creates a sense of agency and sanctuary as the refugees struggle to mesh their domestic world with larger systems of political mandates. Within a camp or an emergency zone it marks

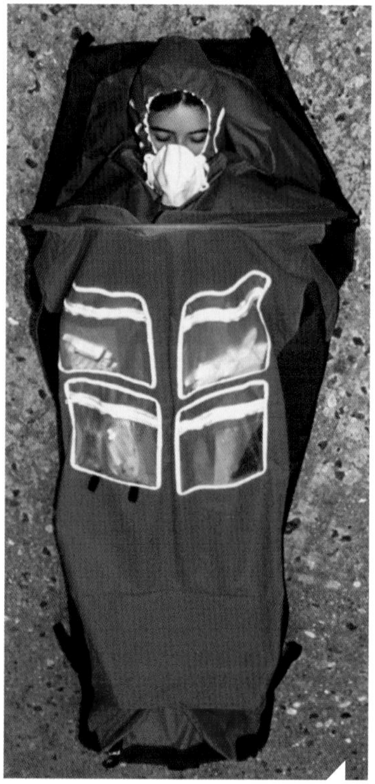

(A)

Intimate Architecture: Lucy Orta's Social Structures

a boundary between public and private domains. In practical terms the units provide the functions of shelter and protection, but the space inside them is a symbolic expression of intimate dwellings. Like a house, they encircle families or individuals with walls of defence, establish points of contact with the outside world and provide spaces that refugees can appropriate as their 'home'.

As a response to the crises of the Gulf War, Orta began *Refuge Wear* to address human suffering on a global scale. Unstable political environments, famine and war resulted in growing numbers of refugees and displaced persons. Orta produced a series of drawings to articulate suggestions for an emergency solution to the homelessness many of these people now faced. Based on the drawings, Orta later fabricated the series of multi-purpose shelters that she eventually gave the generic title *Refuge Wear*.

Refuge Wear went on to become synonymous with clothing and shelter made for extreme conditions. The prototypes had the potential to provide vital mobility and waterproof shelter for the Kurdish and Albanian refugee population; to provide temporary protection and shelter for the victims of natural disasters such as the Kobe earthquake; to address the needs of Serbian civilians in the wake of the NATO bombing; and in the worst extreme function as burial bags in the Rwandan genocide crisis.

Orta's remit to highlight the problems of marginalized groups challenged the issue of social visibility, as she continued to stage a programme of events related to *Refuge Wear* in urban centres. These interventions often cemented social solidarity as they focused awareness on the problems of homelessness, and fostered a drive to redress the issues.

[A] Left Orta's garment-cum-shelters enable refugees and homeless people to reclaim personal space.

[B] The staging of a social bond is one of the common themes connecting Orta's various projects. Her *Nexus Architecture* interventions use clothing to link individuals both literally and symbolically.

(B)

The events received critical acclaim in the art world, who dubbed them 'relational aesthetics' because of their universal message and interactive properties.[7] Orta regarded these public forums as her first 'interventions'. 'It's about taking the art outside the institutional venue and into the street,' she said. 'It's also about developing a team and initiating ideas and seeing how they can develop afterwards, on their own in society.'

Body Architecture

Following her *Refuge Wear* interventions of 1992 and 1993, Orta expanded her protest from the predicament of disenfranchised individuals to encompass the larger problems of displaced communities. Her *Body Architecture* series developed with the protective principles of *Refuge Wear* in mind, but advocated interdependency rather than seeking individual solutions. *Body Architecture* heralded a new direction in Orta's work; she shifted her focus away from the microcosm of the individual to the macrocosm of the community, from practical protective clothing to communal modular habitations. These garments interconnect the wearers as they attach to each other, embodying the principle of solidarity so central to Orta's thinking.

Within the rubric of *Body Architecture*, Orta developed different prototypes that establish physical links between individuals, symbolizing the myriad ties that can be forged emotionally, intellectually, socially and spiritually. Some of the individual *Body Architecture* pieces she creates resemble ski suits or overalls, others recall the hooded shapes of *Refuge Wear*. These are designed as modular units that can be combined in configurations of four to form a single construction. As four units are taken off the body and zipped together they create a four-person tent that can be easily dismantled and rebuilt. Made of aluminium-coated polyamide and equipped with pockets and compartments, the tent is waterproof and aerodynamic, held in place by supporting posts and secured to the ground by pegs along its base. Other *Body Architecture* prototypes are connected to form *Nexus Architecture* interventions, detailed in the following section.

In its inherent abstractness, *Body Architecture* seems to have more resonance with the future than

(A)

Intimate Architecture: Lucy Orta's Social Structures

the present. It defines space with a quality that often seems to be transcendent and immaterial. Their hi-tech fabric domes and tent-like structures suggest physical and psychological refuge within a larger protective enclosure. As they zip together they constitute one membrane; the individuals meshed within it share resources, support and intelligence. Reflecting on its significance in a social context, the French cultural theorist Paul Virilio concluded that *Body Architecture* constitutes a metaphoric remedy for the problems facing society today: 'The precarious nature of society is no longer that of the unemployed or the abandoned, but that of individuals socially alone. In the proximate vicinity our families are falling apart. Ones individual life depends on the warmth of the other. The warmth of one gives warmth to the other. The physical link weaves the social link.'[8]

As Orta relates technical innovation to humanitarianism, her *Body Architecture* covers the same theoretical ground as Shigeru Ban's vision for habitation modules and Future Systems' proposals for temporary homeless shelters in London. The desire to create a sense of interrelatedness in space informed much of the Team X output, who clearly recognized the necessity of facilitating social unity within architectural space. Aldo Van Eyck's orphanage in Amsterdam, built in 1960–1, achieved a similar dynamic of group cohesion and community solidarity through an interconnected sequence of domed family units, all united under a continuous roof.

That architecture can be considered as a potent influence on human behaviour attests to the compelling roles that buildings have assumed in literary works. The architectural entities depicted in Ayn Rand's allegorical masterpiece *The*

^A^The interventions Orta stages take her work beyond the confines of the gallery to the areas where social renewal is needed. The *Refuge Wear* shown here defines the wearers against the urban landscape, bringing marginalized individuals into sight once more.

Fountainhead, in Rem Koolhaas's urban thriller *Delirious New York* and in the sepulchral confines of *The Overlook* hotel in Stephen King's novel *The Shining*, reveal architecture's ability to shape thoughts and stir emotions. Orta's work seems to represent architecture and human existence in equivocal terms, transacting a synergy between her structures and the bodies of the inhabitants. *Body Architecture* extends to forge a degree of symbiosis between the wearers as they rely on each other to make up the remaining parts of the whole. In an unexpected reversal, Orta is using architectural principles to dictate the behaviour of the inhabitants rather than merely structuring it to serve individual needs.

While Orta interprets the body's architecture as an external surface, she also considers it to be a part of a system of tiers that envelop the body in various layers. Underwear, layers of outer clothing and anoraks continue to be expanded by additional surfaces; after the anorak comes the sleeping bag, followed by the tent, after which comes the container. 'Fashion is essentially a system of many layers of protection in which we wrap or cocoon ourselves,' Orta said. 'They hold the potential to define identity and our place in society.' Viewing each outer surface of her work as a second skin, Orta transfers texts, symbols and images onto the fabric to voice statements of identity and solidarity, like personal sentiments and subcultural affinities expressed in tattooing.

In addition to its spatial coherence, *Body Architecture* also provides a framework in which individual narratives can be expressed textually. Texts and images are often a point of entry into the meaning of Orta's work, sometimes evocative of the logos and packaging essential to consumerism. Yet in their humanitarian meaning, Orta's graphics subvert the concept of branding. A brand is considered to be 'a prefix; a qualifier of character', sentiments that also summarize the motives behind Orta's signature graphics and the messages they convey.[9] Her graphics can be likened to advertising with nothing to sell, intended to provoke questions rather than propose solutions. They implant ideas into social consciousness to trigger spontaneous actions rather than to achieve predetermined objectives. Orta breaks new ground to incite social and personal transformations, using physical, often intimate, contact and voluntary participation rather than the dogma of slogans and brands.

The shifting codes of meaning captured in the intertextual manifestations of *Body Architecture* function as a recording device that captures and organizes their cultural meanings over time. In forming a lo-tech record, they recall the pre-digital archives that served as depositories for the accumulation of time and knowledge, a system used by libraries, institutions, museums, academia and other discursive centres of knowledge. Like these archives, fashion and architecture generally serve as objects that reflect culture and society, around which people congregate to examine and interpret their meaning. *Body Architecture's* capacity to create an archive in itself reveals the inherent space for intellectual investigation it also creates.

The Nexus

Of all Orta's projects, *Nexus Architecture* seems to be the most emblematic of her approach. More symbolic than functional, *Nexus Architecture* takes its name from 'nexus', meaning a link or a tie, or a linked series or group. The series is made up of individual outfits termed *Collective Wear* that emulate the hooded body suits worn by Greenpeace activists during anti-nuclear protests. Unlike the Greenpeace suits, which were made to be worn individually, Orta's suits have attachable tubes of fabric that zip the wearers together in a single garment.

Nexus Architecture is intended to function as an antidote to the type of social fragmentation

Intimate Architecture: Lucy Orta's Social Structures

described by the architectural theorist Neil Leach as 'the placelessness of contemporary society'.[10] As 'difference' is subsumed within a single totalizing vision, it can breed a certain intolerance to anything that does not conform to the same vision, promoting the marginalization of individuals even further. As parts of the city fragment and mimic a village, they break down the model for a unified urban fabric, dividing it into neighbourhoods and subsequently subdividing into autonomous units.

The individual units of Orta's *Nexus Architecture* link the wearers together at the front and the back of the garments. The collective garment they form can include a few people or hundreds of them, forming a many-membered organism. Orta interprets the tubes of fabric connecting the individuals to one another as a literal representation of a 'social link', made visible to those outside the workshop as the participants tour the streets wearing it. *Nexus Architecture* interventions have been staged in Europe, the United States, South Africa, Bolivia and Mexico, joining together over one hundred people in a single column as they trek across nature or process through the urban landscape. Within its shared spaces, *Collective Wear* encourages physical contact and co-operation among its wearers, as well as an exploration of individual feeling and movement.

Part of *Nexus Architecture's* expression of collectivism manifests through events and workshops that compliment the interventions. These are typically planned to facilitate the sharing of skills or as an expansion of knowledge that brings people together to raise awareness of key issues. *Nexus Architecture* encourages the collaboration of marginalized social groups, which in the past has mixed migrant labourers, the homeless and inner-city teenagers with local participants. With a focus on forging interrelationships and new perceptions of personal and cultural identity, the collaborations redefine the way that diverse groups are able to communicate and interact with each other. Orta transports an established matrix from one workshop to the next but looks into the local environment to find the themes, materials and construction techniques used by the group. She creates a forum that enables the work to evolve as artists and participants establish a working relationship and an awareness of common concerns.

As part of her participation in the Second Johannesburg Biennale, Orta created a workshop that employed thirteen migrant labourers to produce their own *Nexus* links, leaving them free to make the aesthetical and planning decisions for their own suits, instilling a notion of individuality into each. She explained: 'None of the participants knew how to sew at all but learned the skill during the course of the workshop. So it was about passing on a skill, how to make a garment, but at the same time making them aware of how they can work together as a team to create something and give them the possibility to manifest something. Afterwards the women took the initiative to find work using their sewing skills. In turn, they were able to teach the skill to other women, creating a continuous chain that illustrated the message behind the links perfectly.' The links formed by the attachable appendages linked thirteen different individuals in a self-sufficient entity that signalled the power of the collective body over the isolation of the individual.

One of the *Nexus* workshops facilitated the transatlantic construction of a mobile shelter, bridging the diverse experiences of teenagers from the Arc-en-Ciel foster home in France with the students from the Sonia Delaunay High School in France and adolescents from the Henry Street Settlement arts programme on New York's Lower East Side. These workshops did not include the public interventions of the *Collective Wear* actions, but focused on exploring the role of art as a collective activity that progressed with the active participation of each group. Each participant produced an individual panel of fabric that would be attached to the others and form the walls of a mobile shelter. Mirroring the collective body formed by the individuals linked together in *Collective Wear*, the teenagers symbolically produced a collective entity that brought the individual members of these diverse groups into a collective whole. The success of this long-distance interaction later inspired Orta to develop 'fluid architecture', the interactive website that provides an international forum for people throughout the world to participate in the workshops, which is detailed later in this chapter.[11]

Even after the garments are taken off, *Nexus Architecture* continues to suggest a possible model for living together in a communal formation that encourages individual expression and mutual support. *Nexus Architecture* reveals that the community is made up of individuals and the individual, like an urban dwelling, is not an autonomous element, but an entity rooted in its connection and interaction with the larger whole. The community of workshop participants is established through such connections, each enriching the individual and facilitating a sense of inclusion.

Nexus Architecture is an evolving architectural and social configuration that expands the collective principles behind Orta's *Body Architecture*. Although these evolved through her experimentation with portable structures, the design does not facilitate the same wearability that most of her other prototypes do. The installation comprises the aluminium-coated domes Orta refers to as *Primary Structures*, interconnected by *Nexus* extensions. Each dome has space for up to three people and room for folding tables, chairs, or plinths. The *Primary Structures* are positioned in a hexagonal shape encircling a central space that provides a forum for community workshops. The hexagonal layout provides the structural axis from which further *Primary Structures* can radiate. These constructions, together with the participants, create the feel of a nomadic community, which Orta appropriates to create a dialogue among all members of the group.

The *Nexus Architecture* projects were also championed by Paul Virilio, who applauded their capacity to confront the disintegration of social bonds in today's society. For several decades Virilio had observed the gradual erosion of the family unit and the disappearance of what he

(A)

Intimate Architecture: Lucy Orta's Social Structures

describes as 'humanitarian values'. Virilio parallels this social decay to the disintegration of collective units, as the role of the individual begins to take precedence over humanitarian concerns: '(Orta) is designing collective wear at a time when divorces are on the increase. It is a sort of marriage via clothes, designed to prevent people from tearing themselves apart. It is extraordinary that, at a time when single-parent families are becoming the norm, Lucy Orta is designing collective wear where parents and children wear the same garment. This is like a metaphor symptomatic of the state of society.'[12]

Virilio's critique highlights some of the political dimensions of Orta's work. Although Orta is adamant that her work is not based on political protest, the social and spatial ordering expressed in her architectural structures could also serve as a model for a pluralistic, democratic Europe free from the issues of nationalism provoked by the European Union. It is surprising that such models are necessary at a time when humans celebrate the perception of freedom, emancipation and autonomy, but individuals appear to be regrouping in somewhat threatening configurations – evident in the phenomena of street gangs, subversive cultures, fascist groups and terrorists.

Nexus Architecture garments are inscribed with images and texts, yet voice a critique against brand culture and image making as they circulate in a society dominated by slogans and visual iconography. Echoing the textual features of Clark's *Roupa corpo-roupa* and Oiticica's *Parangolés*, Orta regards the exterior surfaces of the garments as *tabula rasa* onto which she inscribes her signature communiqué.[13] But while the *Parangolés* were

[A]Orta held a *Nexus Architecture* workshop in Johannesburg in 1997, using the concepts behind her work to stage a social bond between people and teach them new skills. As the participants learned to sew their own garments they also made interpersonal exchanges.

[B]Individual sleeping sacs join to a collective hub that functions as a collective arena.

(B)

imprinted with defiant expressions such as 'I embody revolt', 'I am possessed' and 'From adversity we live', Orta's work projects statements of empathy and solidarity.

The outer shell of *Nexus Architecture* sports images and texts to broadcast messages of their own, interpreting the communication potential inherent in all clothing as a form of visual and verbal packaging. One of the prototypes Orta showed at the Venice Biennale in 1995 featured the clear-cut statement: 'Me, I've got a lot to say.' Orta borrowed this expression from a participant in her first *Identity + Refuge* workshop. Each Nexus intervention includes this declaration, articulating that the wearer, whether marginalized by society or not, is claiming their right to voice individual views. As participants customize their individual outfits in Orta's workshops they rediscover themselves by 'writing' their identities. Such messages move beyond literary form, expressing in symbols the human angst that was previously passed over in silence.

Brand culture goes hand in hand with marketing and mobility, and packaging, the means of carrying the message to its destinations, has a dual role. The primary function of packaging is to facilitate transport, and its secondary role is a strategy to market the product. As the *Nexus Architecture* motifs convey information, they also reproduce this approach. In the way that packaging draws consumers, Orta uses texts to draw members of society towards problems that are continually avoided.

Nomadic Cities

If, when making a presentation on *Report on the City 1 and 2*, Rem Koolhaas actually did state 'there have been no new movements in urbanism since Team X and Archigram', he had obviously not heard of Lucy Orta. As her work continued to radiate beyond the individual and small collectives, Orta developed a system of flexible, modular structures that mimic an architectural axis able to grow in size according to population. Unlike a series of buildings that would remain bound to a specific place, *the Connector Mobile Village* forms the basis of a mobile community. The work facilitates a modular social network in which individual units can connect together in a variety of configurations, forming sites for habitation, education or exhi-

(A)

bitions. Individuals can attach and detach at will to join different parts of the community or reformulate the entire network. 'I wanted to engage the individual *Body Architecture* units I call "Survival Sacs" within the structure of an architectural hub to create a forum where individuals could gather and retreat to separate spaces when they need to,' Orta explained.

The Connector is an infrastructure that forms the basis of an architecture that is permanently evolving. Based on both independence and interdependence, it formalizes Orta's concept of an open network for social space. Like the works in her *Body Architecture* series, *The Connector Mobile Village* is designed to promote inclusion and encourage community activities among groups as they work together on a specific project, or engage in leisure and recreation. In this respect *The Connector* is akin to the ancient Succoth – a tent erected in the midst of fields for the ritual feasting and celebrations following the harvest of crops. After the event is over, *The Connector* is disassembled and taken away by the participants. Its assembly and subsequent disassembly does not leave behind the sort of building waste or demolition residue typical of prefabricated housing – making *The Connector* a natural resource in itself.

Whether erected in an urban milieu or in the natural environment, *The Connector Mobile Village* does not necessitate any changes to the landscape around it. In the current drive towards systems of open architecture, *The Connector* echoes the principles of folding architecture as it blurs, blends and intermixes with garments, structures and the landscape. The use of textiles and the construction of home through the principles of architecture and the

[A]The symbols that Orta uses can be likened to packaging or urban graffiti as she inscribes the fabrics with texts, symbols and images that mimic tattoos, branding and advertising.

[B]Survival Kits containing necessities and practical tools are also branded with messages of solidarity.

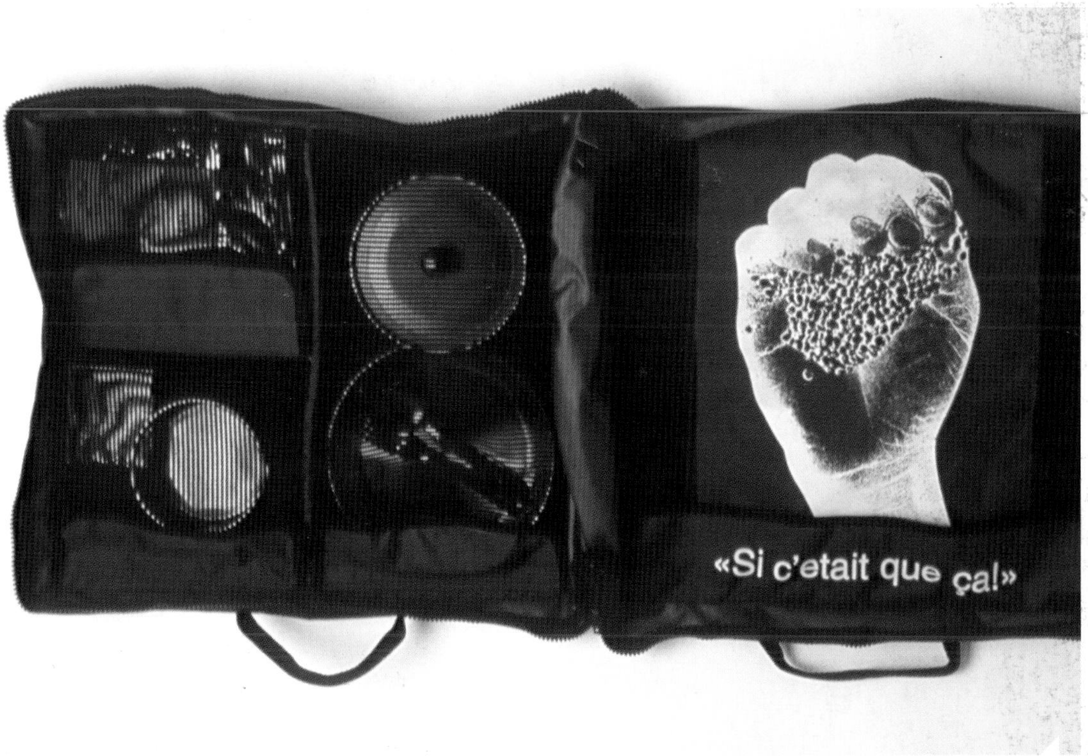

(B)

community it houses were placed into a theoretical context by Gottfried Semper, who interpreted the woven carpets hung from the frames of nomadic tents as early architecture. Although superseded by walls, Semper never considered these textiles to have been lost completely, identifying vestiges of their weaves in the patterns of brickwork and mosaics. The textile panels used in Orta's work revive the fabric containers of early architecture, harking back to the essentially nomadic experience that bonded wandering communities. *The Communicator* fabricates a physical container for both material and cultural content, engaging the wanderers directly and encouraging them to linger.

Orta's *Life Nexus Village Fête* is also an architectural and social configuration that draws on the architectural principles expressed in *The Communicator Mobile Village* and the interconnectedness of *Nexus Architecture*. While these evolved through the principles of wearable garments, the designs are not fully wearable. *The Life Nexus Village Fête* comprises the *Primary Structures* mentioned above, interconnected by *Nexus* extensions. The *Primary Structures* are positioned in a hexagonal shape encircling a central space (foyer) that provides a forum for community workshops. The hexagonal layout provides the structural axis from which further *Primary Structures* can radiate. These constructions, together with the participants, create the feel of a community festival, an atmosphere Orta generates to establish a dialogue among the group.

Beyond metaphors for connection, *The Communicator* also points towards modes of survival in the cases of social and demographic dislocation experienced by refugees. Orta responds with an environment that provides spaces for survival in private areas for sleeping, eating and washing, instantly creating a ready-made village. As *The Connector* produces a frame for spatial meaning, it also facilitates an environment for communication, support and solidarity. 'It's important that the nodes can adapt to include all members of a family, since large families may be split up in emergency shelters or social housing,' Orta said. 'As the community travels they can take these shelters with them for as long as they need to. Hopefully

(A)

Intimate Architecture: Lucy Orta's Social Structures

they will represent the promise of a permanent home later on.'

'The Connector Mobile Village is also a means of keeping social units together,' Orta explained. 'Like a family who can come together in the central node then sleep in their own Survival Sacs without disconnecting. That is very important for parents and children so that they aren't separated.' Orta addresses the vulnerability of children living under extreme conditions by designating space to re-create the security and intimacy they had had in their own homes. *Connector* modules can be customized by and for children with fabrics, textures and colours to create personalized environments.

Orta is not alone in addressing the needs of humanity with mobile dwelling spaces. A range of American and European artists are basing their work on the 'containerization' of living space, exploring the overlaps between architecture, urban planning and transitional systems to realize a fully self-sufficient and mobile social space. In addition to those artists mentioned in chapter 6, artists such as Joep van Lieshout's projects, for example, roam from site to site in the guise of mobile help centres, while Krzysztof Wodiczko created a series of *Homeless Vehicles* to provide marginalized groups with a 'street tool' that transports the basic necessities of a survival economy. Alicia Framis, Tobias Rehberger, Jorge Pardo, Plamen Dejanov and Swetlana Heger also ground their art practice in the social dimensions of collective action and the understanding of itinerant communities. Like the goals of *The Connector Mobile Village*, their work aims to give marginalized groups a forum for public presence and speech, delivering the 'platform' to people who are unable to reach centres of power.

[A]Gloves and sleeves are sewn into this modular dome (made as part of the *Modular Architecture* series) as a symbolic expression of reaching out or sharing resources.

[B]As modular units interconnect they unite individuals in an architecture framework that provides the basis for community.

(B)

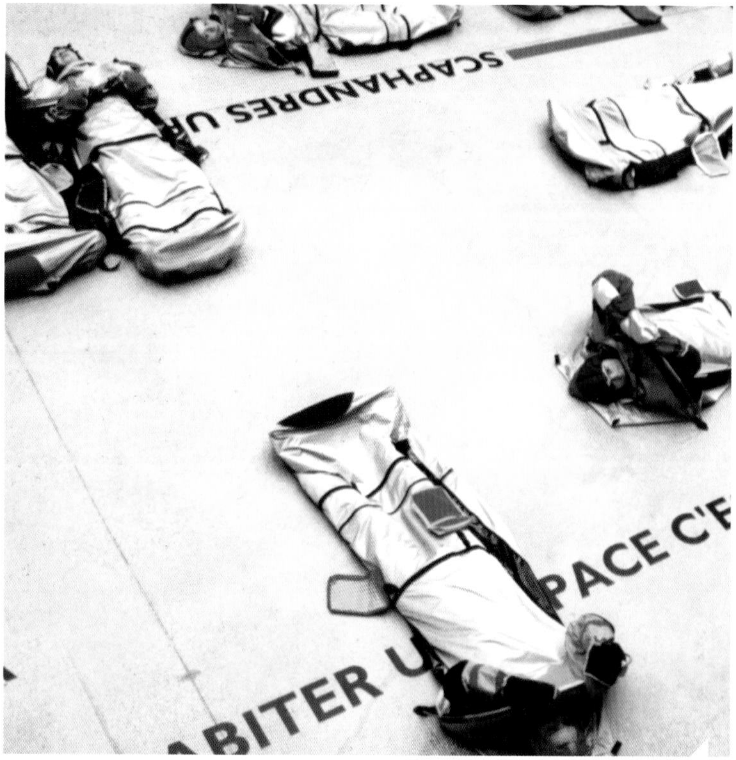

(A)

Modular Architecture

Orta continues to move beyond the concept of an autonomous, separate self to give the individual refuge in the collective whole. Like *The Connector Mobile Village*, *Modular Architecture* addresses the individual's need to share space and extend the warmth and security of one's own space with others. 'I wanted to explore the systems that encapsulate individual bodies, and challenge them with a system that connects and interconnects individuals,' Orta explained. 'There is a sense that putting modules together unites people, making them aware they can exist as individuals but also as components of the whole.'

Modular Architecture amplifies fashion's primary function as shelter, and signals fashion's capacity to assume the functions of modern dwellings. It combines the communal principles of *Body Architecture* with the protective function of *Refuge Wear*. *Modular Architecture* consists of temporary, portable dwellings made up of individual sections, panels or units that can be combined to make a number of different forms, or simply worn as protective clothing. Square, triangular or rectangular in shape, individual panels can be joined and configured into several core designs: geometric domes or modular igloos are created by joining six or eight triangles, while four-sided panels can be fashioned into rectilinear cabins. Square panels can also be rolled into tubes to form the *Nexus* links between the *Collective Wear* suits.

Mirroring the principles of architectonic modularity, any one component can be removed and replaced without affecting the rest of the system. The individual pieces can be rearranged to transform one item into myriad designs, or whole panels

LE LIEN PHYSIQUE TISSE UN

(B)

[A+B] Orta's exhibition at the Cartier Foundation in Paris came to life as ten dancers animated and interconnected the *Modular Architecture* pieces. At times the dancers moved as a collective body, aligning their routines with a painted grid covering the floor. The performance generated the effect of collapsed boundaries as the dancer's movements erased the margins between their bodies, the architectural modules and the surrounding space.

replaced to alter the function of the piece. The *Nexus* links connect the igloos, domes and cabins and the wearers in a single system. In its functionality, the system observes the rules corresponding to the matrix of Western architecture, mirroring the Greek and Roman traditions that underpin the modules prevalent in modern architecture. Yet, workshop participants can determine the dimensions of *Modular Architecture* according to site-specific projects, breaking away from formal measurements and traditional techniques. 'In moving beyond uniform heights and dimensions,' Orta explained, '*Modular Architecture* also addresses the concept of a universal, unchanging order of individual and social realities, and the extent to which these values continue to apply.'

The body suits included in *Modular Architecture* feature modules of body parts; that is, gloves, gloved sleeves and hoods that can be attached, unzipped and interchanged. Pockets and compartments can also assume the guise of modular components – facilitating the sharing of goods and resources once again. Ten modules can be zipped together into a single sleeping tube that circulates body heat and produces an expression of unity as they act as a single entity. Orta regards the wearer's movements as those of a multi-faceted mechanism, mirroring Leibniz's theories on the mechanization of the body. In his theory of Monadology, Leibniz described the body not as a machine in itself, but as a mechanism made up of many machines, considering organs and body parts as devices in themselves. A model for expression in contemporary aesthetics, the concept of the monad is viewed in terms of folds of space, movement and time, like the interrelatedness of the body and the *Modular Architecture* structures supporting it.

Orta staged a dance performance at the Cartier Foundation in Paris in 1996 in conjunction with an installation of her work in the gallery. Ten dance professionals donned *Modular Architecture* outfits and choreographed a mobile version of the installation as they moved through the gallery. As they explored the space of the gallery they also explored the spaces of the *Modular Architecture*, moving through the domes and cabins and investigating the spaces of the structures they

(A)

were wearing. Arm modules were unzipped or extended as the dancers interrelated the architecture to the body and their bodies to one another. They articulated their collective body through its alignment with a painted grid covering the floor. The effect was that of collapsed boundaries, as the dancer's movements dissolved the margins between the bodies and the architectural modules.

Modular Architecture highlights the potential to rethink many of the limitations of architecture as well as fashion. Conceiving of modular systems of architecture offers inhabitants the means to expand and customize their environments, recalling Richard Buckminster Fuller's vision of manufacturing whole rooms for the home that could be purchased and installed like appliances. Buildings would have greater potential to expand laterally without affecting the ground beneath them, and pre-equipped units could replace outmoded living areas. Likewise, garments can evolve to create self-controlled environments that provide the wearer with flexibility, holding the means to create whole wardrobes based on a system of modular segments that can be rearranged in myriad designs, or form panels that can function as modular sections. Worn-out modules can be renewed, and styles can easily be reconfigured by interchanging the modules. This could enable designers to offer customers the range of clothing combinations found in a large collection of separates, while only manufacturing several core designs. While the economics of mass production make it prohibitively expensive to manufacture small numbers of individual designs, producing large numbers of a small range reduces production costs considerably.

[A+B]Acknowledging that the social function of a dining room or restaurant extends beyond its built structure, Orta uses the cultural practice of 'the meal' to create a space for interaction among the people it brings together. Staged outside the confines of architecture, a meal can be transacted in the street or any public space to facilitate exchanges and interactions.

(B)

Accepting the rationale of *Modular Architecture* is to dismiss the belief in an unchanging order of relationships between individuals, societies and the environment around them. Orta has identified the fragmentations evident in the society around her, making her response through a modular structure that redefines them as components in a universal system. It provides an architectural solution to the limitations of physical space while extending the body's mobility and potential to interact within larger systems. As a result, *Modular Architecture* holds the potential to redefine the boundaries between clothing and architecture, outlining a system that interprets garments as built environments in themselves and also a part of a larger one.

Making a Response

The workshops and interventions mentioned previously make strong statements about clothing, humanity, individuality and communality, but they are also intended to identify new forums for bringing people together. Critics often have difficulty finding a term that encapsulates the full range of Orta's practice, typically interpreting it as art installations, relational aesthetics, architectural prototypes or even fashion collections. While aspects of Orta's work can be explained in these terms, the very depth and breadth of her practice collapses such categorical denominations of media and genre one into the other. It is the staging of the social bond itself that binds each project, threading through the concepts of refuge and solidarity to weave an interactive platform for participation and dialogue.

'My motivation is to communicate,' Orta explained. 'To communicate a new art form which can involve all sorts of genres, from performances, interventions and object-making to installations and multi-media. But at the same time, to bring to the fore some social awareness through the objects, dialogues or discussions.' Orta achieves this by encouraging active participation from diverse members of the community, engaging with them in the same spot where she identifies the need for social change in the first place. Squatted buildings, shelters for the homeless, schools, universities, art galleries, theatres and even the street have became the locus for these events. Orta incorpo-

Intimate Architecture: Lucy Orta's Social Structures

rates a range of diverse media, including food and clothing along with images, texts and sound recordings. Orta's 'hands on' method of social bonding gives a contemporary sense to the concepts of activism and social obligation that many activists previously regarded as outdated.

Orta explores the function of architecture and the purpose of clothing with unremitting persistence, re-examining the functions of the spaces contained within them. But while the *Body Architecture* projects create dwellings to reshape and redefine points of interaction between individuals, Orta recognizes the need to build relationships beyond them, extending her practice to spaces whose wearers are unlikely to don her garments. Examining the role of a restaurant or cafeteria reveals that its social function extends beyond its built structure – it is the cultural practice of the meal that creates a space for interaction among the people it brings together. Staged beyond the confines of architecture, a meal can be transacted in the street or any public space to facilitate exchanges and interactions. Like the migrant workers who learned sewing skills and shared them with members of their community, Orta brings people together in the street in the hope that they will re-create the social bonds in the public spaces where they are needed most.

One of Orta's most acclaimed interventions did not feature garments or architecture, answering the body's need for sustenance instead. Entitled *All in One Basket: A Reflection on Hunger and Food Waste*, the intervention was held at the Forum Saint-Eustache des Halles in Paris in March 1997. Orta developed the idea the previous summer when she saw television news coverage of French farmers protesting against European Union agricultural legislation by tipping trailers of fruit onto the highways. Disturbed by these images, Orta realized that, in a less dramatic manner, the Paris market traders also dumped fruit and vegetables at the close of the markets. She responded by organizing the collection of leftover produce in the Les Halles quarter of Paris, and asking a celebrity chef to cook it. The food was served on a buffet and passers-by were invited to eat. The people of Les Halles, whether rich or poor, participated in a demonstration of gastronomic recycling and exchange.

The *All in One Basket* project led to Orta's incorporation of food into other projects. She demonstrated how emergency meals could be provided in times of crisis in an event titled *70 x 7, The Meal*, staged at the Kunstraum gallery in

^Orta's Mobile Interventions raise awareness wherever they travel.

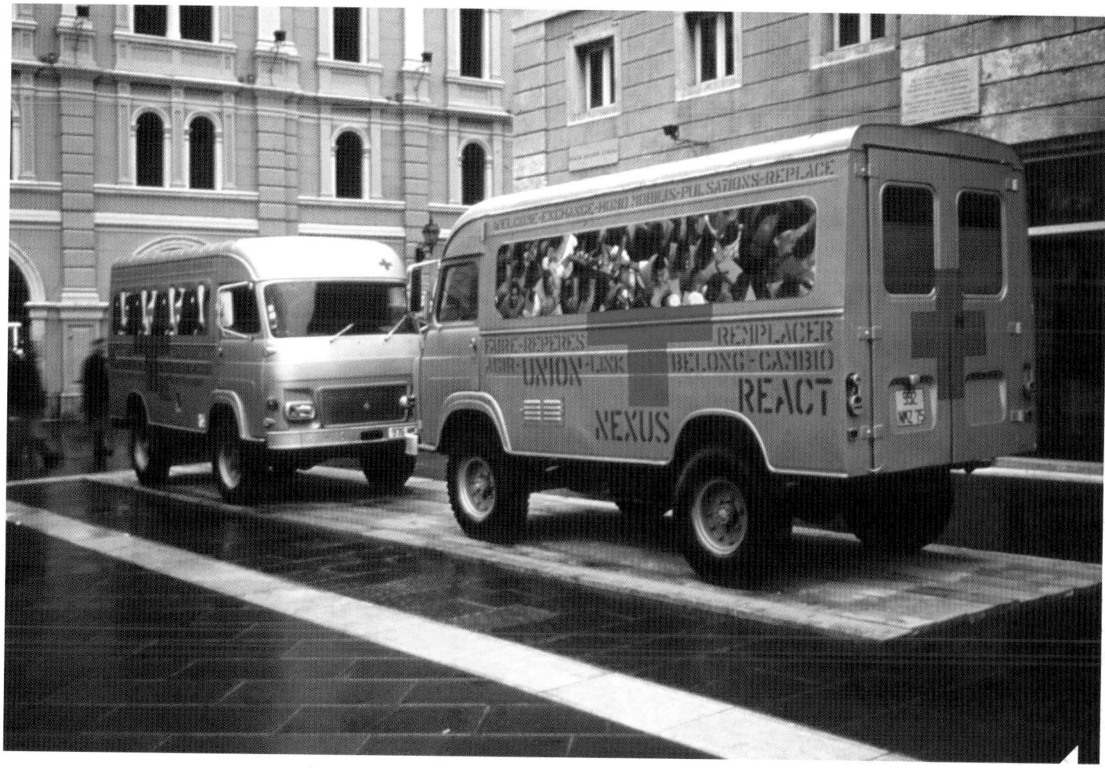

(A)

Innsbruck, Austria. The project was, according to Orta, 'the third act in a series of actions that bring the community together via the ritual of a meal thus creating links and engaging the lives of the broader community'. Orta chose '*70 x 7*' as a symbol of the infinite, taken from a biblical context. Orta's ambition is to transform the symbol into reality by organizing meals that could expand exponentially in multiples of seven to accommodate an infinite number of guests. *70 x 7* consists of an extendable seventy-metre tablecloth set with 490 Limoges dinner plates manufactured specifically for the work. The Kunstraum then organized a series of meals for multiples of seven guests, using surplus produce from local farmers.

Orta has held other relational works outdoors: in the cultural milieu of Tschumi's Parc de la Villette in Paris, in New York's SoHo district where she staged a fashion show outside the Salvation Army on Spring Street and outside the perimeter wall of a prison in Metz. For her 'Earth Day' installation at Parc de la Villette, Orta constructed a mobile unit she dubbed *Citizen Platform* as a vehicle for gauging individual opinions on environmental concerns. By asking the park's visitors to write messages relating to the practice of recycling, Orta created a social response to an urgent ethical need. '*Citizen Platform* was set up to work more or less like *Nexus Architecture* does, but this time the participant was confronted with a mobile architecture made of metal rather than fabric and asked to engage with it through written communication rather than wearing it,' she said. 'It was also a follow-up to the food project at Les Halles where people discussed food wastage – another example of something that should be recycled but isn't.'

As the park's visitors appreciated its landscaped green spaces and fresh air they were confronted with the reality that environmental awareness was essential to maintain it. The messages they wrote were pre-addressed to the mayor of Paris, appealing for improved recycling programmes throughout the city. The response was overwhelming – hundreds of messages were collected and passed on to the mayor's office as a demonstration of collective solidarity. Based on this initial success, the mobile unit will continue to travel the city until definite changes in the

Intimate Architecture: Lucy Orta's Social Structures

city's environmental policies have taken hold. The project drew awareness to the fact that each public area in the city has the potential to act as a platform, transforming into a space that can represent the collective voice of the city.

In another intervention, Orta questioned what a forgotten coat hanging on a peg or an abandoned pair of shoes could tell about the person who wore them, and asked what they could mean to the next owner. Recalling Heidegger's insights into the origins and owners of the boots painted by Van Gogh, Orta considered the original source and future potentials of the discarded clothing she would recycle, giving new life to objects earmarked for disposal. It was in this context that Orta's intervention *Identity + Refuge* with the residents of the Salvation Army shelter in Paris was organized, setting up a sewing workshop to recycle second-hand clothing into new garments for each of the residents. The shelter's storeroom housed a surplus of clothing that was transformed into new and original garments in the workshop, creating a tailor-made wardrobe for residents who usually had no other choice but to salvage second-hand clothing for their own use. When the workshop concluded, Orta organized a fashion show of the regenerated clothing, enlisting the participation of students from a local secondary school to model them.

One of the aims of the workshop had been to give residents the means to reclaim their self-esteem through the items they wore, giving them the capacity to create a wardrobe that they regarded as comfortable, appropriate and even fashionable. Orta encouraged the residents to reconsider their appearance and their individual roles in society, which she hoped would boost their self-esteem and personal identity. The collective task also transmitted a message about human creativity; the garments made by the residents resulted from their own creative inspiration that they may not have realized existed previously. Performed with the tools and materials at hand rather than through mechanized production, the task of making the garments also constituted the sort of work-oriented creativity that Lévi-Strauss identified as *bricolage*.[14] *Bricolage* also identifies the 'events' that result when basic materials are transformed into more refined products, which in this case manifested as both the workshop established to convert rags into beautiful clothing and the self-awareness created among the residents. Lévi-Strauss argued that, 'to understand a real object in its totality we always tend to work from its parts', identifying art in the spaces between creative production and technical skill.[15] The concept of 'art in the spaces' is a perfect metaphor for Orta's interventions, which in this context revealed parallels between the new lease of life produced in the abandoned clothing and the new lease of hope experienced by the residents.

The sewing workshop balanced structure and event, enjoining the physical act of making the clothes with the sensate, bodily experience of wearing them. Through the garments, new visions of life were projected by the makers for the wearers, as if the old clothing represented ambitions not possible to relay by pen and paper, word or gesture. Lévi-Strauss identified such expressions as signs, maintaining that the bricoleur communicates in ciphers that update the previous meanings of the materials with a new message. 'Signs can be opposed to concepts,' he wrote, 'signs allow and even require the interposing and incorporation of a certain amount of human culture into reality.'[16] Likewise, these recycled garments are unique in their capacity to reveal much about the social conditions that necessitated their production in the first place.

Orta went on to create events that would bridge the gap between the confined residents of a penal institution and the free inhabitants of a nearby town in a work titled *Commune Communicate*. Like the platform for discussion set up at La Villette, Orta created a dialogue among members of the public and the inmates at Metz Prison – a discourse between the inclusive group of society and the excluded 'other'. 'I wondered about the prisoners' feelings of isolation and at the same time their rigid scrutiny by the prison administration,' Orta said. 'The public world has little knowledge of their closed world. It was important to them that they communicate with the world outside.' Orta met with the prisoners and discussed their daily routines, their feelings about the world outside and their hopes for the future. The prisoners designed a set of folding tables and suitcases that featured photographs of the prison environment: the patch of blue sky overhead interrupted by helicopter-deterrent wires, the rusted entry gates that had recently been set alight in a prison protest, the interior façade of the concrete prison wall and regulation clothing bearing the stamped logo of the prison.

The inmate's communiqué was set up on the streets of Metz where passers-by could stop and listen to the recorded messages made by some of the prisoners for broadcast to listeners outside, sending good wishes to the people of the town or lobbying for rights and reforms to the French penal system. The recordings enabled the listeners to visualize the prisoners' perspectives and gain an understanding of their isolation. 'Many of the passers-by sent messages back to the prison on postcards, expressing their support or their curiosity,' Orta said. 'Back at the prison the messages were circulated among the inmates, who were happy to have direct communication with people in the town, which they received with nostalgia and humour, but sometimes with a little sadness too.' Although the prisoners were locked into their exclusion, the aim was for them not to lose their individuality in a collective mass. *Commune Communicate* helped some of them to rediscover, in the strength of the group, the spatial organization of society that continued to provide hope.

Fluid Architecture

There is nothing more cutting edge today than the pooling of minds into an immense, interdisciplinary collaboration. Cyberspace, as a realm of intersecting practices, produces a virtual space in which concepts can be represented digitally and presented on an interactive platform. The Internet's wider technological role within material culture stimulates the potential for new interactive formats, reflected in a gradual shift away from traditional methods of meeting in face-to-face forums. This practice is already widespread in design and architecture; now Orta is exploring new developments in multimedia technologies to launch her interactive platforms on the Internet. Web interactivity, though still dependent on photo-based media, makes this new information-based approach to her work possible.

Cyberspace has a revolutionary role that extends far beyond that of the workshop, intervention, seminar or gallery exhibition. Advances in technology enable Orta to engineer connections and interfaces that unite fashion and architecture within an art forum. Orta launched the 'fluid architecture' web platform in 2002 as an adjunct to her 'studio-orta' website to boost the scope for participation and take the scale of projects in a new direction altogether.[17] Fluid architecture is a forum where art, architecture and fashion merge and interact with a range of ideas reflecting activism, philosophy, solidarity and communality. The site features elements of sculpture, intervention, performance, fashion and architecture, underpinned by a series of visual and textual narratives that reveals a synergy between them all.

Orta is not moving away from object-based practice, but reproducing key elements of her workshops and creating interactive displays and webcast exhibitions through her digital archives and digital film projections. The site constitutes a body of work in itself, using a variety of contemporary media to create a new visual language for communication and interaction. The website's interactive technology enables visitors to contribute in real time to a workshop being held in a different time zone, or just log on and observe the participants' progress and interaction. Use of the Internet and digital technology transcends the boundaries of time and space and overcomes the problems of geographical distance, making the projects available to more spectators than could ever be accommodated in a workshop. Visitors can also view video recordings of previous projects held in the site's digital archive, read texts, or listen to soundbites. Visitors are encouraged to send messages to the participants or to each other, creating an editorial space where ideas, opinions and critical feedback are circulated.

The concept behind the site combines contemporary aesthetics and technological innovations in a multimedia environment that facilitates communication and exploration. 'Fluid architecture is a work that is developed and advanced, but by no means finished,' Orta explained in a seminar presentation made to the students and faculty of the London College of Fashion shortly after the site was launched. 'It creates a continuous forum and an open network for participation and a positive critical interface.' Orta also anticipates that the visitors' perceptions of her work will identify areas that parallel her practice or inspire new approaches to the issues she addresses. 'I tend to think of it as an exchange process too, a site where constant change mimics the fluidity of the sort of concepts I'm working with,' Orta explained. 'There is a fluidity of shape and form that takes the workshops in new directions.'

The site represents a body of infinite folds and surfaces that twist and weave through compressed time and space. As visitors access the home page and 'unbuckle' its initial protocols, a series of origami folds open out, each segment representing different projects in Australia, France, The Netherlands and England. Once selected, each individual fold unpacks a virtual tour of a project or workshop, revealed cinematically through time-lapse photography accompanied by a soundtrack of participants' voices describing their experiences of the workshops or interventions. A fluid narrative of panoramas, people, places and projects overlaps ambient sounds and brings written texts and moving images into the foreground. The visitor engages with a simultaneous experience of reading, listening and watching that mirrors the dynamics of the workshops themselves. The website can also include experimental designs and works in progress, or showcase tangential projects that may not relate directly to a workshop or an intervention.

Making these projects interactive and available to the public reduces the traditional degree of separation between artist and spectator. Fluid architecture's interactive platform deliberately challenges the traditional concept of authorship, questioning the role of the artist as the work is enhanced and expanded by a range of contributors. Central to the site's methodology is the reversal of the web visitor's role as a passive spectator, transforming them into participants or users who co-author the work through interaction with it. Orta's affinity with cyberspace heralds an exciting future in a landscape of visual technology as fluid architecture breaks with traditional systems of design and interaction. The website demonstrates how the traditionally separate entities of art, architecture and design are blurring in the virtual realm, just as they do in the real world.

In a body of work spanning more than a decade, Orta has created a unique genre that transcends denominations between fashion, architecture and traditional art practice. She discusses, debates and rethinks the traditional principles of social structures, introducing new ideas that have a profound engagement with society, urban planning, cultural heritage and political and ecological policies. Her work reveals the extent to which perceptions of space play a crucial role in the construction of urban identity, whether it is condensed and compressed to serve individual needs or expanded to encompass the whole of society.

The common denominator linking Orta's different projects is the staging of a social bond. As she locates the points of isolation, indignity and indifference in urban society, Orta rethinks the principles of fashion and architecture and highlights their value as a platform for social responsibility. By using them as the starting point for the transformation of the individual and society, her work initiates social metamorphosis through unexpected media. Fusing the respective spaces of architecture and fashion with art, technology, philosophy and interactivity results in a series of actions and events that forge lasting connections between groups and individuals. The potency of her temporary environments signifies a shift in prerogative from the empowered to the disenfranchised, manifesting an awareness of individual needs that will have lasting effects long after their original construction is forgotten.

Intimate Architecture: Lucy Orta's Social Structures

[1]Lucy Orta was interviewed by the author.

[2]See Guy Debord, 'Theory of Dérive', in K Knabb (ed) (1989),*The Situationist International Anthology*, Berkeley, CA: Bureau of Public Secrets.

[3]Born near Birmingham in 1966, Orta has been active in Paris since 1991, where she now lives with her husband, the Argentinian artist Jorge Orta. Though based in Paris, she is a Professor of the London Institute and holds the Rootstein Hopkins Chair at the London College of Fashion, simultaneously heading the Man & Humanity Masters Degree programme at the Eindhoven Design Academy in Holland. She remains active as an artist and exhibits her work in galleries and museums around the world.

[4]Quoted in Jean Paul Bourdier and Nezar Alsayyad (ed) (1989), *Dwellings, Settlements and Tradition*, New York: University Press of America, p40.

[5]Victor Shklovsky (1965 edition), 'Art as Technique', *Russian Formalist Criticism: Four Essays*, Lincoln, NB: University of Nebraska Press, p12.

[6]Carlos Basualdo (2002), *Hélio Oiticica: Quasi-Cinemas*, Ostfildern-Ruit, Germany: Hatje Cantz Publishers, p140.

[7]See Orta (1998) in *Process of Transformation*, Paris: Editions Jean-Michel Place.

[8]Orta (1996), *Refuge Wear*, Paris: Editions Jean-Michel Place.

[9]See Jane Pavitt (ed) (2000), *Brand New*, London: V&A Publications.

[10]Neil Leach (ed) (1999), *Architecture and Revolution*, London: Routledge, p155.

[11]See www.studio-orta.com/fluidarchitecture.

[12]Basualdo, *Hélio Oiticica*: *Quasi-Cinemas*, p140.

[13]In Orta, *Refuge Wear*, p12.

[14]See Claude Lévi-Strauss (1968 edition), *The Savage Mind*, Chicago, IL: University of Chicago Press.

[15]Lévi-Strauss, *The Savage Mind*, p23.

[16]Claude Lévi-Strauss, *The Savage Mind*, p20.

[17]www.studio-orta.com/fluidarchitecture.

Notes

Fashion Photography

P187_P188

Very few fashion photographs fail to include images of architecture. A flick through *Vogue*, *L'Officiel*, *Nylon* or *Tank* will reveal a wide range of architectural signifiers, regardless of whether buildings are actually present in the photographs or not. Establishing a sense of place is essential to anchoring the garment to the fashion image, and the structuring of an image – by virtue of its definition, scale or lighting – has the effect of framing human existence. The staging of place as a tangible experience is the fundamental task of architecture; its first duty is to demarcate the human's habitation in the world. Yet architecture is also a product of human expression, a vehicle for voicing concepts and ideas. Framing and articulating architecture is equally essential to fashion photography, which provides a coherent context for the images' narrative.

(A)Anders Edström's photography is a far cry from the glamour photography of mainstream fashion. Edström strips away many of the superficialities imposed by traditional fashion photography, intending to evoke the hidden realities of the urban world, if not those of fashion itself.

(A)

Fashion
Photography

[A]

ARather than represent the interior as an idealistic backdrop, Edström often photographs an unkempt backdrop of smoke-tinged walls, graffiti or crumbling architecture. The presence of the decaying interior in fashion photography is typically a visual expression of resistance to dominant fashion.

Fashioning Architecture

The representations of architecture featured in fashion photography are distinct from the canon of architectural photography. Classical representations of architecture enable the viewer to transform the experience of otherness and estrangement into the positive feeling of domicile. Certain architectural styles are elevated to the level of the exemplary, their reproductions presenting the built environments as images of rationality, harmony and order. The authority of architectural photography derives from its emphasis on the public realm and its belief in architecture's potential to create an ideal city.

Modern architecture, in fashion photography, is coordinated like an outfit, and ready to be worn. The parallels between architecture and fashion styles in photographs suggest that contemporary buildings should be 'worn' like fashionable clothing, as if the general attitude towards clothing should determine current attitudes towards buildings. These representations suggest that fashion may be gaining insight into the function of architecture – or perhaps architecture is inviting the world of fashion in? Buildings are traditionally read in terms of architectural style, but the perception of 'fashionable' architecture suggests mutable façades rather than sustainable architecture. In this sense, clothing is not understood as an accessory to urban architecture, but its very condition.

Richly intertextual in content, fashion photographs juxtapose garments, models and architecture to create a sense of place. In a photograph, as in the world, a building or a built environment reveals its own significance. As a system of symbols, the architecture represented in fashion photography continues to be infused with symbolic and allusive values that construct place as abstracted, distant and romanticized. As a setting, the urban environment represents an experience that exceeds our capacity to describe, represent and record it. Consequently, it is always experientially infinite: streets, buildings and inhabitants do not end at the edges of the frame, they continue as a network of streets, buildings and urban life. All photographers depicting the built environment unknowingly step into this unfathomable territory as the gaze of the lens captures the expressive characteristics of architecture. The photograph's subtle – or obvious – representation of these characteristics inexplicably entwines them with the moment, event, scene or mood created in the image.

Architecture's allegorical function in photography follows an established photographic tradition of depicting physical space as a metaphor for states of mind; as in all literature and the visual arts, representations of inhabited realms rouse the type of fantasies described by Bachelard as 'images that give mankind proof or illusions of stability'.[1] The pioneering photography of Nan Goldin typically frames empty spaces as a metaphor for loss, while equating deserted streets with danger and destitution. Darkness and shadows evoke the miasma of drug use, or signify sexual violence, depression and death. Goldin's work, which was heavily inspired by August Sander and Diane Arbus, has been a pivotal influence over a wave of photographers who staged fashion shoots in a number of derelict, dangerous and abandoned urban sites.[2]

This aesthetic was associated with a number of fashion styles, including grunge, heroin chic, urban decay, deconstruction and reconstruction. Irrespective of the garments' style, they are often abstracted or 'blurred' in an expression of dynamism or movement; in many cases they are obscured entirely against a background of decay. More recently, representations of techno fashion often include an urban backdrop, using the characteristics of the non-place to establish their relationship with urban systems.

While the new crop of fashion photographers is influenced by art films and documentary styles, they are also united by an unmitigated desire to capture the outward

Fashion
Photography

(A)

^Roland Barthes once concluded that photography created a purely superficial context intended to deny reality. Edström's photography inverts this claim, as his work is representative of the neo-realism emerging in fashion imagery today.

expression of youth culture, a look sometimes described as 'the present'. This fashion photography is a far cry from the glamour photography of Louise Dahl-Wolfe, Helmut Newton, Irving Penn and Richard Avedon, and more recently the work of Karl Lagerfeld and David LaChapelle, all of whom use flattering lighting to show models and garments to their best advantage. With their focus on 'the present', this new generation of photographers attempts to strip away the superficialities imposed by traditional fashion photography, which has been criticized for denying reality rather than enhancing it. By comparison, models, garments and architecture are intended to evoke the hidden realities of the urban world, if not those of fashion itself. In many respects their work responds to the critique of photography pursued by Barthes, who concluded that photography was staged to deny actual reality, representing only the semiotics of a purely superficial social context.

This photography relates a number of contradictory ideas about the city, and questions the significance of the youth culture superimposed on the decaying image of the urban realm. Many youths of the 1990s forged their identities in a culture of hypervisibility, attempting to reconcile their individual body images with those of media ideals, often expressing an uncomfortable relationship to drugs, alcohol and food. The urban youth of the 1980s and 1990s grew up with the ubiquitous backdrop of surveillance systems and the invisible threat of terrorism, with the growing problem of homelessness ejecting many young people into the street. As the city was photographed collapsing in disorder, architecture was associated with its ruin – dispelling modernist notions that architecture held the power to achieve mastery over the individual and the built environment. As a result, this held certain implications for fashion. No longer represented as a device for masking the flaws of the body and the crises of the psyche, its uncertain meanings completed the dark narrative of the city's decline.

Urban Decay

Modern urbanism once held the promise of the future. Architectural plans were devised to create urban matrices premised on constant renewal and development, where networks of people and individuals could live and interact with ease. Such ideals manifested in the visual and spatial frameworks of an entire generation, who grew up to witness the gradual collapse of social housing and urban centres once considered hallmarks of modernist progress. Likened more to heterotopias than to Utopias, the urban realm of the 1990s was characterized by disintegration and decay, in turn related through narratives in film, music and contemporary art. The theme of urban decay had intersected fashion years earlier, initially in the storylines of the 1960s and 1970s fashion images taken by photographers such as Bob Richardson and Guy Bourdin. This tradition was revived in the 1990s, in the work of photographers like Anders Edström, John Akehurst, Corrine Day, Davide Sorrenti and Terry Richardson.

Many of these photographers do not work with fashion exclusively, connecting more directly with fine-art photography than other aspects of their profession. They are characterized by profoundly urban sensibilities and the ability to witness and represent daily life with an artistic consciousness. Many of their images use architecture as a means of domesticating space, or make it responsible for allowing the city to collapse in ruin. Their interpretations of the inner city make reference to certain types of urban place: the wasteland, as discussed previously with reference to Margiela's projects in chapter 1; the modernist dystopia, in which vestiges of iconic modernist architecture appear sinisterly frozen in time or desecrated completely; the fragmented interior, manifest in abandoned, uninhabited, or surreally 'normal' dwellings; and the 'bomb sites' that mark destruction so absolute they resemble the aftermath of a seismic event. Such destruction is characterized by a lack of architecture, its absence further emphasizing the loss of control and order.

'Images invite comparisons: they are constant reminders of what we are and might with effort yet become,' wrote Mike Featherstone.[3] The dissonance of seeing abandoned buildings represented photographically produces mixed messages that leave the viewer unsatisfied. Even more so, the juxtaposition of haute couture and derelict architecture sours fashion's glamorous allure. Yet it projects a desire to experience danger and excess, even if it is only found voyeuristically in the image. It represents an excess so extreme that it cannot be lived within the parameters of traditional fashion space, leading the spectator into the heterotopic spaces where it exists.

The camera of Swedish photographer Anders Edström captures many forms of urban decay, ranging from the dereliction of crumbling buildings to the metaphorical despair evoked by the decline of the city. His models appear to regard their surroundings with indifference, as the abstractions and seductions typical of fashion photography are replaced by a counter-culture of urban realism. The architecture of the urban place does not stand outside the frame of the image, but becomes part of the story. The street itself seems ever present in Edström's work; he frames models walking the pavement, crossing the street, moving between shop façades or pausing to survey the cityscape around them.

In Edström's fashion editorial for the British magazine *Dazed & Confused*, a young model waits on a street corner, pulling a 1970s-style cap close to her face as she arcs a classic trench coat around her body. She is photographed dramatically against the Gothic arches of a church behind her as she stands beside a modern shop façade dominated by two plate-glass windows reflecting the terrace of pristine Georgian houses that stand opposite. While Edström photographs an intersection of fashion looks a crossroad of architectural styles is unintentionally captured in the background, amplifying the blend of retro and cutting-edge garments worn by the model as he blends architecture from different eras with fashion from different decades.

In his photography for a Miu Miu advertising campaign, Edström captures a solitary girl walking amid familiar London streetscapes. Dressed in grey, taupe and black, the fashion colours she wears are those of the city itself: the

^A^Today fashion photography is moving away from traditional stereotypes of beauty and the norm of idealized settings. As both designers and photographers alike begin to deconstruct fashion imagery, they are widening the scope of models and the types of locations used in fashion photography.

(A)

Fashion
Photography

(A)

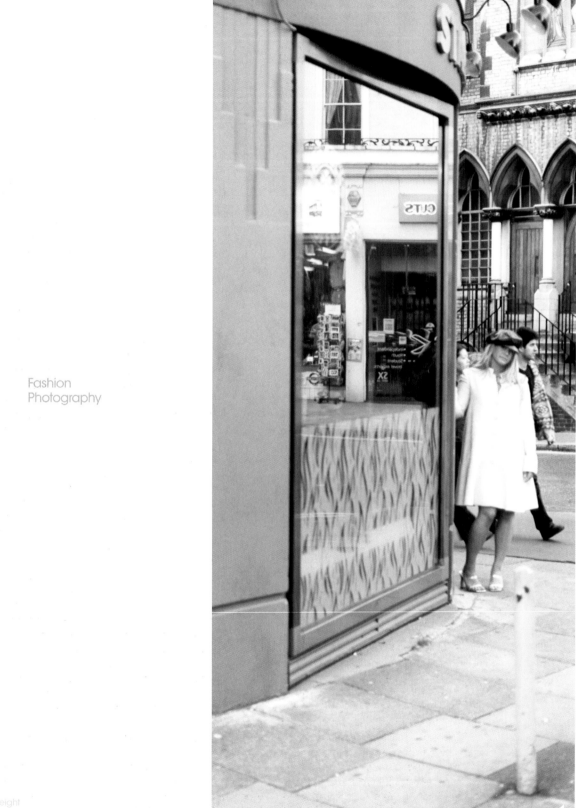

^Dressed in retro styles, a model is framed between the Gothic arches of a church and a modern shop façade whose plate-glass windows reflect the Georgian house that stands opposite. As the image captures an intersection of fashion looks and a crossroad of architectural styles, it amplifies the blend of retro and cutting edge garments worn by the model.

grey of the concrete paving stones, the black lines demarcating the spaces in between them, the browns and beige of the brickwork around her. In each image she appears withdrawn; she stares vacantly towards the camera against a blurry background of residential buildings, or stalks purposely between two railings. Rather than fading into the background, the street itself frames her movements. The visual effect lies somewhere between the street and the interior, suggesting the dualities of interior and exterior characteristic of the nineteenth-century arcades of Paris described by Baudelaire.

In one of the Miu Miu images, a façade of closed shops is evident. The shutters are drawn, closed, rendering the glass behind them invisible. Yet the model herself deliberately projects an air of detachment, her mood mirrored in the street around her. Again, the juxtaposition of modern architecture with period buildings sit... mod...

Such a sense of realism evokes a mood more emblematic of cinema than typical fashion editorial, connecting Edström's expression with a documentary tradition. 'The urban environment is not a symbol to me and my photographs are not political,' he explained. 'I just try to photograph spontaneous moments in between my artistic vision and the model's unstaged movements. I don't pose the model but try and trick her into being natural.'[4]

Photographing an autumn/winter 2000 fashion editorial feature for *Purple* magazine, Edström returns to an urban shopping district. Once again, the shutters are tightly closed – this time the model leans against them, but like the girl photographed in the Miu Miu campaign, she stares vacantly into the street beyond. Her stance and gaze recall the self-absorbed isolation of the model pictured in Helmut Newton's 1975 photograph of Yves Saint Laurent's 'Smoking', as she affected the ambiguities of the city in her emotional remoteness and androgynous silhouette. The model is alone and yet watched; she refuses to return the ca... gaze, or seek ref... her.

...rgette ...e is a setting ..., and the model's rigid stance presents a seemingly impenetrable façade to the camera.

Edström's models seem to be a part of the world they are photographed in, the street around them connected to their everyday life. Edström acknowledges this world is also inextricably linked to his own, and translates his own urban lifestyle into imagery. 'I like to use the environment around me. Because I live in London the London street is a part of the picture,' he explained. 'I don't try to make any comments with my pictures but that's unavoidable as everything is a choice rather than a non-choice.' The images draw the spectator into them, generating a familiarity that makes it difficult to gain distance and evaluate the meanings and identities such images contain. They transmit a fiction of stability in a 'reality' of insecurity, the reassurance they project fails to soothe the contradictions and anxieties of the urban environment or articulate the identity of the model.

The interlocking narratives of street life and fashion style share similar objectives but can be shockingly different. The juxtaposition of elitist brands and prosaic architecture demonstrates a clash of extremes and reveals the predominance of contradictory signifiers in visual culture. Images like this seem to suggest that the urban wasteland is the natural habitat of couture fashion, yet this tenuous connection is not ...at the photographer had envis...aged. From Edström's perspective, the dialogue between the clothes and the cityscape evolves spontaneously, unfolding in the eye of the viewer. He does not deliberately

(A)

[A+B] Representations of cutting-edge fashion often include a city backdrop, using the characteristics of the non-place to establish a relationship with style subcultures. The images project a desire to become part of the fast-paced urban scene, even if it is only found voyeuristically in the image.

anchor his subjects to any particular setting, but presents the clothes in the context of his everyday surroundings. 'I don't think the urban environment is a backdrop or a look to me either,' he said. 'It's just a part of the picture.'

Heroin Chic

> 'While fashion photography is based on the fact that something can be more beautiful in a photograph than in real life, it is not surprising that some photographers who serve fashion are drawn to the non-photogenic.'
> Susan Sontag[5]

When Alexandra Shulman became editor of British *Vogue* in 1992, the magazine began to feature the type of grunge and street-style looks typical of urban decay. At the time, this type of iconography was more typically associated with publications like *i-D*, *Dazed & Confused* and *The Face*. Published in the pages of Vogue, a magazine many women consider to be the bible of gorgeous living, Heroin Chic was interpreted by many readers as a documentary style that captured a 'behind the scenes' image of the fashion world.

British photographer Corrine Day, whose work has been acquired by museum collections around the world, was one of the first to photograph models in the world of their daily existence. Eschewing the norm of rendering models and garments as sublime offerings, Day's work presents brutal accounts of decay and desolation, disrupting the norm of 'closed' fashion images with fixed meanings. Her work portrayed harsh realities of drug use and shocking sexuality, unfolding against a characteristic backdrop of barren interiors, smoke-tinged walls, dirty bedrooms and peeling wallpaper. This look was notoriously known as 'Heroin Chic', assigning Day with a reputation for glamorizing drug addiction – an accusation she summarily dismissed.[6]

Fashion imagery has long been dismissed as narcissistic and superficial for its representations of traditional beauty and perfection. Yet, there has been intense resistance towards the trend to construct what Rebecca Arnold succinctly terms 'harsh visions of realities'.[7] 'I always wanted to get the truth in photographs, the personality of how people really are,' Day explained. 'Fashion is blind to that.'[8] The rhetorical strategies of Day's representations invite the viewer to understand the visual language of the object interior as resistance to dominant fashion. Rather than providing a passive background for the language of con-

'Edström's models appear to regard their surroundings with indifference, replacing the abstractions and seductions typical of fashion photography with a counter-culture of urban realism. Urban architecture does not stand outside the frame of the image, but becomes part of the story.

(A)

sumerism, Day scrutinized the framework of the interior for signs of dissent and gave voice to its resistance, refusing to camouflage them in the guise of glamour and consumerism.

The men and women in Day's images disrupt the narratives characteristic of fashion photography by reclaiming the body as their own. Day typically styles her photographic subjects in their home environments, fragmenting representations of the domestic interior as an idyllic backdrop. As Day's models enact a regime of explicit drug use, sex acts and visible bodily abjections, they disrupt the usual signs and signifiers associated with the photographed interior. Our voyeurism is made uncomfortable as Day's representations suppress the usual fantasy of the fetishized interior. In her study of Day's work and the Heroin Chic phenomenon generally, Arnold noted: 'We are denied our aspirational voyeurism, and given only images of human frailty; and this is profoundly jarring and unsettling.'[9]

Day's work draws heavily on representations of architecture, framing the body amidst an alternative signifying system that voices an anti-fashion critique. Like the photographs of Harlem in Bruce Davidson's book *East 100th Street*, Day's work connects with a tradition of urban photography intended to uncover hidden truths and, to a certain extent, record a vanishing moment for posterity. Day's fascination with interior architecture appears to construct emblems or constitute expressive gestures, communicating within a relay of signs between the interior and the garments. While derelict architecture and dirty, downtrodden interiors are seldom shocking in themselves, the desolation and fragmentation they project is shocking in its hyperreality. Susan Sontag, in her analysis of the photographic subject, noted: 'Poverty is no more surreal than wealth; a body clad in filthy rags is not more surreal than a principessa dressed for a ball.'[10] Yet, the image of a waif living on a scrap heap is somehow more 'real' than the juxtaposition of elegant dress and luxurious décor. Such unwelcome realities are too poignant to stage, too painful to digest.

As Day pushed the boundaries of fashion photography away from traditional stereotypes of beauty she also unravelled the

Fashion Photography

masquerade of the setting both inside and outside representation, succeeding in widening the scope of models and the types of locations used in fashion photography. Arnold summarized the vision Day has created: 'We seem to be witnessing private scenes that are themselves ambiguous, crystallising silent fears that reinforce the sense of lack that pervades consumerist culture, instead of providing comforting visions that welcome our gaze.'[11]

Fashion imagery can provide a window on another world. While the lure of advertising and the seduction of consumption generate superficial identities and aspirational lifestyles that seem within reach, for most men and women they are not. The idealized fashion visions promoted by the media seem all too real, yet clash abruptly with the alienation and fragmentation encountered in large cities. Urban Decay and Heroin Chic represent what the media are reluctant to show – that modernity, society and domesticity are spiralling into decline. As the social framework that modern architecture was intended to mediate crumbles, the seductive luxury of fashion fails to offer solace and solutions.

The photographic representations of Urban Decay and Heroin Chic conjure illusions of their own. The effect is that of hyperrealism, a phenomenon Baudrillard identified as the marker of a society in crisis, one that ultimately takes refuge in images as it struggles to recover from the loss of what it once believed to be real.[12] In the hands of photographers like Edström and Day, realism becomes a metaphor for the structure of human existence, a discourse of resistance and refusal that rejects the fantasy of glamour and prestige dominating the fashion industry. The representations of architecture in Edström and Day's respective images reflects the contradictions of urban life, marking the crisis rather than attempting to reconcile it. As architecture is identified as part of the fashion image, it presents a gesture towards a new understanding of fashion. The fragmentation it projects reveals blind spots we would rather not look at, relating the proof of a reality that only photography can provide.

^Urban signifiers and architectural elements are often abstracted into an expression of dynamism or movement that blur or obscure the garment. This reveals the potency of the urban realm in making a fashion statement.

(A)

[1]Gaston Bachelard (1994 edition), *The Poetics of Space*, Boston, MA: The Beacon Press, p17.

[2]See Nan Goldin (1996), *I'll Be Your Mirror*, New York: The Whitney Museum of American Art/Zurich: Scalo.

[3]Mike Featherstone, 'The Body in Consumer Culture', in Mike Featherstone, Mike Hepworth and Bryan S. Turner (ed) (1991), *The Body: Social Process and Cultural Theory*, London: Sage, p178.

[4]Anders Edström was interviewed by the author.

[5]Susan Sontag (1979) *On Photography*, London: Penguin.

[6]President Clinton condemned the rise of 'Heroin Chic' in a press statement in May 1997, following the fatal drug overdose of 21-year-old Davide Sorrenti, a fashion photographer also associated with the Heroin Chic genre.

[7]Rebecca Arnold (1999), 'Heroin Chic', *Fashion Theory* 3(3), p280.

[8]Leslie White, 'Wasted', *Sunday Times Magazine*, 17 September 2000, p28.

[9]Arnold, 'Heroin Chic', p289.

[10]Susan Sontag, *On Photography*, p58.

[11]Arnold, 'Heroin Chic', p280.

[12]Jean Baudrillard (1994), *Simulcra and Simulation*, Ann Arbor, MI: University of Michigan Press, p26.

Notes

Fluid Form

The laws of gravity and human proportion dictate that a building, like a garment, should be assembled according to certain rules. Fashion designers also interpret clothing according to spatial limitations, their construction skills paralleling those of an architect or an engineer. Both fashion and architecture revolve around existing form, and therefore require an understanding of mass as well as space. Dwellings and garments rely on the scale of the human form to signify their dimensions more than they do other structures, but invariably, existing buildings and preconceived standards of dress determine their result. Today, architectural visionaries and a new breed of fashion designers are thinking beyond such limitations, creating structures that are independent of pre-existing designs, defined only through their mandate to accommodate the human form. Typically these innovations do not resemble any other designs in their respective disciplines, but their resemblance to each other is often uncanny.

P205_P206

Perhaps the first example of this type of aesthetic is the congruency between the spaceship and the spacesuit. While the spacesuit did not resemble any other form of dress, its physical and technological links to NASA's spacecrafts were immediately apparent. The mechanics of space exploration made it necessary for the functions of dwelling and clothing to be unified in a single object, bringing fashion and architecture closer together. Spaceships and spacesuits relied on materials that would encapsulate the occupant in durable materials; offering protection, but more importantly containing life-support systems. Space travel would not have been possible without high-performance textiles such as Mylar, PVC, Teflon, fibreglass, Gore-Tex and nylon, which were widely used in the construction of the spacecrafts and the spacesuits alike. Space-age fashion expressed a new mythology predicated on changes in technology and lifestyle, unfolding against the visionary architectural prototypes of Archigram, Kenzo Tange, Team X and Frank Lloyd Wright.

Fashion, for many, the most tangible expression of a futuristic lifestyle, spawned new ideas about the future of cities and urban architecture. Many were conceived as metropolises built in glass, silvery metal or white concrete, mimicking the shiny and silvery vessels designed for space exploration that were coated in titanium, aluminium and other metals. Their luminous surfaces appealed to the sensibilities of artists, fashion designers, architects and industrial designers, securing a place in the visual culture of the 1960s and 1970s. American fashion designers such as Tiger Morse and Deanna Littell began designing garments made from Mylar and nylon, while, in Paris, Yves Saint Laurent, André Courrèges, Pierre Cardin and Paco Rabanne pioneered the use of space-age materials to sculpt, mould and construct their 'futuristic' visions.

Paco Rabanne used aluminium to craft chain-mail dresses and headdresses suggestive of an urban warrior. They were so intricately made that they resembled pieces of chain mail more than clothing, and so futuristic they inspired Alexander McQueen to create a contemporary version for his spring/summer 2000 collection almost three decades later. Yet their design contained an architectural signature; much of Rabanne's work relied on processes more typical of building construction than fashion design. Like Cardin, Rabanne sparked a new direction for fashion design and construction that came into its own several decades later as a new generation of designers created garments that are glued, stapled, soldered or laser-cut. The diversity of the tools and processes available contributes to the development of new aesthetics. Fashion's appropriation of architectural principles has even impacted on textile creation, often the starting point of a garment's design, introducing a range of nonwoven materials made from plastics, rubber and metal.

Aluminium had been popular among modernist pioneers, such as the architect Otto Wagner, long before it was appropriated by fashion. By the 1920s and 1930s, aluminium had become the material of modernity used in the avant-garde furniture of Marcel Breuer and Le Corbusier, and by the 1950s Mies van der Rohe was exploring the potential of steel plates in his buildings, which he eventually clad in anodized aluminium. The vogue for reflective surfaces today has culminated in the burnished buildings designed by Frank Gehry and the shining peels of Daniel Libeskind's Imperial War Museum (2002). Both architects deployed reflective surfaces to include viewers and environments in the work's meaning and ever-changing aesthetic. Reflective buildings mirror the landscape around them and intensify the light they reflect. They create mirages, illusions and deceptions, obscuring the gaze and diffusing the meanings they project to the viewer. In narratives from Ovid's *Narcissus* to Lacan's mirror stage, reflective surfaces possess a transformational power. Lacan argues that they are our first experience of illusion.

Alexander McQueen, in his spring/summer 1996 collection, included stainless steel-spattered textiles to create garments with the fluidity of silk but the reflective appearance of metal. Designing a dress with a hood that fully masks the face of the wearer, McQueen transformed the body into a reflective membrane that inverts the spectator's gaze. Mark Eisen designed metallic vests for his spring/summer 1996 collection, combining the aesthetic and material qualities of metal with cutting-edge fashion. Robert Cary-Williams's 'Mirror Dress' boxes the body into a series of rectilinear mirrors that flex between leather straps as the body moves, while Yeohlee's use of silvery fabric melts the contours of the body into a shimmering streak of movement. The paradox of mirrors is that while we consider them to be reflective, reliable surfaces, we are never actually able to see those surfaces.

Many non-reflective 'space-age' materials feature in a variety of fashions today, ranging from sportswear to cutting-edge innovations. Designers like Yeohlee and Vexed Generation produce overcoats and jackets coated with a Teflon film, creating an invisible barrier against wind, rain and dirt, while the reinforced surface of Chalayan's Remote Control Dress recalls the resilient exoskeleton of the spacesuit.

The first generation of space-age materials gave way to a range of reinforced weaves or non-woven fabrics made from glass fibres, or polyester-based membranes. Architects use them as bui[illegible]ding materials for membrane stru[illegible]res, mobile pavilions and speci[illegible]çades.

Tensile [illegible]ne structures were de[illegible] earnest from the 19[illegible]e 1980s, architects [illegible]bric structures as progr[illegible] technology with th[illegible]erform with the same [illegible]nventional buildings. [illegible]mbranes are usually meshed over a series of lightweight aluminium portal frames or stretched across fixed structures to expand their size or provide additional protection. The pavilion of Nuage Léger at La Défense in Paris is secured by cable supports, while the Hong Kong Tourist Authority's two-storey mobile pavilion uses hydraulic lifts to raise an inflatable structure containing an open atrium in the centre. Structures such as these can also be supported and sustained by pressurized air, as double layers of fabric are inflated and pressure is maintained by an air-supply system. These can create complete environments, and are typically used as

^Junya Watanabe often morphs, blurs or mutates typical fashion shapes to create silhouettes that are both striking and forward-thinking. Watanabe's radical forms can usually be traced to new developments in architecture or to the innovations found in textile technology.

(A)

Fluid Form

sports complexes and mobile housing, or exhibition pavilions like those designed by beech.media.architecture mentioned in chapter 3. Inflatable stages for outdoor music concerts, fantasy structures at amusement parks and floating pavilions recall the pressurized environment of the spacesuit and the inflated probes and satellites orbiting the earth.

As the space age presented a vision of the future, it provoked debates of how the role of architecture would take shape in the future. The drive towards sustainability, already a central principle of modernist discourse, unfolded in new materials and new design techniques, as well as aesthetics. Historically buildings were read in terms of architectural style, but modernist architects aimed to eliminate the ornamentation and detail viewed as 'fashionable' in favour of an enduring style that would be antithetical to fashion.

By the 1990s, examinations of sustainable architecture had escalated beyond debates about ornamentation and patterns of habitation to re-evaluate the architectural forms themselves and the new paradigms they characterized. Digital technology had a profound impact on the type of structures that could be created materially and theoretically. Blobs, folds, waves, spirals and twists are terms used to describe the range of tilted forms, unusual shapes or interstitial structures reflected in the new architectural paradigm of digitally created buildings. Many of the texts that refer to the growing movement of virtual architecture describe it as 'cybertecture' or 'hypersurfaces'. Rather than being characterized by specific formal characteristics, the new paradigm reflects a more general shift towards a hybrid, in-between space. The architectural plans that result are generally referred to as 'blobitecture' or 'blobmeisters', with very few of them actually manifesting as built structures.

These new questions of style and form parallel many of the aesthetical and construction issues in fashion today. Their approach is enacted in a vocabulary of shapes and forms similar to those employed by conceptual fashion designers. As fashion designers explore new expressions of physical space and materials, their garments parallel the blobs, folds, waves, spirals and twists of architecture. Applied to fashion, this architectural paradigm is a new visual language that categorizes the shapes and forms of avant-garde fashion and the work of cutting-edge designers. In the sections that follow, four new architecture

[A]Hussein Chalayan uses tulle to create unusual forms and textures.

[B]In both fashion and architecture, reflective surfaces have always represented a futuristic aesthetic.

[C]The textured fabrics designed by Thea Bjerg cocoon the torso in fractal forms.

(A)

(B)

(C)

paradigms and the architectural device known as transparency will be examined in terms of their congruency with historic and contemporary fashion, revealing a new direction for each.

Blobs

One of the most radical innovations to emerge in the built environment in recent years, 'blob' architecture is designed with the aid of computer-animation software. Blobs banish the tyranny of T-squares, true angles and rectilinear planes, creating formless, primordial shapes often described as 'biomorphic' and 'invertebrate'. The evolution of blob architecture coincided with a fashion aesthetic that eschewed conventional cuts and traditional proportions, decentring the premise that garments should contour the body's outlines or conform to a vertical axis. These fashions explore the mutability of structure and material, mutating the fashioned form into radical new shapes.

Despite the unprecedented pliancy and mutability of blob architecture, transferring the complex, curvilinear computer images of the blob from the virtual to the physical is met with considerable difficulty. While the construction emphasis is on variation, blob designs tend to look remarkably similar, and few have explained how their relationship to the built environment will unfold, other than as a collage. Although their unique forms are intended to displace simple, spherical shapes such as the cones and cylinders employed by Vitruvius and Le Corbusier, how construction processes will engage with these new principles is not yet clear. Currently, the blob functions as a metaphor for new developments in construction and engineering that will introduce another paradigm altogether.

Leading proponents of blob architecture include visionaries such as Greg Lynn, Ben van Berkel and Caroline Bos, Jesse Reiser, Lars Spuybroek, Uneko Umamoto, Hani Rashid and Lise Ann Couture, who mutate, morph, blur and fold basic shapes into flowing sequences of surging contours. They regard the crisscrossing matrix of existing cityscapes as uncomfortable and inefficient, proposing fantastic new landscapes of globular grids and pseudo-organic asymmetry. One of their aims is to produce an environ-

Fluid Form

(A)

^Chalayan eschews conventional cuts and traditional proportions, decentring the premise that garments should contour the body's outlines or conform to a vertical axis. He sculpts tulle around the body to create a dense silhouette while ensuring a free range of movement in the model's arms, legs and neck.

ment of multiple readings that overlaps existing structures with prophetic forms and new systems of living. While fashion's aims may be less ambitious, the new construction principles and aesthetic sensibilities presented by 'blob' garments are redefining the fashion landscape. Although a few of them can be interpreted in terms of deconstruction or unconstruction, the majority of them are impossible to categorize by fashion terminology alone.

Designing according to the premise of the blob initially appears to bring clothing and architecture closer to the human form, as fashion designers begin to interpret the contours of the body as evolved blobs. But often the finished designs ignore preconceived notions of the body's boundaries, expanding them through padded inserts or voluminous extensions. Blob garments suffuse geometric shapes with expressive meanings, creating structures that are planar, tiered and at times independent of the body rather than cradling it. Many of McQueen's designs amplify the body's structure by exaggerating the axis of the shoulders or the natural posture of the hips, reinterpreting the body as a series of roundels or hoop shapes. In his spring/summer 2001 collection, McQueen extended a plume of feathers from the surface of the body to a point nearly one metre in front of the wearer, distorting her natural body shape into that of a humped insect. Rather than overlapping, the feathers furled into ridges and caverns along the garment's surface, moving the silhouette even further away from classical feminine shapes. McQueen's 'White Sprayed Dress' for his *#13* collection (spring/summer 1999) was a voluminous white cotton gown secured under the arms by a wide leather belt, resembling a skirt and crinoline secured at the armpits rather than the waist. The effect was that of a woman's body without a torso, seamed together in a surreal jumble of arms, waistline and long legs that compressed the human form into a circular top shape.

McQueen's arcing silhouettes recall Issey Miyake's 'Koma' or 'Spinning Top' dress from 1975, which expanded the body's verticality into a lateral cylinder as the dress's tiers spun colourful circles around the body. As the wearer turns and rotates the twirling tiers transform the body into a perfect cone shape, 'blobbing' the body's mass downward. Miyake seems to have redistributed the balance in his autumn/winter 2000 collection, which cushioned the wearer's shoulders, arms and torso in protective padding. Reminiscent of the Michelin Man's bulging layers, the garments bulked out the midriff and the sleeves as they redistributed the body's mass around the torso.

Blob architects seek to decentre perspective and deprivilege any single viewpoint, creating a system of architecture that has no intrinsic front or back. The contours of blob architecture simultaneously curve forward or move back on themselves. Spectators can trace points of egress and points of origination, but categories of vantage points collapse one into the other. The sculpted tulle dresses Chalayan made for his *before minus now* collection (spring/summer 2000) express similar principles. Removed from the body, its points of egress are identifiable, penetrating the outlines of a dress premised on a sculptural study of mass and void. Chalayan's tulle dresses are expressions of the natural landscape, never intended to function according to the codes and signifiers of conventional fashion.

The textile artist Maria Blaisse creates highly unusual garments by manipulating technologized materials and abstractions of form. In her 'Moving Back' and 'Black Circles' garments of 1996, Blaisse sculpted membranes of vacuum-formed industrial foam around the movements of the body, creating garments that could be contracted or expanded alternately into concave or convex shapes. Blaisse related elements of simple spherical form to the body with materials that could be moulded

Fluid Form

into shapes independent of the body, allowing the wearer to move freely within them. Using a system of special clips, the garments could be shaped into a multitude of permutations by the wearer, endlessly reconfiguring it into a range of shapes and silhouettes. Moving Back and Black Circles exemplify the impact of blob architecture, as their design genius transmutes a single basic 'formless' garment into transformable shapes and function. While the spaces between the wearer and the material constitute voids, they are not integral to the garment itself. They constantly change shape and position as the garment moves with the body.

Marianne Kooimans is a Dutch fashion and costume designer based in the US, who creates garments by redistributing volume around the body. Kooimans studied landscape architecture before moving into fashion design, and structures her clothing along the verticality of the body to create ridges, pinnacles and topographic paths in fabric. Kooimans subjects her textiles to heat treatments and chemical processes in order to create dense textures that shape the garments' silhouettes and mould them into place. Her 'Bubble Skirt' from 1995 positions large hollow petal-like panels in the garment's front that balloon the wearer's shape forward. The panels move as the wearer walks, charging the skirt with dynamic movement. Kooimans has also designed streamlined eveningwear that covers the wearer from neck to ankle in vertical pleats. She counters this strict, body-hugging form with billowing sleeves that seem to encase the wearers' arms in a series of bubbles that continually change shape as the wearers rotate their shoulders and elbows.

The US-based fashion research lab International Fashion Machines (IFM) are pioneering blob garments that morph shape and size but remain snug against the body of the wearer. Based on a nylon fabric woven with fibres of the shape-memory alloy Nitinol, IFM have created the 'Shape Shifting Dress', a highly elasticized dress capable of changing shape as temperatures rise and fall, but returning to its original shape as temperatures stabilize. Nitinol, an acronym for Nickel Titanium Naval Ordinance Laboratory, is a family of intermetallic materials that contain a mixture of nickel and titanium.

Nitinol's 'shape-memory' properties permit the fabric to expand and contract, enabling the dress to shorten and lengthen when temperatures fluctuate. 'The sleeves and hemlines could be programmed to shorten as soon as the room temperature becomes a few degrees hotter,' explained Joanna Berzowska of IFM, one of the dress's developers.[1]

Because Nitinol can also be blended with other materials, it gives clothing the capacity to morph in many different directions under a variety of temperatures and conditions. Clothing takes on the properties of an ever-changing landscape, and mirrors the mutability and versatility of blob architecture. As a material Nitinol exemplifies the principles of blob architecture as it continually redistributes its mass to change shape. Because the blob is charged with matter it constitutes the opposite of the void. As architects create empty spaces for habitation within their structures, so too do the fashion designers detailed here conceive of spaces for wearable habitation amid the mass of the extraordinary shapes they create. McQueen's White Sprayed Dress retains its shape through the massing of multiple layers of tulle while Miyake's Spinning Top ensemble juxtaposes the substance of the tiers with the whirling air required to elevate them; both deploy mass to define shape rather than creating empty volume.

Thierry Mugler's 'Apron Dress' from his spring/summer 1991 collection meshed the wearer between padded bolsters in a dress that doubled the girth of a traditional gingham apron. The boundaries between the dress and the model's natural shape were unclear, and the padding seemed to balance the vertical axis with horizontal extensions. Yamamoto's 'Reversible Fitted Coat With Net Yokes' (autumn/winter 1995/6) created the opposite effect. The shapelessness of the coat enveloped the wearer's limbs and drew an amoeba-like outline around the body. Yamamoto's coat was the exact opposite of one of the iconic images of fashion's engagement with architectural principles, that of Marimekko's 'Kikapuu' dress. Kikapuu covered the body in a rectangular sack that extended from the ankles to the wrists, shaping the garment within four right angles and two sets of parallel lines. Yamamoto's coat turns its back on such precise symmetry, just as blob architects disavow the rhythmic geometry of the cityscape.

Olivier Theyskens's 'Cape Ensemble' (autumn/winter 1999) rolled wide bands of fabric around the upper body, looping them into roundels and spirals that recalled honeycomb cells. Yoshiki Hishinuma's evening ensemble from his *Pêché Originel* collection (autumn/winter 2001) also comprised bands of fabric, which were meshed within a semi-transparent fabric. Two rows of identical bands extend sideways from the breasts, capping the arms as they form sleeves. The neckline is puffed, recalling a seventeenth-century ruff, extending upwards around the head to simultaneously form a headpiece and a collar. The skirt balloons from the hips, taking on an inflated appearance, capped by seamed spines angled dramatically around the hips. The body is at once cocooned and distorted as distinctions between the head, neck and chest are blurred, and the proportions of the hips are angled rather than merely expanded.

Pia Myrvold imbued her *Hypermix* and *Cyberware* collections with graphic representations of the blob, which she featured as prints and motifs that give the blob a textual dimension. In collaboration with Karim Rashid, Myrvold printed a range of patterns and abstractions created by Rashid onto her textiles. Rashid is the brother of Hani Rashid, who, together with his partner Lise Ann Couture, pioneers the potentials and possibilities of blob architecture to antidote the Cartesian spaces architecture struggles to move away from. Myrvold's juxtaposition of Rashid's shapes gives them a sensual textuality, leading the eye to recognize the contours of the body expressed within the rounded configurations of Rashid's designs.

Ultimately Myrvold is more interested in the application of blob technology than the forms them-

Fluid Form

selves. 'What makes blob architecture appealing to me is that the new technology makes it possible to produce series of multiples with random alterations that will vary from piece to piece,' she explained. Such technology promises to redefine the meaning of 'one-off' pieces as mass-produced goods can be given uniquely individual characteristics.

Blob architecture proposes bodies of work rather than individual projects, and visionary new systems that will not be restricted to architecture alone. As design is understood to be a discipline with social, political and cultural dimensions, new movements create opportunities to rethink cultural shifts and conditions that collapse the boundaries between fashion and architecture even further.

The Fold

A fold changes everything. It brings surfaces together while simultaneously dividing them, or bends them one into the other as it organizes the space they occupy. Although it is simplistic in form, the fold has many parts. It is transacted both materially and visually, and premised on repetition and plurality. The fold is understood in terms of surfaces, yet the void manifest within its central recess is ever present. A fold constitutes a move from effective to affective space; folding is a description of activity, intended to flow smoothly and continually with no evidence of ambiguity or interruption. It is not a crease.

The concept of the fold appeals to architects and fashion designers alike. As they strive to move beyond highly figured and easily identifiable shapes, the fold represents the possibility of locating new shapes within old forms. Timeless in its scope and stylistic in its appeal, the fold is a visual gesture that is strongly coded in visual culture as a surface and an action that are found throughout the world. As an expression of form, the fold produces its own architecture by creating a site that enfolds structurally. A folded plane can provided shelter, or be adapted for the human form as clothing.

The fold gained currency in contemporary thought with the publication of Gilles Deleuze's polemic text *The Fold*. Deleuze viewed the material and metaphorical world in terms of folds of space, movement and time, interpreting aesthetics as a body of infinite folds and surfaces that twist and weave through compressed time and space. This mode of thought interpreted the 'modern' subject as a nomadic entity, perpetually engaged in the process

A+B As he strives to move beyond highly figured and conventional shapes, Watanabe uses a simple folding technique to create new construction methods.

C Yeohlee relies on a simple folding technique to structure this coat and fasten its lapels.

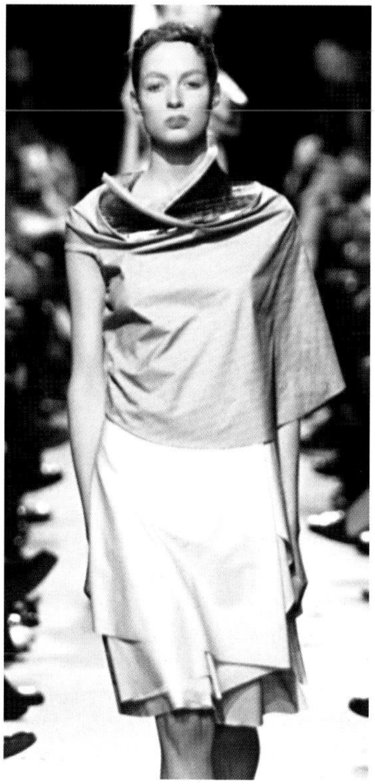

(A)

(B)

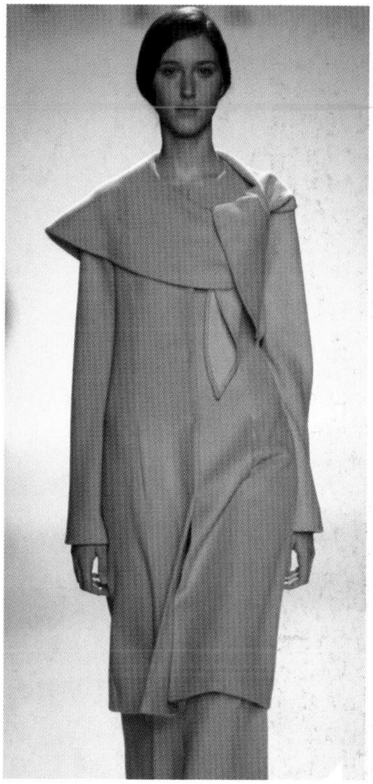

(C)

of transformation. The constant change of architectural styles and the mutability of fashion are both expanded by this model.

Deleuze traced the fold through Leibniz's writings, relating it to the concept of the infinite expressed through the philosophy of the Baroque, using Leibniz's theories as a framework for his own analysis of contemporary visual culture. Deleuze accessed the fold via one of Leibniz's metaphors of Baroque architecture, described as a montage of moving between an uninhabited lower floor bathed in bright light, and a darkened, sealed upper floor resonating as if it contained an orchestra. By charging the layers of structure with alternating quietude and vibration, Leibniz highlighted the dualities inherent within individual spaces even as they were 'folded' into a single structure. Expressing this relationship between philosophy, architecture and visual culture not only works to position one in relation to the others, it reveals that each is already present in the others.

The work of fashion designers embodies and expresses the characteristics of the Deleuzean fold. Their craft is based on the constant draping and folding of fabrics and materials around the human form, itself viewed as a mobile fold. As humans insert themselves into the folds of the garments they wear, they charge static planes with energy, as Leibniz's imaginary spaces aligned the static 'seen' with the dynamic 'unseen'. Likewise, architectural space unites diverse areas while providing the means to keep them separate. Deleuze opened the relationship between form and function by applying the fold as a model of decoding the relative meanings of surfaces, identifying expressions of structure, voids, dissection and ornamentation.

In its most literal sense, the fold is a demonstration of organization that compresses the surface area of materials into a more compact shape. In Japan, the fold is considered to be an art form, with the practice of origami likened to fine art. Origami expresses the act of folding as an underlying spatial continuum, with each individual fold representing ever more complex spatial arrangements. Watanabe explored origami techniques in his autumn/winter 2000 collection, producing a series of billowing dresses

(A)

(B)

that cocooned the wearer in otherworldly creations. Intricate origami folds were woven into the fabric to spin a honeycomb weave into a feather-light dress that appeared almost to float on the model.

In architecture, origami has been a source of inspiration for the multi-layered topography of skyscrapers and subscrapers, and a model for creating systems that are intended to be continuous but not uniform. Mies van der Rohe's high-rises expressed a mechanical continuity, the folds of his exterior detailing and structural supports presenting the illusion of stacking, infinite repetition and perpetually folding planes. A combination of stacking and accordion-like folding is found in Koolhaas's model for the Bibliothèques Jussieu in Paris (1993), containing a sloped interior boulevard that connects all floors in a single gesture. Each floor wraps a bit of its structure into the floor above and the floor below, blurring distinctions between them as the model's core spirals upwards in a seamless structure.

Libeskind's Summer Pavilion for London's Serpentine Gallery (2001) translated origami folding into architectural principles, exemplifying the strength that folding structures can have. The Pavilion was a fold of flat aluminium sheets that interlocked for support. Its metal seams were cut on a diagonal axis, and the exposed interior supports were also positioned on the diagonal. Toyo Ito designed a pavilion for the Serpentine Gallery the following year, which went a step further to fold the façade and the underlying supports into a single plane. 'There is a tendency in architecture today to hide structure,' Ito explained, 'but in the pavilion you can see everything

[4]Toyo Ito's pavilion for the Serpentine Gallery in London folded the structure's façade and the underlying supports into a series of single planes.

[5]Daniel Libeskind used a family of folded surfaces to design this pavilion. As an expression of form, the fold produces its own structure and is merely adapted architecturally.

since the intention was to integrate the surface and the structure. In a modernist sense of structure you prefabricate as much as possible at the factory, then take the materials to the site and finish the building there. My task (was) to fold structure and skin in both technology and theory.'[2]

Chalayan's 'Poppy Dress' (*Ventriloquy*, spring/summer 2001) combines many of these elements in a garment constructed with irregular, interlocking planes in the torso, and series of overlapping folds in its skirt. Chalayan's choice of fabric featured a grid pattern that wound its way around the skirt and up into the torso and shoulder areas. A panel of printed fabric in the dress's front depicted a poppy field, placing life-size poppies near the garment's hem that became smaller in size as the pattern travelled inwards to the waist. The print gave the illusion of depth as the printed image appeared to vanish into the torso.

The definition of an edge is one that is pondered by architects, philosophers and fashion designers alike. Deleuze described the edge as the severing of the inside and the outside of built form, while Loos, who demanded the full disassociation of inner and outer, made this distinction clear in his work.[3] Both architecture and fashion emphasize their outermost layer, and the polemics of their representations continually question if these should be considered as envelopes designed only to conceal, or as membranes that reflect and express their interiority. Although previous chapters have also examined this argument, the debate gains new currency with the concept of the fold. As the inner and the outer are regarded as the folded sides of a single surface, they counter the notion that a garment's border constitutes a rim. Invariably, garments contain seams; although they may be finely joined, their edges remain discernible as they unite two separate planes. Concrete architecture, with its seamless surface, can easily mask such edges and joins. Zaha Hadid tends to suppress doorframes and window ledges and make any superficial trim flush with the surface to create an unbroken, edgeless surface.

A pleat is a fold, but it is also an edge of another kind. In garments pleats are aligned in a fold, then folded into a seam and stitched in place. As they overlap tiny voids are created; as they extend outward and unfurl a wider surface area is made visible. As fabric pleats are held in place along the seam, the rest of their length is animated by the wearer; they exemplify Leibniz's model of the seen and the unseen, the dynamic and the static.

Pleats have decorated architecture for several millennia. The fluting of Ionic columns was traced to the drapery of ancient Grecian statuary by James Laver, who identified parallels between the pleated folds of long tunics and the vertical ridges sculpted into temple columns.[4] Both are intended to increase the apparent height of the surface, with the pleated texture of columns breaking up their dense appearance to convey a sense of lightness. While no evidence exists to verify their interrelatedness, it is significant that the style characteristics are present in both the architecture and dress of the period.

Fashion pleats can be traced back to the ancient Egyptians, and their popularity in fashion has continued unabated. Since his *Mutant Pleats* collection (autumn/winter 1989), Issey Miyake's textile pleating techniques have become his signature. Miyake uses pleats to create a textured cadence across the garment's surface as rhythmic as the stretch of columns across a classical portico. The pleats' faceted surfaces erupt in peaks and folds, or as fragmented panels that abstract and flatten the contours of the body. Miyake's pleats were initially woven into the fabric, but later processed by machines to enable them to support themselves in directions perpendicular to the folds.

Architectural pleats layer and expand the surface of a building as layers of veiling generate a sense of compression or continuity. The split-

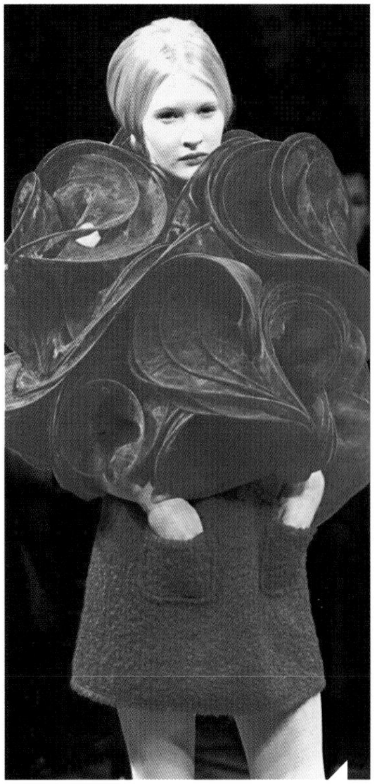

(A)

(B)

level stacking of floors in multi-storey buildings can constitute an extended pleat as the architect folds each floor into the other. Diller + Scofidio's competition entry for the Eyebeam Atelier/Museum of Art and Technology winds a vertical ribbon of flooring through the structure's shell. As the ribbon travels upward it levels into horizontal planes before winding back on itself, creating many different floors of various heights and levels as it moves upwards. Each of the ribbon's pleats enfolds an entire storey, creating walls and ceilings as well as individual floors. As the pleating divides the space it reveals the essential connections and interconnections between the frame and the material itself.

All folds will unfold eventually, even pleated ones. The material imprints and traces that remain designate patterns, figures and shapes, while metaphorically unfolding the nature of inner and outer, limited and unlimited. While the surface holds the potential to contain infinite folds, the notion of unfolding is infinite too. Each unfolding opens up further folds, which in being unfolded reveal further folds, without discovering the locus of a true beginning or a true ending. The concept of a folding space reveals the potential for textual modules to be continuously folded onto and into each other – continuously leading to fresh insights into surfaces and spaces shared by architecture and fashion.

Twisting

Twisted, rotated and twirled surfaces are present in both architecture and dress. Architecture has long had a signature vocabulary of coiled, intertwined shapes, while the cutting techniques that wind and spiral swathes of fabric into flowing fashions are a more recent phenome-

[A+B] Watanabe twists and coils fabric around the upper body to create forms that are both sculptural and architectural.

[C+D] Inspired by the twisted buildings of Karel Vollers, Shelley Fox began rotating panels of fabric around the body to develop a range of visionary shapes and silhouettes.

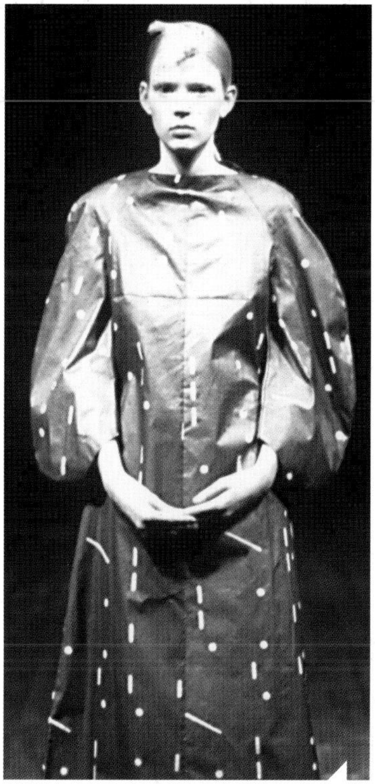

(C)

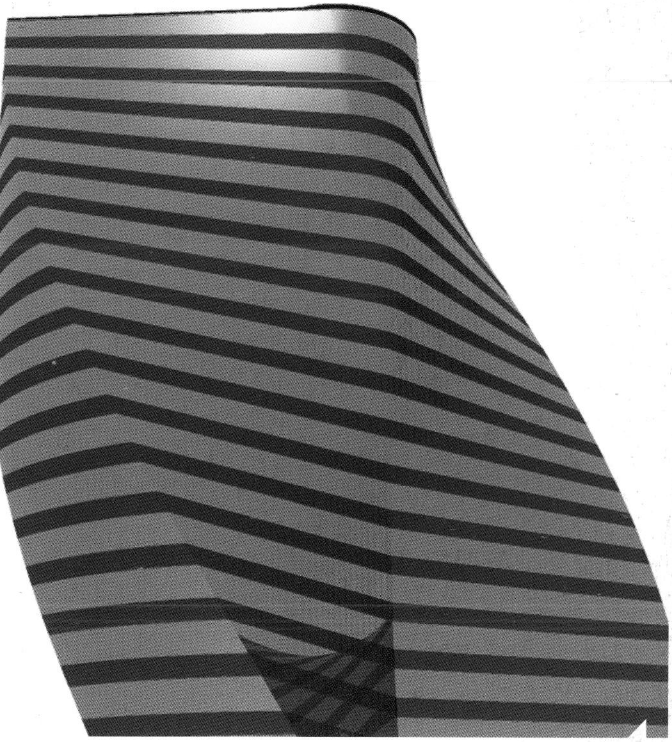

(D)

non. Madeleine Vionnet, the celebrated Parisienne couturier of the 1920s and 1930s, invented the influential bias cut by shearing her fabric along the diagonal of its weave. Vionnet's cutting techniques resulted from her project to create free-flowing fashions that would free clothing from the limitations of the fabric's vertical and horizontal axes, enabling it to spiral around the body.

Charles James followed Vionnet's example, but shaped garments by twisting and spiralling their seams rather than rotating the fabric panels. James's curving darts and spiralling seams created sculptural garments regarded as 'human architecture' due to the robust construction principles that reinforced their shapes. James's tubular down jacket of 1938 was conceived as a wearable shield, a contoured exoskeleton that, like a shell, seemed to maintain its shape without the presence of the human body. Padded coils spiralled elegantly from the jacket's lapel to its back, also curving from the shoulder and following the line of the arm.

Oscar Niemeyer, and the other architects who designed Brasilia, conceived of a sculptural modernist style that rotated both the façades and the structures underpinning them into twisted formations. Turns and twists characterize the signature sloping designs created by Antoni Gaudí, while more recently, Santiago Calatrava, Frank Gehry and Shin Takamatsu have also built twisted structures. Gehry's Guggenheim Museum in Bilbao (1997) brought twisted surfaces to world-wide attention, paralleling a fashion aesthetic pioneered by Miyake, Kawakubo and Yamamoto. Vestiges of their meandering sensibilities are easily identifiable in much of Japan's contemporary architecture; Kisho Kurokawa's Fukui City Museum of Art (1993–6), features winding contours that trace building's outline. The museum culminates in a top-heavy tower that resembles an inverted cone. Both the tower and the building's outline seem to have inspired the twisted glass façade of Comme des Garçons' Tokyo boutique, and perhaps several of the collections themselves.

Watanabe's unconstruction garments wrap lengths of fabric around the wearer, held in place by coils of wire spiralled around the body or looped into wide arcs

^As Karel Vollers moves beyond orthogonal architecture to pioneer new structures for buildings, his work inspires fashion designers to rethink traditional construction techniques. Vollers is developing a system that rotates a building's structure as well as its volume, even twisting the window frames and glass panels to achieve dynamic tension throughout the entire construction. Likewise, fashion designers and textile engineers are twisting fabric to breaking point as they strive to take the bias cut in a new direction.

Fluid Form

(A)

and flat discs. In one garment, Watanabe fans vertical pleating around the neck and torso, sculpting it to the body by using the coils to 'close' the pleats as they encase the wearer's neck. Other clothes rely on the coils to control the shaping of the garment's proportions, following and reinforcing the twists of the fabric. Some coils suspend the fabric panels horizontally rather than buttressing them against the body, loosely draping the fabric in wide folds. Watanabe's coils mimic the metal blades of Schlemmer's 'Screw' costume for his Triadic Ballet, which imitated a ribbed metal blade rotating around the body from the waist to the knee.

The British fashion designer Shelley Fox discovered the twisted buildings designed by Karel Vollers, one of The Netherlands's leading architects. Vollers has developed a new method for creating twisted and bent façades that simplifies the techniques already in use by architects like Frank Gehry. Fox was fascinated by Voller's ability to create surfaces constructed of straight lines and varying rotations; her own work pioneers such innovations as she creates unique garments that are virtually impossible to copy.

Fox's garments have always presented a challenge to conventional fashion thinking, as she applies mathematical principles to her designs in order to balance their construction against the geometry of the body. 'It's a bit like being an architect,' Fox said. 'I look at the minimum requirements. In the case of an architect it's to construct a building. With a garment, it has to go over the head or round the head; the arms have to come through and be able to move, same with the legs. In a way those are my only constraints. There's going to be other limitations later on, so I try and get rid of them in the beginning. Like a house needs a door, you need to get in and out, and after that it is how it's achieved that is open to interpretation.'[5]

Vollers has designed a basic vocabulary of shapes and techniques that can be employed by architects, industrial designers and fashion designers to twist and expand simple forms. Vollers experimented with various tordated building models, eventually developing two main designs: the 'Tordo' and the 'Twister'. The Tordo features only a single bent façade, with its other sides remaining rectangular. The Twister resembles a fully twisted helix, with all façades rotated in the same direction. Some of Fox's felt panels parallel the tordated surfaces manifest in Voller's architecture, while her seams can consist of straight lines with different rotations, or twist back on themselves to pull panels of fabrics into unconventional configurations.

Geometry is echoed in the angled shapes and circular silhouettes of Fox's tops, skirts and dresses; the fabrics are rounded from the collar into the shoulders, arcing around the elbows to meet the forearms or the wrists. The look is raglan in shape, but the sleeves create wing-like half circles hovering over the arms and shoulders or draped behind them. Some of Fox's creations hang loosely on the body, the asymmetry of their cuts weighting one side in order to twist the garments around the body. Fox's 'Circle' skirt is actually a circle of fabric with a discreet slit cut directly into it; the waist is an opening in the centre of the material that twists around the wearer's hips. 'We kept working with that idea until we did a version of the skirt with two or three waists in them,' Fox explained. 'It can be worn like a regular skirt by stepping into the waist in the very centre, because the fabric will hang symmetrically. Wearing one of the waists closer to the edge makes it hang asymmetrically for something more unusual,' she explained.

The Dutch-born American designer Ronaldus Shamask created deceptively simple spiralling silhouettes characterized by the refined elegance they convey. His 'Red Spiral Coat' was constructed from two panels of fabric fused together by seams that spiral across its back. The neckline and the sleeves are joined in another twist of the spiral, absorbing the body of the coat, the collar and the sleeves in a unified whole. Like the sweep of the Guggenheim spiral that folds and connects the building's layers and tiers, Shamask's Red Spiral Coat twists its seams through the different sections of the coat to link them.

Shamask's 'Cello' blouse is considered to be a design classic. Shamask adapted the hollow vessel of the musical instrument for wear on the body, constructed from spiralling seams that pay homage to the cello's contoured shape. Shamask plotted its panels and seams architecturally in order to construct a contoured shape that would stand independently of the body. Shamask uses graph paper to plot his dress patterns and the pleating system of a dress to fabric, effectively plotting a life-sized elevation. Shamask also built three-dimensional models to perfect the form of his Red Spiral Coat. Commenting on his collects to Susan Sidlauskas in 1982, Shamask described the principles underlying his work: 'It is architecture, as it attempts to create habitable structures,' he said. 'I relate to my work as both an art and a science; my imagination and aesthetic are constantly guided, and occasionally tempered, by systematized investigations into the properties, possibilities and limitations of the materials I work with. I employ what I consider to be a "reasoned" conception of beauty, concentrating on cut and proportion and eliminating any solution not justified by the logic of my conception.'[6]

Blurring

For architects, the last few decades have been characterized by an absence of clarity. Architecture is no longer a question of sheltering, nor is the articulation of form its overriding goal. Contemporary architecture brings together the complex worlds of fashion, interior design and spatial planning, becoming an extension of urban architecture and a hybrid of all four. Ultimately, the structures that result undermine conventional definitions of architecture, questioning where the boundaries between architecture and non-architecture are drawn.

Fashion too, as we have seen throughout this book, reconfigures itself as it absorbs other forms and forges new relationships with the built environment. As items of clothing articulate their potential function as shelter, they blur the boundaries between fashion and architecture; as they transform into backpacks and sleeping bags they express their nomadic functionality; inflating into furniture and mattresses, their connection with interior design is revealed. While fashion's mutability

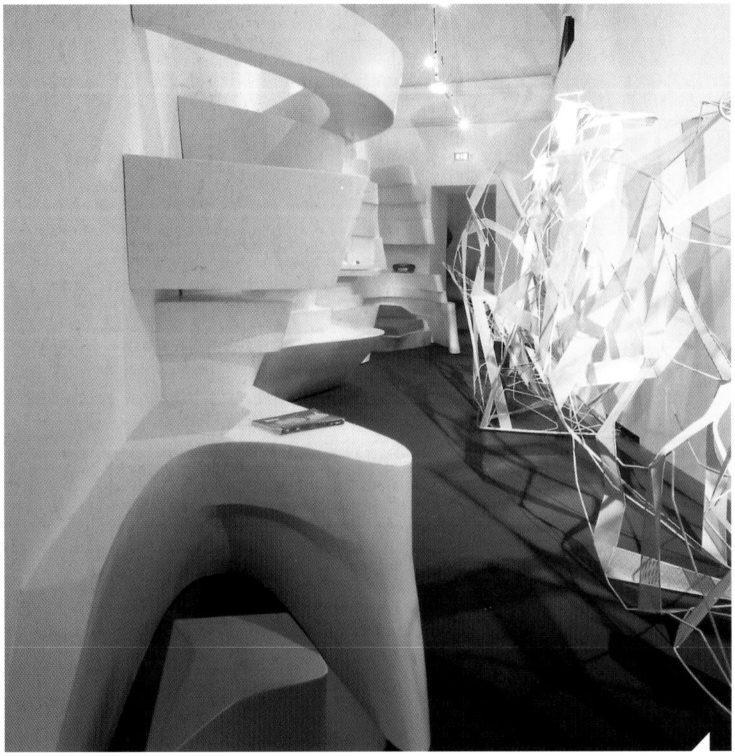

(A)

Fluid Form

enables it to truly integrate with these other disciplines, it redefines the respective boundaries between each. The resulting objects contain a heightened level of functionality, yet the meaning of their hybrid forms is not clear cut, it is blurred.

Blurring manifests in urban places as well as in objects. Architectural structures can be built according to the pre-existing orientations of an environment, incorporating its history, typography, climate, materials and construction, and yet remain conspicuous. Blurring brings together diverse elements and creates new ways of combining them. In deconstructing and reconstructing vintage fashions and contemporary styles, their respective aesthetics and representations blur into a fragmented whole. Blurring is also an articulation and reshaping of existing systems; as designs become more unstructured they become more fluid.

As architecture is approached from different perspectives and critically considered by other genres, its formal vocabulary collapses into other forms. Although modernist architecture is deliberately abstract it is not necessarily blurred. The work of such visionaries as Alison and Peter Smithson, Team X and Archigram explores ways to transform architecture into a social tool, and yet blur these ideological principles with the haptic and sensory experiences of everyday living. Buildings such as Gaudí's Casa Battló (1904–6) are intended to evoke sculptural forms, blurring art and architecture. Likewise, Gehry's collage of binoculars and copper trees makes the Chiat/Day/Mojo Building (1989–91) a blur of postmodern architecture and pop art. The sweeping, sculptural surfaces of Eero Saarinen's TWA

[A] Zaha Hadid's *Latent Utopias* installation, she designed an environment of 'suggestibles' that lent themselves to a multitude of readings. Some surfaces suggested a desk, table or work surface, while lower levels evoked a bed or couch.

[B+C] Simon Thorogood's fashion 'Suggestibles' are sculptures that evoke the shapes of garments or vestiges of fashion as they question the conventions of clothing design.

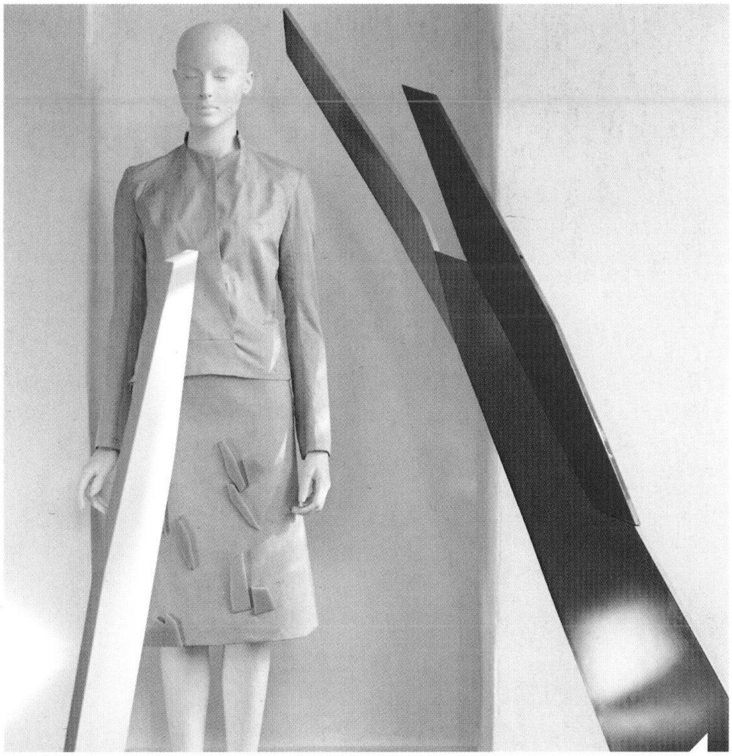

(B)

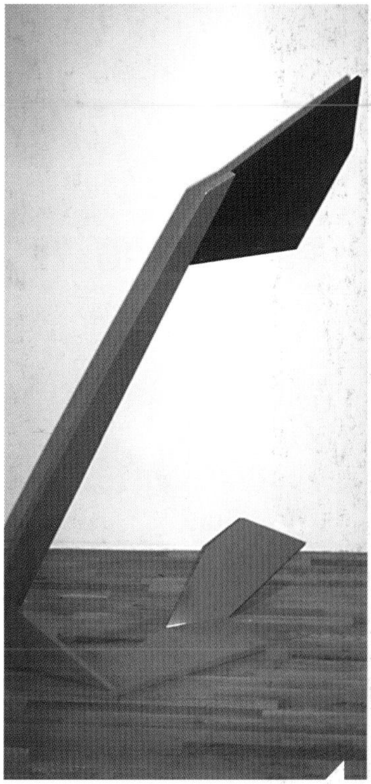

(C)

Building in New York (1962) were conceived as a metaphor of flight, charging the structure with symbolic values that would broadcast the airline's sensibilities. As a result, the building blurs artistic vision with architecture and promotional ambitions, without collapsing the boundaries between them.

For Diller + Scofidio, the architects behind the Blur Pavilion, the landscape is not a fixed condition. Their vision of blurring an entire building into the landscape manifests as a temporary attraction for the 2002 Swiss Expo, as a media centre at the base of Lake Neuchâtel in Yverdon-les-Bains, Switzerland. Set beside a lake, the building is intended to look like a cloud suspended above a watercourse, rather than be immediately identifiable as a man-made structure. This is achieved by forcing lake water through thousands of high-pressure spray nozzles attached to a framework of steel cables and rods. The resulting mist envelopes the framework in what appears to be a sphere of vapour, hiding any trace of the building within it. Set several hundred metres from the shore, the pavilion is accessed via a long ramp. Visitors are provided with special raincoats to keep them dry as they walk through the spray.

The clarity of Zaha Hadid's buildings is often startling; but while they are distinct from the landscape and free of historical references, their interior spaces are often conceived as spatial fields rather than areas intended to facilitate one specific activity. 'When you think of house you realize it is a given concept,' explained Patrik Schumacher. 'We want to create condensed fields in the landscape whose meanings can be interpreted in a range of different ways.' The evidence of blurring in Hadid's work is subtle, often transacted by suggestion rather than in explicit terms. Hadid's installation for the *Latent Utopias* exhibition at the Landesmuseum Joanneum in Graz, Austria in 2002, presents a giant wall relief with dramatic recesses, gentle contours and inverted folds. The semi-abstract, moulded surfaces of the relief are designed to evoke an apartment that has been 'unfolded' and flattened into a single plane. The folds, niches, recesses and protrusions follow a formal logic that triggers a series of semi-functional shapes that

Fluid Form

hint towards potential use as a bed, sofa, desk, kitchen work surface, etc. As the spectator discerns their functional uses, the shapes move from blur to clarity and back again.

Inspired by the concept of forms that can represent multipurpose objects or remain vague to be completed in the mind of the observer, Simon Thorogood produced a body of work for the British Council's *Personal Space* exhibition shown in a London gallery. Thorogood's fascia theme related to an earlier project at the Judith Clark Costume Gallery, where Thorogood presented nine constructions and two garments from his spring/summer 2001 collection to explore the idea of clothing as a wearable home.

As Thorogood considered the different elements of the body and individual space, the words fashion, architecture, signs, colour, interior and apparel came to mind, which he merged into an acronym; 'fascia'. He discovered that it also existed as a real term, meaning bands of fibrous tissue between groups of muscles, or a distinctive band of colour on an insect or plant. Thorogood replicated some of the panel components from the design of the Stealth aircraft and fitted them together in freestanding sculptures. 'I thought of these pieces as "suggestibles" of clothing; visitors to the exhibition could wander around them and complete them as garments in their imaginations,' he said.[8] The pieces could also be tilted onto their sides to be used like armchairs, or stacked together to form soft walls, sculptural installations and interior 'sky-lines'.

The future axis of fashion and architecture does not seem set to take the shape of physical buildings and tangible garments alone, but also suggestibles of them. As these blurred forms unfold they clarify the interrelatedness of the built environment and its textile counterparts.

Blurring forms often makes them appear mysterious, rearticulating familiar shapes in strange and unusual guises. While the end result is intended to be sculptural or poetic, the forms they take can appear incongruous, perhaps deliberately unrecognizable. This practice parallels the method of 'making strange', a tactic that designers employ to introduce a new function found in an existing form or reinterpret the meaning of its characteristics. 'Both contemporary fashion and architecture rely on the concept of "making strange",' Schumacher explained. 'They defamiliarise the object so that it can assume a different function.'

[A]Chalayan often redefines typical proportions to morph one garment into another form. This top blurs the definitions between a normal shirt and a straightjacket.

[B]Pia Myrvold creates transparent sheaths around the body to enable its contours to remain visible. Likewise, architects use transparency to highlight a building's structure and create a viewpoint into its core.

(A)

(B)

In Zaha Hadid's architectural designs, Schumacher creates otherworldly structures that defy conventional categorization; taken out of context, the shapes of their houses, museums and office buildings could be mistaken for abstract sculpture or concrete landforms. The Terminus and Car Park they designed in Strasbourg, France (2001), appears to be a smooth field punctuated by series of contrasting rectangular strips, or a poetic gesture of land art created in the midst of a provincial European terrain. To reduce it to the signifiers of an ordinary car park must be strangely disconcerting for both the spectator and the driver alike.

'The work of Dirk Bikkembergs compares to our project for Vitra,' Schumacher explained, referring to the former fire station transformed into a chair museum for one of Europe's leading furniture manufacturers in 1993. 'Bikkembergs twists and reorientates his jackets, reversing the standard proportions of tailoring. One jacket has a new type of buttons that are scaled down to the smallest possible size, so they have to be reversed to be fastened.' The Vitra project scaled down the pre-existing building and constructed a new building to inject the site with vitality and innovation. Like Bikkembergs's take on the standard menswear blazer, the Vitra project makes an exciting form more accessible by creating secondary structures and reconsidering points of egress.

Fashion designers such as Rei Kawakubo, Martin Margiela, Hussein Chalayan, Jean Paul Gaultier, Thierry Mugler and John Galliano are renowned for the radical collections they design, morphing familiar garments into strange permutations. Mugler turns his models into insects, birds and even machinery; his 'Harley Davidson' bustier was designed complete with headlights, wing mirrors and handlebars with which the model could steer herself. Margiela's collection of enlarged clothing transformed everyday garments into objects of uncanny fascination: a 1960s cocktail dress and a pair of destroyed jeans were enlarged by 200%, becoming big enough to accommodate two wearers; a pair of sunglasses was enlarged by 148%, making them almost unwearable. Margiela enlarged his 'Grey Wool

Fluid Form

Pea Coat' by 150%, his 'Sleeveless Jacket' by 148% and his 'Prince of Wales Check Jacket' by 157%, giving their pipings, buttons and motifs surreally large proportions.

While the forms of conventional garments and traditional buildings are familiar, the process of their formation often remains mysterious to the people who occupy them. In fashion, some designers take steps to communicate the garment's construction history – which fashion normally takes steps to erase – in terms of its 'lived' experience. The intention is to make the wearer aware of the methodology behind a garment's production, dispelling the mystique associated with tailoring. As deconstruction architecture reveals its construction process, it juxtaposes form and formation in a single gesture. By showing the structure that underpins the building's formation, it is the form that remains mysterious as it initially presented an unconventional aesthetic.

In terms of her own fashion sensibilities, Zaha Hadid's approach to architecture and her dress ethos are one and the same. Hadid is a devotee of Japanese fashion designers. She often wears Issey Miyake jackets upside down, so that the neckline cinches her waist and the jacket's bottom hem frames the neck and shoulders in a vast swathe of material that suggests flowing lapels or a raglan shape. By making a jacket 'strange' it becomes an abstraction that can function as a cape or a mantle, a formal top or a comfortable, casual blazer.

Miyake is committed to pioneering shapeless designs that can be transformed by the wearer or made strange through a variety of devices. His 'Wind Coats', for example, are described as being a 'free' style due to the design characteristics that enable them to expand and contract into a variety of configurations. The coats can be wrapped around the body like a duvet, billow with the blowing wind and fall back into shape. To a large extent the Wind Coats designate the wearers as their creators as they determine the shape of the coats. For Miyake, these are the characteristics that bring modernism to clothing and, for him, that characterizes freedom.

Blurring proposes new ways of thinking about architecture, presenting new ideas about what architecture can represent. Blurring creates an awareness that architectural design involves more than just materials and static forms, that it does not necessarily have to have specific boundaries. But as it blurs boundaries between figures it simultaneously clarifies them, highlighting a dynamic and movement-based approach to form shared by fashion and architecture alike.

Masking and Revealing

Transparency, one of the dominant metaphors of twentieth-century architecture, is almost the antithesis of fashion design. While architects primarily visualized modernity in terms of glass and steel, transparency and sheen, and materials inherently devoid of pattern, texture and ornamentation, fashion designers rely upon such devices to mask the flaws of the body. The traditional woman of fashion has always been 'added to', padded and enhanced through layers of fabric and camouflaged by motifs. The body consciousness of the 1980s briefly stripped away the bulky opacity of fashion in favour of streamlined silhouettes, then quickly introduced shoulder pads and Wonderbras before flirting with corsetry and bustiers in the 1990s.

Modernist architects regarded transparency as both a metaphor and a material. It represented political openness, democracy and the new state; visionary ideals, futuristic materials and conduits for exchange as it conveyed the literal means of seeing through walls. Transparency has always been a driving force in the development of work of many renowned architects. From Mies van der Rohe's visionary glass skyscrapers to Norman Foster's Reichstag renovation (1999), from Brinkman and Van der Vlugt's Van Nelle factory to Dominick Perrault's Bibliothéque Nationale de France (1995), transparency has figured as a key element of both architectural designs and ground-breaking construction projects. This relationship between transparency and vision is one that is often overlooked in cultural discourses, but rarely criticized for its shortcomings. The fact that modernism is virtually synonymous with glass inadvertently linked the material to visual transparency, while the presence and emergence of other types of sensual transparencies tend to be hidden from view.

The ideological goal of transparency expressed in the architecture of public spaces would seem to be the total transparency of information, a strategy deployed by the power elite to create a sense of order and rational structure. In *The Production of Space*, Henri Lefebvre argued that such spaces actually sustain the illusion of transparency rather than negate it, deploying luminous, tangible and 'real' characteristics to counter it. 'Transparency is deceptive, and everything is concealed,' wrote Lefebvre, pointing out that, 'space is illusory and the secret of the illusion lies in the transparency itself'.[9] The public access granted to these spaces designates them as realms of 'known' experience, their 'real' characteristics intended to disrupt the gaze and prevent it from looking beyond the periphery, or even focus on the margins. At the same time, the issue of transparency renders a high degree of uncertainty; the evidence that public space could contain hidden agendas at all would reveal the mythology behind them, disrupting the belief that these spaces are the locus of 'known' experience.

The phenomenon of transparency in architecture was explored by Colin Rowe and Robert Slutsky in 1954, who borrowed from cubist ideas to define two approaches to transparency in architectural practice: the literal and the phenomenal.[10] Rowe and Slutsky focused on the practical and theoretical representations of visual transparency that evolved through modernism, concluding that the symbolic meanings ascribed to both were virtually indistinguishable. Cubism had also been a source of inspiration to couturiers such as Paul Poiret. Vionnet, who expressed themes of transparency in her body-conscious designs, subtly revealed the wearer's anatomy without exposing the body. While her form-fitting creations were not intended to articulate social mandates, her work paralleled the modernist approach to materials and methodology evident in the architecture, philosophy, film and art of the period.

Schiaparelli made her fashion debut in 1927 with her

trompe-l'oeil knitwear, which featured sailor's tattoos, and also the skeleton jersey, which gave the women wearing it the appearance of being seen through an X-ray screen. Famous for her surrealist fantasies, Schiaparelli also designed 'glass clothes' made in a brittle transparent plastic along with Cinderella-like transparent slippers. Schiaparelli's use of transparency was intended to underscore the garment's structure, but also created the illusion of nudity that was every bit as risqué as the glass edifices designed by modernist architects.

Transparency gained momentum in fashion during the 1960s as plastic dresses and see-through garments became popular, and daring shapes were designed that heightened body consciousness. Pierre Cardin designed boldly coloured jersey tunics, into which he carved geometric shapes. These corresponded to fitted tops or cat suits worn underneath that contrasted the body's surface with the outer shell, layering a façade over the body-hugging designs underneath. In the New York boutique Paraphernalia, Betsey Johnson collaborated with Warhol to create plastic clothing and garments with reflective surfaces. Deana Littell used transparent materials to make a range of clothing, including incandescent evening coats. Tiger Morse, also based in New York, was credited with initiating the transition from transparency to psychedelia, which ended the craze for transparent clothing as fashion moved in a new direction altogether.

Transparency resurfaced in fashion at the turn of the new millennium. McQueen presented classically cut shirts and trousers in his spring/summer 1996 collection, transformed through the transparent materials they were made in. McQueen took the theme of transparency a step further in his 'Red-glass Slide anc [illegible] rich Feather Dress' (spri [illegible] er 2001), which was cor [illegible] two thousand m [illegible] ed from hip-bone [illegible] rom a surgical supplie [illegible] slide is hand-drilled and individually painted red. 'The significance of the glass is that it is about putting the body under a microscope,' McQueen told Susannah Frankel. They are red because, 'there's blood beneath every layer of skin'.[11]

Japanese designer Kei Kagami is a graduate of architecture who worked with Kenzo Tange in Tokyo before pursuing a career in fashion. He gave transparency full reign on the catwalk, manifesting as

(A)

[A]The links between the skyscrapers of modernist architecture and the slim, streamlined silhouettes of modern fashion are made apparent by Myrvold as she transforms architectural images into avant-garde motifs.

elaborate dresses constructed from strands of translucent thread, sophisticated skirts and tops cut in beautiful diaphanous fabrics, and futuristic garments made from transparent zips. Kagami also presented a glass skirt and a glass bustier in his spring/summer 2002 collection during London Fashion Week. The glass exposes the inner layers of the garment, presenting a modern view of the body; it was exposed, but protected. The glass skirt revealed the fabric's inner surface, displaying how a fitted skirt presses into the folds of the skin, creating tension against the body as it moves with the wearer. Kagami used transparency as an effective means of probing the space between body and material, bringing the intimacies of clothing into public view.

The collection recalled the architecture of modern Japan, especially the Crystal Light (1987) building designed by Masaharu Takasaki, and the lucent structures of Tadao Ando and Toyo Ito. Throughout their careers, they have created buildings characterized by flowing spaces, the satiny sheen of translucent materials, the cloudy transparency and crystalline reflectivity of glass, and the dematerializing qualities of light. Glass skins, structural tubes and floor plates are conceived as vertical or longitudinal lines set at irregular heights throughout their structures; thinner skeletal tubes are expressed as transparent lattices snaking through the building, while vertical glass skins appear to be suspended perpendicularly from the floor plates. Visionary buildings like these are free of the mass and opacity normally expected of architecture.

Like these architects, Kagami seeks to invert the density of structure and form through the transmission of light. Surrounding the human form in light signals a return to its 'natural' state, which Kagami regards as being 'a place of transparent beauty'. Takasaki, Ando and Tange also work according to this premise, taking transparency as a basis from which to create buildings in tune with the forces of nature and the topology of the landscape. Ito described the role of the modern architecture as a 'task to integrate structure and skin both through technology and theory...in the process of this type of design you are not sure what the finished product will be'.[12] Certain zones of their buildings may be hidden to facilitate privacy or conceal structural and mechanical devices, but they are seldom regarded as inherently opaque. These architects often express such exchanges between clarity and opacity in terms of veiling and transparency. In the hands of fashion designers transparency becomes a device for enhancing the body's natural form, while certain zones are veiled with opaque materials to hide them from view.

Aware that the surface reveals more than just the properties of volume and form, architecture traditionally masks its own shortcomings through exterior details and ornamentation. Façades, textures, cladding and even colour are visual and tactile lures to detract the spectator from the mechanics of construction. Surface materials are chosen for their capacity to disguise the structure; their ability to disperse light and mould naturally into the building's own shape are all modes of concealment rather than ornamentation alone.

A fabric surface constructs a second elastic skin to human scale that masks and conceals the body's frame. Body-conscious dress is the equivalent of architecture intended to blur the boundaries between structure and landscape. As dress sits close to the body's contours it emphasizes its shape; corsetry, bustiers and padding are devices that shape and sculpt the body into idealized forms rather than enhancing its natural shape. Some fashions use dress to disguise the body's contours altogether, masking the body in architectural proportions that encase the entire body within a superstructure. Issey Miyake has created garments resembling vestiges of samurai armour, while others recall fencing garb. Miyake designed a solid bustier in cast plastic (autumn/winter 1980) that manipulated the female torso into a classical ideal, while his 'Rattan Armour' (spring/summer 1982) encased the wearer in rounded wicker frame that seemed to move independently of the body.

Medieval ecclesiastical dress, nun's habits, monk's robes and clerical uniforms were designed and ornamented to mirror the churches and cathedrals that they were worn in, connecting their shape and fabric to the architecture they were intended to sanctify. Symbolically, they mask the body within architectural proportions that designate its relationship to the institution it serves. Tudor arches, Gothic transepts and Elizabethan roundels characterize British cathedrals, and their shapes continue to be reproduced in the silhouettes of their clerical vestments. The ceremonial dress of the high church functions like a kind of cladding that transforms the body into an architectural symbol. Worn over clerical robes during religious observances, ecclesiastical vestments articulate the wearer's relationship to the cathedral rather than the institution.

Modernist architecture stripped off the old cladding of preceding centuries to reveal the structural body previously masked by other architectural styles.

But many architects considered transparency to be an overrated quality, advocating the impact of density and solidity as both an aesthetic and an element of construction. The vision of Zaha Hadid Architects signals a move away from cladding and towards unspoiled concrete surfaces that articulate their undecorated beauty rather than masking it. Eschewing paint and ornamentation creates a sense of surface transparency, enabling the building's exterior to be shown as it was constructed without further embellishment. 'Our strategy is to create something very solid, very durable and lasting,' Patrik Schumacher explained. 'Concrete is poured to create a dense, impenetrable mass. We eliminate cladding, surface decoration, window sills and door frames, and also go beyond the decorated surfaces that are vulnerable to being destroyed by wear and tear or the passage of time.'

Modernist buildings rarely achieved true transparency. Though many were devoid of ornamentation or effectively reduced to skeletal simplicity, their forms were often dramatically intensified by the application of paint. A layer of paint forms a seamless skin, a continuous plane that masks the surface as it hides superficial flaws beneath a uniform coating. While a coating is an architectural metaphor for transparency and purity, it actually occupies the space once allocated to ornamentation, without being recognized as a façade or a type of cladding. Irrespective of its thin layer, it is still a skin that sustains the logic of cladding, revealing that modernist architecture continues to engage with many of the mechanisms it attempted to detach from.

Mark Wigley pointed out the ambiguous function of white paint, which deceptively transforms any surface into a signalling device.[13] White paint may appear to project a neutral surface, but its presence in modernist architecture presented a shocking novelty. It emphasized the mechanical smoothness of modern buildings, and highlighted its contrast to the surrounding buildings. Yet just as a coat of whitewash provides a visual link between all the buildings of a Mediterranean village, it also linked the buildings of modernist architecture irrespective of their stylistic differences and geographical locations. The popularity of white clothing grew out of the same modernist sensibilities that assigned the 'neutrality' of white to many twentieth-century buildings.

The effacement of colour in fashion is a complex phenomenon that defies the logic of clothing. As white has come to represent purity and transparency, it has also been likened to ethereal qualities such as honesty, integrity and freedom. In the media, white is compared to the substance of crystals and diamonds and the purity of spring water, ice and snow. The highly symbolic value of white easily projects these meanings into a fashion collection to create a distinctive mood of nascence, and provide a blank canvas where new aesthetics can manifest. White fashions characterized many of the space-age collections of the 1960s, rivalled only by silver as the colour of future horizons.

The concept of masking reinforces the analogy of the architectural surface as a form of dress, and implies that for architecture to become genuinely modern it should adopt the codes of revealing and concealing more common to the conventions of fashion. As the surface of clothing functions as a recording device upon which textualities are registered, so too does the self-imposed mask of architecture reveal its own uncertainties. The dualities of revealing and concealing are constantly shifting, providing architecture and fashion with the means to camouflage the shortcomings of the infrastructures they conceal.

^This dome-like sheath evokes the outline of a nun's habit, which in the medieval period was designed to represent the architecture of cloisters and cathedrals. The female body was masked by the habit's architectural proportions and clearly identified with the church.

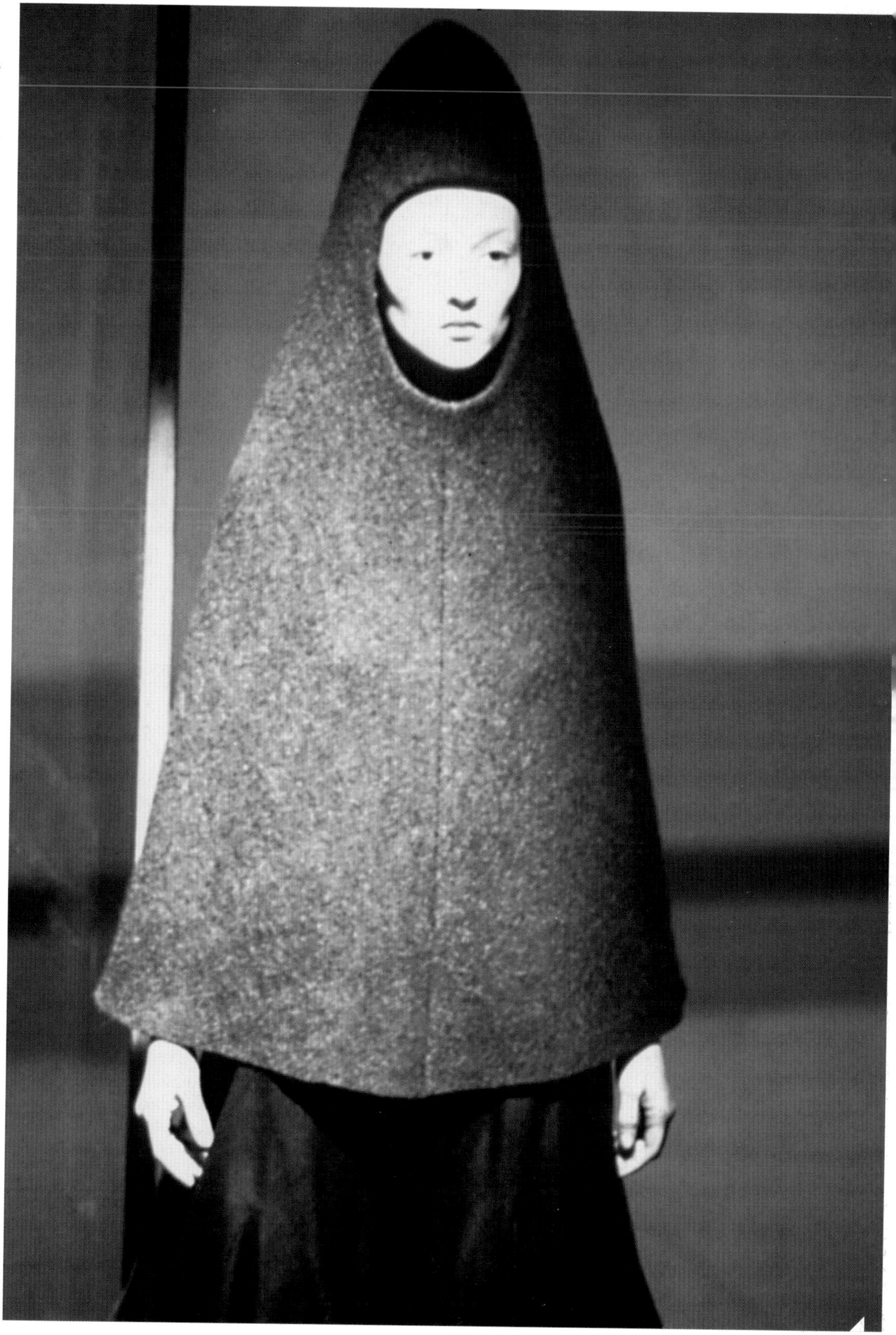

(A)

[1]Joanna Berzowska was interviewed by the author.

[2]Quoted from his talk held at the Serpentine Gallery on 13 July 2002.

[3]See Anthony Vidler (2000), 'Skin and Bones: Folded Forms from Leibniz to Lynn' in *Warped Space: Art, Architecture and Anxiety in Modern Culture*, Cambridge, MA: MIT Press, p230.

[4]James Laver (1948), *Style in Costume*, London: Oxford University Press, p18.

[5]Shelley Fox was interviewed by the author.

[6]Susan Sidlauskas (1982), *Intimate Architecture: Contemporary Clothing Design*, Cambridge, MA: The MIT Committee on the Visual Arts.

[7]See www.dillerscofidio.com.

[8]Simon Thorogood was interviewed by the author.

[9]Henri Lefebvre (1991 edition), *The Production of Space*, Oxford: Blackwell.

[10]See Collin Rowe and Robert Slutzky (1997 edition), *Transparency*, Bern: Birkhäuser.

[11]Susannah Frankel (1999), 'The Real McQueen', *The Independent* magazine, 8 September 1999.

[12]From Toyo Ito's talk at the Serpentine Gallery, held on 13th July 2002.

[13]See Mark Wigley (1995), *White Walls*, Cambridge, MA: MIT Press.

Notes

Select bibliography

P239_P240

Addley, Esther (2002), 'Why the Camera Loves Us', *The Guardian*, 14 September 2002.

Arnold, Rebecca (2001), *Fashion, Desire and Anxiety*, London: I. B. Tauris & Co, p61.

Arnold, Rebecca (1999), 'Heroin Chic', *Fashion Theory* 3(3), p279–95.

Augé, Marc (1995), *non-places*, London: Verso, p107.

Bachelard, Gaston (1994 edition), *The Poetics of Space*, Boston, MA: The Beacon Press, p17, 107.

Balsamo, Anne (1997), *Technologies of the Gendered Body*, Durham, NC: Duke University Press.

Banham, Reyner (1970), *Modern Chairs: 1918–70*, London: Whitechapel Gallery.

Barnard, Malcolm (1996), *Fashion and Communication*, London: Routledge.

Barthes, Roland (1997 edition), *The Eiffel Tower*, Berkeley, CA: University of California Press, p8.

Barthes, Roland, 'Semiology and the Urban Eiffel Tower' in Neil Leach (ed) (1999), *Rethinking Architecture*, London: Routledge.

Basualdo, Carlos (2002), *Hélio Oiticica: Quasi-Cinemas*, Ostfildern-Ruit, Germany: Hatje Cantz Publishers, p140.

Baudelaire, Charles, 'The Painter of Modern Life' in Jonathon Mayne (ed) (1995), *The Painter of Modern Life and Other Essays*, London: Phaidon.

Baudrillard, Jean (1994), *Simulcra and Simulation*, Ann Arbor, MI: University of Michigan Press, p26.

Baudrillard, Jean, 'Is Space Political?' in Neil Leach (ed) (1999), *Rethinking Architecture*, London: Routledge.

Benjamin, Andrew, 'Policing the Body: Descartes and the Architecture of Change' in Neil Leach (ed) (1999), *Architecture and Revolution*, London: Routledge.

Benjamin, Walter (1999 edition), *Charles Baudelaire*, London: Verso, p37, 171.

Benjamin, Walter (1999 edition), *The Arcades Project*, Cambridge, MA: Harvard Belknap Press.

Benjamin, Walter, 'On Some Motifs in Baudelaire Paris, Capital of the Nineteenth Century' in Neil Leach (ed) (1999), *Rethinking Architecture*, London: Routledge.

Benjamin, Walter (2003 edition), in John Osborne (trans) *The Origin of German Tragic Drama*, London, Verso.

Bocco Guarneri, Andrea (2002), *Bernard Rudofsky: A Humane Designer*, Vienna: Springer Verlag.

Bolton, Andrew (2002), The *Supermodern Wardrobe*, London: V&A Publishing, p71.

Borden, Iain, (2002), 'Fashioning the City', *Architectural Design*, (70)6, p12–19.

Borden, Iain, Joe Kerr, Alicia Pivaro and Jane Rendell (ed) (1996), *Strangely Familiar: Narratives of Architecture in the City*, London: E & F N Spon.

Borrelli, Laird (2002), *Web Fashion Now*, London: Thames & Hudson, p43.

Boulton Stroud, Marion (2003), *New Material as New Media*, Cambridge, MA: MIT Press.

Bourdier, Jean Paul and Nezar Alsayyad (ed) (1989), *Dwellings, Settlements and Tradition*, New York: University Press of America, p40.

Bourdieu, Pierre (1984), *Distinction: A Social Critique of the Judgement of Taste*, London: Routledge.

Bourgeois, Louise (1999), *Memory and Architecture*, Madrid: National Museum of Art.

Bowlby, Rachel (1997), *Feminist Destinations and Further Essays on Virginia Woolf*, Edinburgh: Edinburgh University Press, p191–219.

Boym, Svetlana (2001), *The Future of Nostalgia*, New York: Basic Books, p17.

Braddock, Sarah and Marie O'Mahony (1998), *Techno Textiles*, London: Thames & Hudson.

Breward, Christopher (1999), *Masculinities, Fashion and City Life 1860–1914*, Manchester: Manchester University Press.

Caleo, Chiara (2001), 'The Tanagra Larnakes: An Iconographic Analysis', *Anistoriton Journal of History, Archaeology, Art History*, 22 December 2001, p12.

Castle, Helen, 'Catwalk Architecture', in Helen Castle (ed) (2000), *Fashion and Architecture*, Bognor Regis, England: Wiley.

Select Bibliography

Chalayan, Hussein (ed) (2002), 'Featuring Hussein Chalayan', *ABC* magazine, Issue 'C'.

Chernow, Burt (2002), *Christo and Jeanne-Claude: A Biography*, New York: St Martin's Press.

Chung, Chuihua Judy, Jeffrey Inaba, Rem Koolhaas and Sze Tsung Leong (ed) (2002), *The Harvard Design School Guide to Shopping/Harvard Design School Project on the City 2*, Cologne: Taschen.

Clark, Judith (1998), 'Kinetic Beauty: The Theatre of the 1920s' in *Addressing the Century* exhibition catalogue, London: Hayward Gallery Publishing.

Cline, Ann (1998), *A Hut of One's Own*, Cambridge, MA: MIT Press.

Coates, Nigel (2000), *Ecstacity*, London: Booth Clibborn Editions.

Cook, Peter and Warren Chalk (ed) (1999), *Archigram*, New York: Princeton Architectural Press.

Cooper Marcus, Clare (1995), *House as a Mirror of Self*, Berkeley, CA: Conari Press.

Corrin, Lisa (2002), 'The Perfect Home: A Conversation with Do-Ho Suh' in *Do-Ho Suh*, the Serpentine Gallery's exhibition catalogue, p37.

Craik, Jennifer (1994), *The Face of Fashion*, London: Routledge, p4.

Crompton, Dennis (1994), *Archigram: Life and Times of the Archigram Group*, Chichester: Academy Editions.

Crompton, Dennis, Michael Sorkin and William Menking (1998), *Concerning Archigram*, New York: Thread Waxing Space.

Debord, Guy (1995 edition), *Society of the Spectacle*, New York: Zone Books.

Debord, Guy, 'Theory of Dérive', in K Knabb (1989) (ed), *The Situationist International Anthology*, Berkeley, CA: Bureau of Public Secrets, p50.

de Certeau, Michel (1984), 'Walking in the City,' in *The Practice of Everyday Life*, Berkeley, CA: University of California Press.

Deleuze, Gilles (1992), *The Fold*, St Paul, MN: University of Minnesota Press.

Deleuze, Gilles and Felix Guattari (1987), *A Thousand Plateaus: Capitalism and Schizophrenia*, St Paul, MN: University of Minnesota Press.

Din, Rasshied (2002), *New Retail*, London: Conran Octopus, p8, 9, 13, 156.

Dodds, George and Robert Tavernor (ed) (2001), *Body and Building*, Cambridge, MA: MIT Press.

Eisenman, Peter and Charles Jencks (2002), 'The New Paradigm and September 11th', *Architectural Design*, 72(4), p98–106.

Eisenman, Peter and Elizabeth Grosz (2001), *Architecture from the Outside: Essays on Virtual and Real Space*, Cambridge, MA: MIT Press.

El Guindi, Fadwa (1999), 'Veiling Resistance', in *Fashion Theory* 3(1), p58.

Entwistle, Joanna, 'The Dressed Body' in Joanne Entwistle and Elizabeth Wilson (ed) (2001), *Body Dressing*, Oxford: Berg.

Fausch, Deborah, Paulette Singley, Rodolphe El-Khoury and Zvi Efrat (1994), *Architecture: In Fashion*, New York: Princeton Architectural Press.

Featherstone, Mike, 'The Body in Consumer Culture', in Mike Featherstone, Mike Hepworth and Bryan S. Turner (ed) (1991), *The Body: Social Process and Cultural Theory*, London: Sage, p178.

Feuerstein, Gunther (1997), *Androgynous: The Male–Female in Art and Architecture*, Stuttgart: Editions Axel Menges.

Feuerstein, Gunther (2001), *Biomorphic Architecture*, Stuttgart: Editions Axel Mentges.

Foster, Hal (1993), *Compulsive Beauty*, Cambridge, MA: MIT Press, p269.

Foster, Hal (2002), *Design and Crime*, London: Verso, p5, 44.

Foucault, Michel (1977), *Discipline and Punish*, London: Penguin, p200–1.

Foucault, Michel, (1967), 'Des espace autres', translated by Jay Miskowiec as 'Of Other Spaces' in *Diacritics*, (1986), Baltimore, MD: Johns Hopkins University Press, p22–7.

Frampton, Kenneth and John Cava (ed) (1995), *Studies in Tectonic Culture*, Cambridge, MA: MIT Press.

Franck, Karen (2000), *Architecture Inside Out*, New York: Wiley-Academy.

Franck, Karen, 'Yes, We Wear Buildings' in Helen Castle (ed) (2000), *Fashion and Architecture*, Bognor Regis, England: Wiley.

Frankel, Susannah (2001), *Fashion Visionaries*, London: V&A Publications, p158.

Frankel, Susannah (1999), 'The Real McQueen', *The Independent* magazine, 8 September 1999.

Gierstberg, Frits and Warna Oosterbaan (2001), *The Image Society*, Rotterdam: Nai Publishers.

Gill, Alison, 'Deconstruction Fashion: The Making of Unfinished, Decomposing and Re-assembled Clothes', *Fashion Theory*, (2)1, p25–48.

Goldin, Nan (ed) (1996), *I'll Be Your Mirror*, New York: The Whitney Museum of American Art/Zurich: Scalo.

Goulthorpe, Mark (2002), 'Notes on Digital Nesting: A Poetics of Evolutionary Form', *Architectural Design*, (72)2, p20.

Grosz, Elizabeth (2001), *Architecture From the Outside*, Cambridge, MA: MIT Press.

Hadid, Zaha (2000), *Zaha Hadid: Projects*, London: Thames & Hudson.

Heynen, Hilde (1999), *Architecture and Modernity*, Cambridge, MA: MIT Press.

Hollander, Anne (1993), *Seeing Through Clothes*, Berkeley, CA: University of California Press.

Hollander, Anne (1994), *Sex and Suits*, New York: Kodanska, p19.

Irvine, Susan (2001), 'Deconstructing Hussein', *The Telegraph* 5 December 2001.

Jameson, Fredric, 'History Lessons', in Neil Leach (ed) (1999), *Architecture and Revolution*, London: Routledge, p72.

Jay, Martin, 'Scopic Regimes of Modernity' in Hal Foster (ed) (1988), *Vision and Visuality*, New York: The New Press, p3–20.

Johnston, Pamela (1996), *The Function of the Oblique: The Architecture of Claude Parent and Paul Virilio, 1963–1969*, London: AA Publishing.

Jordan, Sandra and Jan Greenberg (2000), *Frank O Gehry: Outside In*, New York: DK Publishing.

Koda, Harold (2001), *Extreme Beauty: The Body Transformed*, New York: The Metropolitan Museum of Art.

Koolhaas, Rem (1998), *S, M, L, XL*, New York: Penguin.

Koolhaas, Rem (2001 edition), *Delirious New York*, New York: The Monacelli Press, p14.

Koolhaas, Rem, Miuccia Prada, Patrizio Bertelli and Michael Kubo (ed) (2001), *Projects for Prada Part 1*, Milan: Prada Foundation Editions.

Kozloski, Lillian (1994), US *Space Gear*, Washington, DC: Smithsonian Press.

Kwinter, Sanford (2001), *Architectures of Time*, Cambridge, MA: MIT Press.

Kwinter, Sanford and Jonathan Crary (ed) (1994), *Interpretations*, New York: Zone.

Kwinter, Sanford (2002), 'Hydraulic Vision' in *Mood River* 2002 exhibition catalogue, Columbus, OH: Wexner Centre for the Arts.

Lacan, Jacques (1992 edition), *The Ethics of Psychoanalysis*, London: Routledge.

Laver, James (1949), *Style in Costume*, London: Oxford University Press.

Leach, Neil (ed) (1997), *Rethinking Architecture*, London: Routledge.

Leach, Neil (ed) (1999), *Architecture and Revolution*, London: Routledge.

Leach, Neil (ed) (2002), *The Hieroglyphics of Space*, London: Routledge.

Leatherbarrow, David and Moshen Mostafavi (2002), *Surface Architecture*, Cambridge, MA: MIT Press.

Lefebvre, Henri (1991 edition), *The Production of Space*, Oxford: Blackwell.

Lehmann, Ulrich (2000), *Tigersprung*, Cambridge, MA: MIT Press, p57.

Leitner, Bernard (2001), *Wittgenstein House*, New York: Princeton Architectural Press.

Select Bibliography

Lévi-Strauss, Claude (1968 edition), *The Savage Mind*, Chicago, IL: University of Chicago Press, p20, 23.

Libeskind, Daniel, 'Traces of the Unborn' in Neil Leach (ed) (1999), *Architecture and Revolution*, London: Routledge.

Libeskind, Daniel (2002), 'The Walls Are Alive', *The Guardian*, 13 July 2002.

Lindstrand, Tor (1998), 'Believing Las Vegas', *Merge Magazine*, Issue 1.

Loos, Adolph, 'Ornament und Verbrechen' lecture of 1908, translated as 'Ornament and Crime' by Wilfred Wang (1985) in *The Architecture of Adolf Loos*, London: The Arts Council.

Loos, Adolph, 'The Principle of Cladding' (as the title of Loos's 1898 essay, 'Das Prinzip der Bekleidung' was translated), Jane Newman and John Smith (ed) (1987), *Spoken into the Void: Collected Essays 1897–1900*, Cambridge, MA: MIT Press, p66–9.

Lovegrove, Keith (2000), *Airline*, London: Laurence King.

Lund, Nils Ole (1990), *Collage Architecture*, Berlin: Ernst and Sohn.

Lupton, Ellen (2002), *Skin: Surface, Substance and Design*, London: Laurence King, p61.

Mallgrave, Harry (ed) (1996), *Otto Wagner: Reflections on the Raiment of Modernity*, Los Angeles, CA: Getty.

Mallgrave, Harry and Wolfgang Herrmann (trans) (1989), *The Four Elements of Architecture and Other Writings*, Cambridge: Cambridge University Press.

Margolin, Victor (1998), *The Struggle for Utopia: Rodchenko, Lissitsky and Moholy-Nagy, 1917–1946*, Chicago, IL: University of Chicago Press.

Markham, Julian, 'E-tail and the Increasing Importance of Retail Innovation' in Helen Castle (ed) (2000), *Fashion and Architecture*, Bognor Regis, England: Wiley.

Martin, Richard (1989), *Fashion and Surrealism*, New York: Rizzoli.

Martin, Richard (1998), 'Yeohlee: Energy and Economy, Measure and Magic' *Fashion Theory* 2(3), p287–93.

McDowell, Colin (2000), *Fashion Today*, London: Phaidon, p428.

McLuhan, Marshall (1994), *Understanding Media*, Cambridge, MA: MIT Press, p119–20.

Mitchell, William (1999), *e-topia*, Cambridge, MA: MIT Press.

Miyake, Issey et al (1999), *Making Things*, Zurich: Scalo Verlag.

Morgan, Conway (1995), *Jean Nouvel: The Elements of Architecture*, New York: Universe Publishers.

Mori, Toshiko (ed) (2002), *Immaterial/Ultramaterial*, New York: George Braziller.

Muthesius, Eckhart (1979), *Hermann Muthesius, 1861–1927*, London: Architectural Association.

Orta, Lucy (ed) (2000), *Refuge Wear*, Paris: Editions Jean Michel Place.

Orta, Lucy (ed) (2001), *Process of Transformation*, Paris: Editions Jean-Michel Place.

Orta, Lucy (ed) (2003), *Body Architecture*, Munich: Silke Schreiber Verlag.

Osman, Michael, 'Mining Autonomy' in Michael Osman, Adam Ruedia, Matthew Seidel and Lisa Tilney (ed) 2002) *Perspecta* 33, Vol. XXXIII, Cambridge: MIT Press.

Pallaasma, Juhani (1996), *The Eyes of the Skin: Architecture and the Senses*, London: Academy Editions.

Papastergiadis, Nikos (2002), 'Traces Left in Cities', *Architectural Design*, 72(2), p45.

Parsons, Deborah (1999), 'Flâneur or Flâneuse? Mythologies of Modernity', *New Formations* 38, p91–100.

Patterson, Richard (2002), 'The Metamorphosis of Tragedy', *Architectural Design* 70(5), p38.

Patterson, Richard (2002), 'The Void That is Subject', *Architectural Design*, 70(5), p73.

Pavitt, Jane (ed) (2000), *Brand New*, London: V&A Publications.

Pawley, Martin, 'Fashion and Architecture in the 21st Century' in Helen Castle (ed) (2000), *Fashion and Architecture*, Bognor Regis, England: Wiley.

Pearson, Hugh (2002), *Contemporary World Architecture*, London: Phaidon.

Pollock, Griselda, 'Modernity and the Spaces of Femininity,' in Nicholas Mirzoeff (ed) (2002), *The Visual Culture Reader*, London: Routledge, p74–84.

Poshyananda, Apinan, 'Undressing Europa' in Salah Hassan and Iftikhar Dadi (ed) (2002), *Unpacking Europe*, Rotterdam: NAI Press.

Quinn, Bradley (2002), *Techno Fashion*, Oxford: Berg.

Rendell, Jane (2000), 'Between Architecture, Fashion and Identity', *Architectural Design* 70(6), p9, 11.

Rendell, Jane, 'Introduction: Gender, Space' in Jane Rendell, Barbara Penner and Iain Borden (ed) (2000), *Gender Space Architecture*, London: Routledge.

Rendell, Jane, 'The Pursuit of Pleasure: London Rambling' in Neil Leach (ed) (2000), *The Hieroglyphics of Space*, London: Routledge.

Richards, Ivor (2001), *Groundscrapers and Subscrapers of Hamzah & Yeang*, Bognor Regis, England: Wiley-Academy.

Rogoff, Irit (2000), *Terra Infirma*, London: Routledge, p30.

Rowe, Colin and Robert Slutzky (1997 edition), *Transparency*, Bern: Birkhäuser.

Rudofsky, Bernard (1947), *Are Clothes Modern?*, Chicago, IL: Paul Theobald.

Rudofsky, Bernard (1965), *Architecture Without Architects*, New York: Doubleday.

Rudofsky, Bernard (1971), *The Unfashionable Human Body*, New York: Doubleday.

Schezen, Roberto (ed) (1996), *Adolf Loos: Architecture 1903–1932*, New York: Monacelli Press.

Schlemmer, Oskar, Laszlo Moholy-Nagy, Farkas Molnar, Walter Gropius and Arthur Wessinger (ed) (1996 edition), *The Theater of the Bauhaus*, Baltimore, MD: Johns Hopkins University Press.

Seabrook, John (2002) 'Nursing Chic', *The New Yorker*, 18 March 2002.

Serraino, Perluigi and Julius Shulman (2000), *Modernism Rediscovered*, Cologne: Taschen.

Shklovsky, Victor (1965 edition), 'Art as Technique', *Russian Formalist Criticism: Four Essays*, Lincoln, NB: University of Nebraska Press, p12.

Sidlauskas, Susan (1982), *Intimate Architecture: Contemporary Clothing Design*, Cambridge, MA: The MIT Committee on the Visual Arts.

Simmel, Georg, 'The Metropolis and Mental Life' in Neil Leach (ed) (1999), *Rethinking Architecture*, London: Routledge.

Sontag, Susan (1979), *On Photography*, London: Penguin, p58, 104.

Sontag, Susan (1991), *Against Interpretation and Other Essays*, New York: Farrar, Strauss and Giroux.

Sorkin, Michael (1998), 'Amazing Archigram', *Metropolis Magazine*, April 1998.

Steele, Valerie (1998), *Paris Fashion*, Oxford: Berg.

Steele, Valerie (2001), *The Corset*, New Haven, CT: Yale University Press.

Steiner, Dietmar (2000), 'Promotional Architecture' *Architectural Design* 70(6), p20–3.

Sudjic, Dejan (1990), *Rei Kawakubo and Commes des Garçons*, New York: Rizzoli.

Surya, Michel (2002), *Georges Bataille*, London: Verso, p3.

Tolla, Ada and Guiseppe Lignano (2002), *Lot/ek*, New York: Princeton Architectural Press.

Trasi, Nicola (2002), *Interdisciplinary Architecture*, New York: Wiley Academy.

Tschumi, Bernard (1995), *Event-Cities*, Cambridge, MA: MIT Press.

Tschumi, Bernard, 'Disjunctions' in Neil Leach (ed) (1999), *Architecture and Revolution*, London: Routledge, p146.

Select Bibliography

Tschumi, Bernard (2000), *Event-Cities 2*, Cambridge, MA: MIT Press.

van Berkel, Ben and Caroline Bos (2001), *Move*, Rotterdam: Nai Publishers.

Vattimo, Gianni, 'The End of Modernity, The End of the Project?' in Neil Leach (ed) (1999), *Rethinking Architecture*, London: Routledge.

Vidler, Anthony (2000), 'Skin and Bones: Folded Forms from Leibniz to Lynn' in *Warped Space: Art, Architecture and Anxiety in Modern Culture*, Cambridge, MA: MIT Press, p230.

Virilio, Paul (2000), *The Information Bomb*, London: Verso, p61.

Virilio, Paul, 'The Overexposed City' in Neil Leach (ed) (1999), *Rethinking Architecture*, London: Routledge.

Visionaire N° 20, *The Comme des Garçons Issue*, New York: Art Publishers.

Vollers, Karel (2001), *Twist and Build – Creating Non-orthogonal Architecture*, Rotterdam: 010 Publishers.

von Maur, Karin (1988), *Oskar Schlemmer*, Stuttgart State Gallery's 100th anniversary exhibition catalogue, Stuttgart: Staatsgalerie/Editions Cantz.

Warner, Michael (2002), *Publics and Counterpublics*, New York: Zone Books, p56.

Warwick, Alexandra and Dani Cavallaro (1998), *Fashioning the Frame*, Oxford: Berg.

White, Leslie (2000), 'Wasted', *Sunday Times* Magazine, 17 September 2000.

Wigley, Mark (2001), *White Walls*, Cambridge, MA: MIT Press, pxx, 9, 11, 13.

Wilson, Elizabeth, 'All the Rage' in J Gains and C Herzog (ed) (1990), *Fabrications: Costume and the Female Body*, New York: Routledge.

Winters, Edward (2000), 'Sacraria, Tragedy and the Interior Narrative', *Architectural Design* 70(5), p84.

Wolff, Janet (1990), *Feminine Sentences: Essays on Women and Culture*, Berkeley, CA: University of California Press, p34–50.

Yamamoto, Yohji and Carla Sozzani (ed) (2002), *Talking To Myself*, Tokyo: Yohji Yamamoto Inc/Milan: Carla Sozzani srl.

Young, Robert (1994), *Mental Space*, London: Process Press, p80.

Picture credits

Opening image: 'My House', photographed by David Lachapelle, reprinted courtesy Art and Commerce.

Page 4: (A) Reprinted courtesy Pia Myrvold. (B) Photographed by Chris Moore, reprinted courtesy Hussein Chalayan.

Page 6: (A+B) Reprinted courtesy Arkadius.

Page 8: (A) Photographed by Jean Françoise Jose, reprinted courtesy Comme des Garçons. (B) Photographed by Chris Moore, reprinted courtesy V&A Museum. (C) Reprinted courtesy Pia Myrvold.

Pages 9+10: (A+B) Courtesy Prada.

Pages 11+12: (A) Photographed by Maria Friberg, reprinted courtesy Maria Friberg. (B) Reprinted courtesy Zaha Hadid Architects.

Pages 19+20: Courtesy Prada.

Page 23: (A) Photographed by Patrice Stable, reprinted courtesy John Ribbe. (B) Photographed by Chris Moore, reprinted courtesy Hussein Chalayan.

Pages 29–30: All images photographed by Anders Edström, reprinted courtesy Anders Edström.

Page 34: Photographed by Michael Maier, reprinted courtesy Michael Maier.

Page 36: (A) Reprinted courtesy Pia Myrvold. (B) Courtesy Paul Smith.

Pages 38+40: Courtesy Prada.

Page 44: Courtesy Paul Smith.

Pages 46–48: All images courtesy Prada.

Page 50: (A+B) Reprinted courtesy Comme des Garçons.

Page 53: Reprinted courtesy Pia Myrvold.

Page 58: (A+B) Reprinted courtesy Pia Myrvold.

Page 67: Reprinted courtesy Comme des Garçons.

Page 69: Reprinted courtesy Concrete PR.

Page 74: (A+B) Photographed by Jean Françoise Jose, reprinted courtesy Comme des Garçons.

Page 75: Photographed by Jean Françoise Jose, reprinted courtesy Comme des Garçons.

Pages 77+78: Photographed by Stuart A Veech, reprinted courtesy veech.media.architecture.

Pages 79–81: All images photographed by Sabina Gruber, reprinted courtesy veech.media.architecture.

Page 82: Photographed by Francesco Valentino, reprinted courtesy Michiko Koshino.

Page 84: (A) Photographed by Chris Moore, reprinted courtesy Hussein Chalayan. (B+C) Photographed by Jean Françoise Jose, reprinted courtesy Comme des Garçons.

Pages 86–88: All images reprinted courtesy Jüdisches Museum Berlin.

Page 92: (A+B) Reprinted courtesy Arkadius.

Page 95: (A+B) Photographed by Dan Lecca, reprinted courtesy Yeohlee.

Page 101: Reprinted courtesy Final Home / A-net Press.

Page 103: Photographed by Natsu Tanimoto, reprinted courtesy Final Home/A-net Press.

Pages 105–106: All images reprinted courtesy CP Company / Modus Publicity.

Pages 110–116: All images photographed by Dan Lecca, reprinted courtesy Yeohlee.

Pages 120–129: All images photographed by Chris Moore, reprinted courtesy Hussein Chalayan.

Page 134: Reprinted courtesy the artist and the Serpentine Gallery, London.

Page 135: © Lucy Orta, reprinted courtesy Royal College of Art, London.

Page 139: Photographed by Dan Lecca, reprinted courtesy Yeohlee.

Page 140: Photographed by Chris Moore, reprinted courtesy Hussein Chalayan.

Page 141: Courtesy of the artist and Lehman Maupin, New York/Serpentine Gallery, London.

Page 142: (A) Photographed by Maria Friberg, reprinted courtesy Maria Friberg. (B) Reprinted courtesy Paulina Wallenberg Olsson.

Picture credits

Page 143: © the Artist; courtesy Sadie Coles HQ, London.

Page 145: Photographed by Toshiko Mori, reprinted courtesy Toshiko Mori, Architect.

Page 146: © Lucy Orta, reprinted courtesy Studio Orta.

Page 147: Reprinted courtesy Jurgen Bey.

Page 148: © the Artist; courtesy Sadie Coles HQ, London.

Page 150: © the Artist; courtesy Sadie Coles HQ, London.

Pages 156–180 © Lucy Orta, reprinted courtesy Studio Orta.

Pages 188–202: All images photographed by Anders Edström, reprinted courtesy Anders Edström.

Page 208: Photographed by Jean Françoise Jose, reprinted courtesy Comme des Garçons.

Page 210: (A) Photographed by Chris Moore, reprinted courtesy Hussein Chalayan. (B) Photographed by Dan Lecca, reprinted courtesy Yeohlee. (C) Photographed by Torben Eskerod, reprinted courtesy Thea Bjerg.

Page 211: Photographed by Chris Moore, reprinted courtesy Hussein Chalayan.

Page 216: (A+B) Photographed by Jean Françoise Jose, reprinted courtesy Comme des Garçons. (C) Photographed by Dan Lecca, reprinted courtesy Yeohlee.

Page 217: (A) Photographed by Sally Tallant, reprinted courtesy Serpentine Gallery, London. (B) Photographed by Helene Binet, reprinted courtesy Helene Binet/ Serpentine Gallery, London.

Page 219: (A+B) Photographed by Jean Françoise Jose, reprinted courtesy Comme des Garçons.

Page 220: (A) Photographed by Chris Moore, reprinted courtesy Abnormal PR. (B) Graphic image directed by Karel Vollers and drawn by Gobel Hellevoort of Hellevoort Visuals, Amsterdam. Reprinted courtesy Karel Vollers.

Pages 221+222: Graphic image directed by Karel Vollers and drawn by Gobel Hellevoort of Hellevoort Visuals, Amsterdam. Reprinted courtesy Karel Vollers.

Page 225: Photographed by Helene Binet, reprinted courtesy Zaha Hadid Architects.

Page 226: (A) Reprinted courtesy Simon Thorogood/ Judith Clark Costume. (B) Reprinted courtesy Simon Thorogood.

Page 228: (A) Photographed by Chris Moore, reprinted courtesy Hussein Chalayan. (B) Reprinted courtesy Pia Myrvold.

Page 232: Reprinted courtesy Pia Myrvold.

Page 236: Photographed by Chris Moore, reprinted courtesy Hussein Chalayan.

Index

P251_P252